W9-BDI-591

Additional Praise for *Us*

"In his previous books, Terry Real awakened us to the fact that most men are not relational; they're in their heads and out of their hearts. In *Us*, he not only elaborates on that thesis but, with the writing of a good novelist, brings his approach to transforming men and couples to life. This book will challenge you to examine how your trauma history and internalized individualism impact your relationships. Share it with your partner and then talk about what it brings up. It may be one of the most painful but also important conversations of your life."

—Richard Schwartz, PhD, developer of the Internal Family
Systems model of psychotherapy

Also by Terrence Real

The New Rules of Marriage

I Don't Want to Talk About It

How Can I Get Through to You?

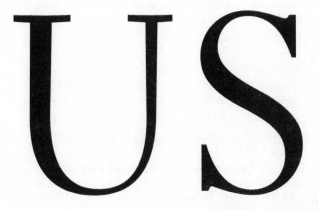

US

Getting Past You & Me to

Build a More Loving Relationship

TERRENCE REAL

Foreword by Bruce Springsteen

goop
press

Rodale

New York

Published in the United States by Rodale Books, an imprint of Random House, a division of Penguin Random House LLC, New York.

rodalebooks.com
RODALE and the Plant colophon are registered trademarks of Penguin Random House LLC.

Grateful acknowledgment is made to HarperCollins Publishers for permission to reprint Chapter 39 of *Tao Te Ching: A New English Version* by Stephen Mitchell, translation copyright © 1988 by Stephen Mitchell. Used by permission of HarperCollins Publishers.

Library of Congress Cataloging-in-Publication Data
Names: Real, Terrence, author.
Title: Us : getting past you and me to build a more loving relationship / Terrence Real; foreword by Bruce Springsteen.
Description: First edition. | New York : Goop Press/Rodale, [2022]
Identifiers: LCCN 2021040825 (print) | LCCN 2021040826 (ebook) | ISBN 9780593233672 (hardcover) | ISBN 9780593233689 (ebook)
Subjects: LCSH: Married people–Psychology. | Couples–Psychology. | Man-woman relationships. | Interpersonal conflict. | Interpersonal relations.
Classification: LCC HQ734 .R283 2022 (print) | LCC HQ734 (ebook) | DDC 306.7—dc23

ISBN 978-0-593-23367-2
Ebook ISBN 978-0-593-23368-9

Printed in the United States of America

Editor: Donna Loffredo
Designer: Jen Valero
Production Editor: Serena Wang
Production Manager: Heather Williamson
Composition: Berryville Graphics
Copy Editor: Janet Biehl
Indexer: Jay Kreider
Marketer: Brianne Sperber
Publicist: Lindsey Kennedy

10 9 8 7 6 5 4 3 2 1

First Edition

To my beloved family, Belinda, Justin, and Alexander.
You are the light in my firmament.

And in memory of the Great Appreciator,
one of the world's best pals, Rich Simon.

Contents

Foreword

This world does not belong to us.
We belong to one another.

—TERRENCE REAL

By my early thirties, I'd become aware enough to know, as things stood, I'd never have the things I wanted. A full life, a home, a wholeness of being, a companion, and a place in a community of neighbors and friends all seemed beyond my grasp. I didn't have the judgment, the courage, or the skills to bring a real life to fruition. I was one of the most successful musicians on the planet, but work is work, life is life, and they are not the same. Even more frustrating, the things that made me good at my job—my easy tolerance, even hunger, for the isolation of creativity, my ability to comfortably and deeply reside within myself and put all my energy into my work for days, weeks, years at a time—doomed my personal life to failure. I lived a lonely but seemingly secure existence. Then at thirty-two I hit an emotional wall and realized I was lost in a deep dark forest, largely of my own making, without a map. So began forty years of trying to find my way through the shadowed trees, down to the river of a sustaining life.

With help I realized, in early middle age, that I was subject to a legacy that had been passed down from generation to generation in my Italian-Irish family. A long and stubborn stream of mental illness and dysfunction manifested itself in my life as a deep, recurring depression and an emotional paralysis. I had a fear of exposing my inner life to anyone besides twenty thousand complete strangers at your nearest arena. The eye-to-eye democracy of real adult love struck fear and insecurity deep in my heart. Meanwhile I could feel my life clock ticking on the things I wanted to do and what I wanted to become.

So how do you transform that legacy? How do you break the chain of trauma and illness whose price is compounded with each successive generation? As Terry says, "Family pathology is like a fire in the woods taking down all in front of it until someone turns to face the flames." Slowly I began to face those flames, mainly because I couldn't stand the idea of failing my own children, my family, in the manner that I felt I'd been failed. And at the end of the day, the way we honor our parents and their efforts is by carrying on their blessings and doing our best to not pass forward their troubles, their faults, to our own children. Our children's sins should be their own. It's only through the hard work of transformation do those of ours who have come before cease to be the ghosts that haunt us and transform into the ancestors we need and love to walk beside us. Working even a small piece of this into my life took a long time, and I'm still a daily work in progress. My children will have plenty of work to do on their own, but we all have to learn and earn our own adulthood.

Looking more broadly, the price we pay as a society for our toxic individualism and patriarchy is our permanent estrangement from one another. If I can't connect to you, I can't connect to us. Whether it's racism, class differences, or any of myriad other social plagues, its cost is always the same: a broken and dysfunctional system that prevents us from recognizing and caring for our neighbor with a flawed but full heart. Terry's writing is loving and kind, clever and strong, and he's written a beautiful and important book, particularly for the moment we are in. It helps lead the way to a more powerful and noble society based on the tenets of love, justice, and respect. He has laid out a process by which we can begin to understand our place in our own families and our society.

I've worked hard, and I've been lucky. Over the years I've found some very good guides through that dark forest and down to that river of life. For my wife, Patti, and me, Terrence Real has been one of those guides, and this book is a map through those trees.

Be safe and journey forward,
Bruce Springsteen

1

Which Version of You Shows Up to Your Relationship?

Have you ever felt as if you were an unwitting passenger in your own interactions? You tell yourself a dozen times that this once you will not lose it with your child, colleague, family member, or spouse. But in the heat of the moment—oh my, there it goes: the unkind word, the raised voice, the torrent of what you "really" think.

Maybe you're not the explosive type. Instead of lashing out, you shut down because you're either disgusted (*I don't need this!*) or overwhelmed (*I can't handle this!*) or both at the same time.

Maybe you're neither aggressive nor withdrawn. Maybe for the most part you're moderate, even-tempered, and sensible — it's just that your partner isn't.

Welcome to humanity.

Your desire is to finally get through to them, or to finally be left the hell alone. But the reins have been ripped from your hands, and you find yourself galloping toward the edge of a cliff. Sometimes you watch it all happen, knowing it's wrong, knowing you don't want to do this. In other moments, you abandon your good intentions altogether, jump right onto the horse's back, and pull on the reins even harder. You scream louder. You shut down even more impenetrably.

Sooner or later—in minutes or hours, days, even weeks— you come to your senses. And then it's time for you to do damage control. Or you both just move on, sweeping the whole thing under the rug. Until the next time.

Aren't you just sick of it? Don't you regret it? This is not how you want to live, and you keep promising yourself that this time you'll be different, or *they* will be different. And indeed, things are fine for a while, maybe even a long while—until she turns away cold and unloving, or until he disrespects and takes liberties again. You just want to get through to that jerk, you have the right, you *need* to be heard! Or you just want to be left unperturbed. Why can't she just accept you as you are? You signed up for marriage, not a lifelong self-improvement course!

It has been said that there are two types of couples in the world—those who fight and those who distance. I'd add a third type: those who do both. One rails while the other shuts down. Hailstorm and tortoise.

I'm a relationship expert who's spoken about and given workshops on superlative relationships to corporations, to the general public, and to psychotherapists around the world. Over three decades, thousands of mental health professionals and corporate coaches have trained in the model of therapy I've created, called Relational Life Therapy, and countless individuals and couples have benefited.

If you find yourself frequently fighting with your partner, if you feel unheard or frustrated, if you often feel underappreciated or overly controlled, distanced from, walled off and lonely, or just poorly treated, this book offers you a completely new way to relate. It's about changing the way you see yourself in relation to your partner so that your life is neither a desert nor a battle. In this book, I am asking you to do something pretty revolutionary, something that will require changing some fundamental parts of your identity—even, for many of you, changing who you think of yourselves as being to begin with.

But I promise it will be worth it—in fact, it's the only way to end the struggle. Too many couples fight repetitively, resolving not much of anything, or one or both of you backs off, so you begin living "alone together." Here you will learn how to reconnect, first to yourself—your feelings, needs, and desires—because great relationships start with your relationship to yourself. Then you will learn the skills of a sophisticated and practical *relationship technology* designed to teach you how to get more of what you want in your relationships with others—how to move past those shadowed trees to the sustaining river of life.

It won't be easy, as I'm guessing you already know. Because if you're reading this book, you probably have firsthand experience with a home truth: relationships can be hell. In the heart-to-heart combat of close relationships, we lose it, in ways large or small, often over and over again. We forget that the person we're excoriating or stonewalling is the one we care about most in our lives. We look at our partner through the wrong end of a telescope, and they seem pitiful or overwhelming or both.

That's where someone like me steps in. I've been advising intimate partners, colleagues at work, and business and social leaders for much of my career. I'm a turnaround guy. People come see me when they are on the brink of disaster, when no one so far has been able to help. I'm a couples therapist specializing in male psychology, gender issues, trauma, and power.

Relational Life Therapy is known for producing deep, permanent change quickly in individuals and in their relationships. It teaches men, women, and nonbinary people how to live skilled relational lives—lives of radically honest, fearlessly assertive, passionate connection to themselves and to those they love. Relational Life therapists break many of the rules we learned in school. We are not neutral, for example. When it comes to responsibility, not all problems are an even fifty-fifty split. We take sides. And we don't hide behind a mask of professionalism. We make a point of being real people, sharing when appropriate from our own journey toward wholeness and intimacy.

This book is an invitation, the same invitation that I and other Relational Life therapists offer our clients every day. It's an invitation to truly master a sophisticated skill set, a technology. It's demanding, I won't lie, but once you learn it, it has the power to catapult you and your partner into a level of closeness, trust, solidity, and joy that leaves the norms of our culture in the dust. Would you like to feel heard? And can you satisfy your partner's need to feel listened to as well? Would you like to remember, even in heated or distant moments, that you and your partner stand on the same side?

Remembering Love

Before you pick up that verbal knife, before you brick yourself in even further, let me remind you that you love this person. And therein lies the rub, my friend. Do you remember, really, in that heated moment when fear or righteous anger courses through your veins, that you love this person? Do you remember it when your body shuts down and, for the life of you, you can barely squeak out a word or two? The sobering answer, if you're dead honest with yourself, is that you do not. In that heated moment, the sweetness between you, the sense of the two of you as a team facing the world together, the sense of *us*, is nearly impossible to locate.

The good news is that the love is still there. The bad news is that it's stored in parts of your brain, body, and nervous system that, in those flash moments, you no longer inhabit. Your endocrine system is on high alert, pumping stimulants into your bloodstream. Your autonomic nervous system—far below your consciousness—is in fight-or-flight, spurring you on or shutting you down. The higher functions of your brain (the prefrontal cortex, the reins) have gone completely offline, while the more primitive parts of your brain (the limbic system, particularly the amygdalae) have decisively taken over.

At those times, the brain is in a state in which the prefrontal cortex is neither connected to nor soothing the subcortical system. Without that soothing and connection, we lose a pause between what we feel and what we do. These more primitive parts of our bodies and brains care only about our personal survival; they have no interest in maintaining the vulnerability of intimacy. *Us* evaporates and becomes *you and me*, adversaries in a cold world of *I win, you lose.*

Us is the seat of closeness. *You and me* is the seat of adversarial contest. *You and me* is great when you are confronting a tiger, but less so when you are confronting your spouse, your boss, or your child. In those fraught moments, what makes it so hard to keep a cool head is a million or so years of evolution, plus one other powerful force: trauma. Trauma pulls you into survival mode, in which you are clenching your fists for the fight or clamping your jaws shut like a fortress. And the more trauma you sustained as a child, the more compelling *you and me* becomes.

If you are thinking, *Well, gosh, I didn't have much trauma growing up*, my answer is maybe. We'll talk about it later. But before you make up your mind, why not settle into my discussion of childhood trauma? Because sometimes it doesn't take much. Depending on your constitution and a host of other variables, it may take only a slight tap on the egg to produce fissures that can last a lifetime.

What's Your Trauma?

When I'm working with a couple, I have one important question in my mind. It's not *What are the stressors?* Stressors—like the pandemic, money woes, mismatched sex drives, kids, and in-laws—are all important, but a well-functioning couple can handle a reasonable amount of stress. The critical question I think about is not even *What is the dynamic, the choreography, between you?* That's also an important question, but it's not the most essential. The central question I ask myself during a therapy session is simply this one: *Which part of you am I talking to?*

Am I talking to the mature part of you, the one who's present in the here and now? This is the part I call the *Wise Adult.* That's the part that cares about *us.* Or am I speaking to a triggered part of you, to your adversarial *you and me* consciousness? The triggered part of you sees things through the prism of the past. I believe there's no such thing as overreacting; it's just that what someone is reacting to may no longer be what's in front of them. One of the blessings that partners in intimate relationships bestow upon each other is the simple and healing gift of their presence. But in order to be present with your partner, you must yourself be in the present, not saturated by your past.

The phrase *trauma memory* is really a misnomer. You don't remember trauma; you relive it. The combat vet who hears a car backfire and suddenly spins around like he's gripping a rifle is not thinking, *Now I'm walking down Main Street remembering combat.* In that flash moment, the vet is viscerally back at war. The past superimposes itself onto the present, fundamentally confusing the mind. When our trauma is triggered, we might physically spring into fight-or-flight mode. Faced with an overwhelming shock — infidelity, for example — I've seen patients gasp and head for the door before they came to in my hallway.

But most of us do not reenact the experience of the trauma itself. Instead, we act out the coping strategy that we evolved to deal with it. You were emotionally abandoned throughout your childhood, and so you've grown into a charming seducer, expert at securing others' attention. Or you were intruded upon as a child, and now you operate behind walls; you are adept at keeping people out. I speak of this compensating part of us as the Adaptive Child.

One of my great mentors, Pia Mellody, spoke of the Adaptive Child as a "kid in grown-up's clothing." The Adaptive Child is a child's version of an adult, the you that you cobbled together in the absence of healthy parenting. Here's a chart detailing the traits of the Adaptive Child, as distinct from the Wise Adult.

ADAPTIVE CHILD	WISE ADULT
Black & White	Nuanced
Perfectionistic	Realistic
Relentless	Forgiving
Rigid	Flexible
Harsh	Warm
Hard	Yielding
Certain	Humble
Tight in body	Relaxed in body

I'd like you to notice a few things as you look at this chart. First of all, see how tight, certain, and black and white the Adaptive Child is? One of my clients said that her Adaptive Child was like a little fundamentalist who lived inside her. This is in contrast to the flexibility, humility, and appreciation of nuance that are characteristic of the Wise Adult—qualities you may also recognize, from the literature on adult development, as those associated with emotional maturity.

There's No Redeeming Value in Harshness

Let's take a closer look at just one of the immature qualities prevalent in our Adaptive Child: harshness. I tell my clients that if they walk away from their sessions with me with just this one concept, they will have spent their therapy money well. Here it is: *There is no redeeming value whatsoever in harshness.* Harshness does nothing that loving firmness doesn't do better.

I once had a client, about seventy, who was a ringer for Clint Eastwood, and indeed, he was a Wyoming rancher. I went over in detail with him that there was nothing of value in harshness, and son of a gun, if he didn't start to cry. Small, manly Clint Eastwood tears, but tears nevertheless.

I said to him, "So you're thinking about how hard you've been on yourself all these years."

"No," he corrected me, "I'm thinking about the damage I've done to my sons."

Meeting Your Adaptive Child

Now just because the Adaptive Child part of you is rigid does not mean it is always outwardly aggressive. You can have an overly accommodating, people-pleasing Adaptive Child. Your Adaptive Child can tend toward superiority, it can tend toward inferiority, or it can bounce back and forth. But whether it's more dominating or withdrawn, it will react pretty much the same way whenever you're triggered. This set point reaction, this relational modus operandi, is your *relational stance*, the thing you will do over and over again when you are stressed.

Take Dan, for example. Dan had a very clear and specific relational stance, the well-worn track of his Adaptive Child. And it was a hairbreadth away from costing him his marriage.

Dan and Julia: A Liar Relents

"I lie," Dan tells me flatly in the first minutes of our first session.

Julia, his wife, fills in, "About everything large and small. Ask Dan what kind of shoes he has on, and he'll tell you they're sneakers."

Funny line, I think, but she's not joking. They're here for a two-day relationship intervention. They and I will spend two whole days together and at the end decide whether they're either back on track or divorcing. This is the last stop for couples on the brink.

Dan is a nice guy, a sweet man. Just don't try to get a straight answer out of him. He loves his wife, and he is by and large a well-meaning person. So, why would anyone in his right mind not be able to stop lying as he does? Because, I hypothesize, Dan isn't quite in his right mind. I don't mean that I think Dan is crazy, simply that he lives his life as his *you and me* consciousness, his Adaptive Child, while mistakenly thinking of himself as a Wise Adult, capable of appreciating *us*. And the culture at large rewards Dan's Adaptive Child. He knows better than to lie at work, but he does twist himself into knots in order to please his superiors. He works eighty hours a week, and he's risen through the ranks of the IT company he works for.

Like many of the clients I encounter, Dan has an Adaptive Child that makes him a great success in the world, but it also threatens to devastate his personal life. That's because the culture at large feeds off of Adaptive Children and is often threatened by mature adults. Our society mirrors the qualities of the Adaptive Child—black and white, rigid, perfectionistic, unrealistic, and unforgiving. This is the culture of individualism, about which I'll have much to say in Chapter 2.

Dan, white, mid-thirties, tells me that he lies to "stay out of trouble," glancing at Julia beside him, who is Black and about the same age.

Maybe, I think, *but perhaps there's more to it.* As we work together, Dan will show me how he handles himself, his relational stance.

"Did Julia bring you to therapy?" I ask Dan at one point.

"Not *bring* exactly, but she certainly strongly suggested," he replies.

"Have you tried to stop lying on your own?"

"Well I've *tried*, of course, but then again, what do you mean by *try* exactly?"

"Have you been struggling a long time?"

"I can't say I *struggle* per se . . ."

After three or four go-rounds, I begin to feel as though I could say the sky is blue, and Dan will tell me it's aquamarine. He's the kind of guy who opens the window in a monsoon, retrieves his soaking wet hand, and says, "There appears to be precipitation."

As a couples therapist, I have three sources of information: what the partners report about themselves and each other, how they behave in front of me, and how I feel witnessing their behavior.

When someone says they do something (like lie), and they then do a version of it right in front of me (evade), I have a fair idea that they are as described. So Dan is a champion evader. He lives out of his Adaptive Child. The Wise Adult inside us doesn't chronically lie. Knowing that, my next question is: What has Dan's Adaptive Child adapted to? How did Dan get bent into his current relational stance of evasion?

"Show me the thumbprint," I say to my students, "and I'll tell you about the thumb." If Dan has a black belt in avoidance, he learned it somewhere. Chances are that throughout his childhood he saw someone who was slippery, after whom he modeled himself; or conversely, he learned the art of evasion in reaction to some caregiver who was practiced in the art of control.

"Dan"—I try an educated guess—"who tried to control you while you were growing up?"

He contemplates this question. "Not my father. He was passive, hardly there."

"Your mother ruled the roost?" I try.

He laughs. "With an iron hand."

"And ruled you . . . ?"

"Well, you see, I was a good actor," he says.

"What does that mean?"

"I was a good boy. A good athlete, good grades, church on Sundays." He smiles, amused. "I put up a good front."

"And what was behind the good front?"

Again, the broad smile. "Well, I guess I must have had a bad back."

"Excuse me?"

"Oh, nothing disastrous. Girls, some drinking, even some weed, coke. But she never knew."

"You kept it low to the ground," I venture.

"Sure. What you don't know can't hurt you."

His motto, I think. *You could emblazon that phrase on his T-shirt.* "Low to the ground," I repeat. "Like your father."

"Sure," he allows. "I can see that."

"So what happened if anyone crossed your mother?"

"Oh"—he shakes his head—"that didn't happen. She was very strict, very religious. Catholic."

"You never saw anyone cross her?"

"No one dared," he answers flatly.

I lean back and regard him. Julia sits beside her husband, as still as a stone.

"So you learned," I tell him.

"I learned what?"

"How to preserve yourself. How to psychologically survive."

All Relational Life therapists know that they must always be respectful of the exquisite intelligence of the Adaptive Child. Lying to his rigid, commanding mother was precisely the thing little Dan needed to do to preserve his sense of self and autonomy. If Dan, as a child, had to choose between checking out, like his father, and singlehandedly taking on his domineering mother, he chose neither.

"I rendered unto Caesar what was Caesar's," he tells me.

"And you took for yourself what was yours."

Dan smiles, not displeased.

"On the side," I tell him.

On the side—that's the problem facing Dan today. In his private life, he still spends money, flirts, has a little drink with the guys—on the side. But as we say in Relational Life Therapy, "Adaptive then, maladaptive now." The same strategy that kept Dan sane and preserved him as a child is about to sink his marriage. It's time for Dan to realize that Julia is not his scolding, controlling mother—and that he is no longer that secretly defiant little boy. It's time for Dan to step into his Wise Adult self—the part of him that can withstand the flood of young feelings that washed over him whenever he sees Julia as demanding, the part of him rooted not in his past but in his present, not the limbic system but his prefrontal cortex. It's time to help him pull out of *you and me* into *us*.

One of the telltale characteristics of the *you and me* Adaptive Child is that it is automatic, a knee-jerk response. It's the Whoosh, the visceral reaction that comes up from the feet like a wave washing over your body. I speak of it as our first consciousness, and I divide it into three reactions—fight, flight, or fix. We all know what fight looks like. As for flight, just a reminder that someone can sit inches away from another and still flee—they just do so internally. We call that *stonewalling*. Finally, the knee-jerk response of fixing is not the same as a mature, considered wish to work on the relationship. Adaptive Child fixers are fueled by an anxious, driven need to take anyone's tension away from them as quickly as possible. Their motto is "I'm upset until you're not."

Dan is neither a fighter nor a fixer. He is a fleer; he flees by lying, omitting, and evading. Now, in our work together, it dawns on him that compliance and passive resistance are not the only two possibilities for him. That might have been true when he faced his mother, but not in his marriage to Julia. Julia has resources—like kindness and understanding—that Dan's mother largely lacked. And Dan now has resources that he lacked as that little boy, like the ability to stand up to his wife, to tell Julia the truth and let the chips fall where they may. I call this *letting the bad thing happen*.

One day about two months into our therapy, Dan and Julia saunter into my office holding hands and smiling broadly.

"You two look happy," I comment.

"We are," Dan tells me.

"We've had a breakthrough," adds Julia.

"Okay," I say. "There's a story here. Tell me."

It couldn't have been simpler, they tell me. "It happened this weekend," Dan fills me in. "Julia sent me off to the grocery store with a list of a few things. True to form, I came back with *almost* everything." They glance at each other. "She asked, 'Where's the damn milk?'" Dan leans forward, peering at me. "And I tell ya, man. Every muscle in my body wanted to say, 'They were out of it.' But instead, I took a deep breath and simply said, 'I forgot.'"

He turns to his wife and says, "And Julia just burst into tears on the spot."

"I told him," she says, "I've been waiting for this moment for twenty-five years."

The Real Work of Relationships:
Moving Beyond the Automatic

My wife, the family therapist Belinda Berman, has a name for the kind of moment Dan experienced. She calls it *relational heroism*—that moment when every muscle and nerve in your body is screaming to do the same old, but through raised consciousness, insight, discipline, and grace, you lift yourself off your accustomed track and deliberately place yourself on another track. You shift from the automatic, thoughtless response, from your *you and me* consciousness, your Adaptive

Child, to something new, something more relational, more connected, more mature. You call on your nontriggered *us* consciousness, your Wise Adult.

The great spiritual teacher Jiddu Krishnamurti once said that true liberation is freedom from our own automatic responses. In our culture, our relationship to relationships tends to be passive. We get what we get, and then we react to it. Most of us try to get more of what we want from our partners by complaining when they don't get it right. That's got to be about the worst behavioral modification program I've ever heard of.

This reactive approach to relationships is inherently individualistic. We have lost *us* consciousness, an appreciation for the whole, and instead we have shifted into *you and me*. We have moved out of our Wise Adult into our Adaptive Child parts. The present-based, most mature part of our brain, the prefrontal cortex, has lost connection with the older fast brain, the subcortical limbic system. Without that connection, you lose a pause between what you feel and what you do.

But my message is that in our reactions, we are not simple passengers. Over time, with training and practice, we can change our responses. We can shift from being reactive individuals to being proactive teammates who, in cooperation with our partner, intentionally shape the transaction between us. This everyday practice is *relational mindfulness*—stopping for a brief moment and centering ourselves. Observing, just as in all forms of mindfulness, the thoughts, feelings, impulses that arise—and choosing something different.

In your close relationships, urgency is your enemy, and breath is your friend. Breath can change your heart rate and your thinking physiologically. On Dan's fateful day, he reached for a different part of himself than his usual. His negative expectation, born in childhood—that Julia would be harsh with him—was contradicted. Neurobiology calls this *memory reconsolidation*; in psychology we call it a *corrective emotional experience*. Dan's frightened expectation was upended by his wife's kind response.

The other word for this is *healing*. And yes, in our relationships, we can heal each other—but not in the ways we commonly think, not by controlling our partners, getting from them what we lacked as children. Rather, we can heal by coming to terms with ignored parts of ourselves. Before we can provide corrective emotional experiences for each other, we must learn how to tend to our own immature parts, to our own reactivity, to our avoidance, our long-suffering frustration. We must master the art of relational mindfulness and retake the reins.

Everyone hears that relationships take work, but few of us have heard what the nature of that work entails. The real work of relationships is not occasional, or even daily: it is minute-to-minute. In this triggered moment right now, which path am I going to take? Rather than being overridden by your history, you can stop, pause, and choose. Moses came down from the mountain and saw that his people were worshipping false gods. Which false gods have you been worshipping lately? Money? Status? Security? Moses looked out at the scene and said, "There is a path toward life, there is a path toward death. Choose life!" (Deut. 30:19). To which I say, "There is a path toward *us*, toward integration, connection, wholeness. And there is a path toward *you and me*, trauma, scarcity, selfishness. Choose connection." But in those fraught moments of choice, you have to know how. The galloping horse of reactivity can pull on you like a relentless law of nature, until you show up to change it.

What follows is a journey toward mastery, from reactivity to responsibility, in those moments of choice. But that journey has a price of admission. Embarking on this path requires that we give up many cherished concepts of the world and of ourselves as individuals, starting with the notion that we are, indeed, individuals to begin with.

The Myth of the Individual

For centuries, Western culture has been dominated by the idea of the individual. And what could make more sense? I exist. I, Terry, this individual person hunched over my laptop, am distinct from others. I am an entity bordered by the perimeter of my body. In fact, the very word *individual* comes from the term *indivisible*. And I end with my skin. Or do I?

Confined within my body, you'll find my brain. Is that where my mind also resides? What is the shape of my mind, and does it end with my body? The great anthropologist Gregory Bateson gave the example of a blind man making his way down the street using a stick. Surely the stick and the information it yielded, argued Bateson, were a part of his mind.

The noted philosopher and cognitive scientist Thomas Metzinger began his exploration of the nature of consciousness by recounting the well-known "fake hand" experiment, which he re-created using himself as subject. Here's how he described it:

The subjects observed a rubber hand lying on the desk in front of them, with their own corresponding hand concealed from view by a screen. The visible rubber hand and the subject's unseen hand were then synchronously stroked with a probe. . . . After a certain time (sixty to ninety seconds, in my case), the famous rubber-hand illusion emerges. Suddenly, you experience the rubber hand as your own, and you feel the repeated strokes in this rubber hand. Moreover, you feel a full-blown "virtual arm"—that is, a connection from your shoulder to the fake hand on the table in front of you.

Perhaps this philosopher's Thomas-ness ended at the tips of his fingers—but at the tip of which fingers, the real ones or the rubber ones? Cognitive science teaches us that what we think of as ourselves derives not from a direct experience but from a collage of sensations and images—self-representations, pictures we have of ourselves. Similarly, we experience the world not directly but rather as it is filtered through our accumulated knowing. We recognize a chair because of its chairness. It fits into a category we already know. Without that cultural knowledge, we would see the world as a newborn baby sees it, as light, shadow, shapes, and smells, coming at us with little or no definition.

In this regard, we are all a type of narcissist. None of us sees ourselves directly—our self-perceptions are filtered through acquired knowledge. Most of us think of ourselves as our bodies, our physical selves. But that image itself is a construction of our minds. Cognitive science reveals that what we call our self is really a changing tapestry of self-representations, images. And the good news is that how we see ourselves and the world may change quickly, dramatically, and with support, permanently.

Psychologists used to think that character, once developed, was very difficult to transform. They assumed that once a neural pathway was set in the brain, it was set. The discovery of neuroplasticity changed all that. We've come to realize that habitual neural networks can open up and re-form—that is, take in new information and restructure. The often-cited phrase is "Neurons that fire together wire together." Or as neurobiologists say, "States become traits." In psychotherapy, neuroplasticity is currently the name of the game. In my practice, I have seen that opening neural pathways can lead to profound change, to brand-new traits and behavior, sometimes in a matter of minutes.

"That would stop me in my tracks."

Ernesto, Latinx and fifty-six, was a rager. He wasn't a physical rager, thank goodness, but he was a screamer, demeaner, a get-in-your-face-and-say-nasty-things verbal abuser. "It just comes over me too fast," he tells me about three-quarters of the way through a ninety-minute one-shot consultation with him and his wife, Maddy, also Latinx and a few years younger. Ernesto sounds like many abusive clients I have listened to over the years.

After meandering around for the better part of an hour, I finally ask him a question that hits pay dirt: "Who taught you how to be nasty and mean?"

"You mean like family?" he stutters. "Well, my mother died when I was eight, and my father remarried. Yeah, I guess my stepmother."

"What was she like?"

Ernesto smiles, shakes his head. "Oh, she was the meanest, worst, most horrible —"

"So, she's the one," I say.

"Yes."

"She taught you how to be this nasty?"

"Yes, I guess she did."

"And what's it like to see that?" I try to catch his eye as he looks down at the floor. Sitting across from him, I can feel his shame, a flush of warmth up his face. "Ernesto?" I ask softly.

He doesn't speak.

"Where are you now?" I ask after a time. "What's going on?"

"Oh," he says, not smiling. "I'm embarrassed. For someone to see me the way I see her." He shakes his head, looking beyond me.

I wonder what he's seeing, remembering.

"I feel mortified," he tells me.

"That embarrassment is what we call healthy guilt, or remorse. If you had felt that up front, it would have stopped you. Make sense?"

He nods, head down.

"Do you have a picture of your stepmother?"

"What, on me? No."

"Can you get one?"

"Sure," he says. "Yeah, I can."

"Good. Here's what I want you to do. You can rage at your wife. I can't stop you. But the next time you're about to blow, before you do, I want you to take out the picture of your step-mother, look her in the eye, and say: 'I know I'm about to do harm. But right now, being like you is more important to me than my wife is.' Say that, and then go ahead and rage if you have to."

Ernesto's head snaps up, and he looks at me. "That's not true. That would stop me in my tracks. She's not more impor-tant than my wife is." He falls silent, reaches out his hand, and places it palm up on Maddy's lap.

She takes his hand, and they gaze at each other. That was almost fourteen years ago. Ernesto has not raged since.

Neurobiologists tell us that it takes two things to unlock and open up a neural pathway. The first is that the implicit must be made explicit. Sometimes you need help seeing what you don't see. But you must be open to the feedback. Second, there must be some sort of recoil, a sense of discrepancy, of "Oh no, I'm not sure I really want to keep doing that."

In my interview with Ernesto, I helped make the implicit explicit by putting into words his replay of his stepmother's behavior. Ernesto supplied the recoil. After that he had, ac-cording to current research, about five hours to take in new learning and begin to forge a new neural pathway: "Oh my goodness, I will not replicate the awfulness I grew up in!"

In that moment of recoil, Ernesto awoke to *us*. This was the woman he loved he'd been yelling at. What had he been thinking? With my help, he shifted out of his left hemisphere into both hemispheres. He was led by the relationality of the right brain, but the practical wisdom of the left collaborated as well. With my help, he remembered the whole, the relationship of which he was a part. This is our optimal state in relationships.

Ernesto shifted from his Adaptive Child—the immature part of him that absorbed his stepmother's rage and discharged it—into his Wise Adult. He borrowed my prefrontal cortex until he woke up his own. Put most simply, he borrowed my brain. We do this for one another all the time. Current research clearly indicates that we are not walled-in, freestanding individuals. Our human brains—in fact, most mammals' brains—are built for co-regulation.

The Relational Brain

Interpersonal neurobiology is the study of how our brains and central nervous system form through our relationships in childhood and how relationships impact our neurobiology as intimate adults. What we're finding out is that the mind exists in a social context. Partners in close relationships co-regulate each other's nervous systems, cortisol (stress hormone) levels, and immune responsiveness. Secure relationships lead to increased immunity and less disease, to say nothing of lower scores in depression, anxiety, and higher reported general well-being. Insecure relationships stress you out and can make you ill.

Research has substantiated what most parents know intuitively, that the neurological development of infants and young children depends on loving, stimulating social interaction. From the first weeks of life, infants actively seek and elicit connection. Parents provide what one psychoanalyst called a "good enough holding environment" for the child. A toddler falls off his bike and looks to the expression on his caretaker's face to see how bad the scrape is. Parents routinely soothe children, lending them perspective—*this pain won't last forever*—and emotional modulation. According to the pioneer infant observational researcher Ed Tronick, "Child developmental researchers use the term *neuroarchitects* to describe caregivers of young infants. A baby's earliest relationships determine the nature of the wiring—they literally build the brain."

Every day in my office, I see what happens to people who didn't, as children, receive help modulating their emotions. Generally, they're cut off from their emotions. Without ancillary help from a grown-up's nervous system, they did—and still do—find emotions, theirs and often yours, overwhelming.

"I Relied on Myself."

Paul, white and forty-eight, crosses his ankle on top of his knee and drums his fingers absently on his horizontal leg. His wife, Cheryl, also Caucasian, fifty-five, has had it with him. He is too closed off, too unintimate. She needs more. And yet, Paul assures me, he came from a normal, happy childhood. No one screamed at him or hit him or bullied him, he tells me. I've heard this before, and at this early point in the session, it's difficult to ascertain whether Paul grew up in an unloving home or just a quiet one.

I ask, "So who did you turn to for comfort or reassurance when you were hurt or scared?"

"Why," he muses, "I don't recall turning to anyone. I relied on myself."

"From what age?"

"Pardon?"

"How young were you when you first learned to take care of it yourself?"

"I don't know," he says. "As long as I can remember."

"Right," I tell him. "You shut the door on feelings so long ago, you don't remember. But you didn't come out that way. Further back than your memory stretches, you did reach out to your parents once or twice for solace, and their response led you to conclude that depending on them, emotionally, was a bad idea."

Paul shifts in his chair, listening.

"With no one there to help modulate your feelings, you did a very smart thing as that little boy. You shut them down. Closed a door on them."

Paul is a type-one love avoidant, someone who, in today's psychological parlance, would be classed as having an avoid-ant dismissive attachment style. Paul lives behind walls because he grew up in a family where everyone lived behind walls, so what's the problem? Being emotionally shut down is normal to Paul. And if he lived alone, he'd be fine, but he isn't alone. He has a wife and a bunch of kids, all of whom need him. The problem for Paul is that we humans cannot be surgical with our feelings. If you open up to one feeling, they all come. Cheryl is knocking hard on Paul's door. But opening up his heart to her means reopening the door he firmly closed as a child. He is routinely subject to emotions, but he doesn't have the tools to identify them.

"You left your feelings," I tell him in a later session. "They never left you. They've been percolating the whole time. You just need help connecting to them again and naming them."

I have to teach Paul how to have emotions. He needs them to share with his wife. For some time, she's been feeling bored with their marriage, she confesses later in the session. Paul needs to share his emotional life with Cheryl, and he needs to become interested in Cheryl's emotional life as well. All this requires help because when little Paul fell from his bicycle, the adults looked away or stared at him without expression.

I tell Paul about passive abuse, emotional neglect. His issue is not that something is present (like sexual energy or rage) that shouldn't be; rather, it's that things that should be there aren't: guidance, comfort, sharing. More children are removed from homes because of neglect than because of violating abuse. If you want to see clearly what happens to infants and young children when connection is withheld, watch any of Dr. Ed Tronick's "still face" experiments on YouTube.

"Here's what you see," I tell Paul, recommending a Tronick video to him. "The taped vignette starts off great. You see Mother with a young child on her lap, one and a half, maybe two. The boy holds a toy brontosaurus, and the dinosaur feeds the mother, and the mother eats the imaginary food offered by the toy. Mother and child murmur together. Then suddenly the mother turns her head away and freezes. Nothing hostile, no cues to the child, just a completely blank still face. Two minutes. That's how long the whole thing lasts.

"It's an excruciating two minutes to sit through. At first the young boy runs through an increasingly desperate repertoire of eliciting behaviors. He coos and murmurs, holding the dinosaur up to the mother, trying to get the mother to eat again, to engage. When nothing works, the child moves into 'protest behavior.' He yells, screeches, arches his back. Finally, the little boy just decompensates. He starts rocking, he's crying, drool drips from his mouth as he rams the back of his head into his mother's body over and over again.

"Two minutes," I tell Paul. "And just how many minutes do you think you endured?"

Paul, as a child, missed out on synchronicity. When a caregiver repeatedly interacts with a child, it elicits a strong biological response, whether alleviating distress or causing pleasure. Connection floods the child with oxytocin and a cascade of the body's own endogenous opioids, securing the attachment. All that sounds great, but as Dr. Tronick repeatedly warns, real relationships are messy. Between caregiver and child courses an endless repetition of harmony, disharmony, and repair.

Furthermore, connection is hardly a one-way street. In one of Dr. Tronick's videos, a dysregulated infant arches its back and bawls. Frazzled, the mother gets frustrated and glares down at the baby in her arms. Instinctively the infant lifts its tiny forearms in front of its head to shield itself from mother's angry face. The whole sequence takes thirty-five seconds. Just as infants' nervous systems respond to their parents, children regulate their parents' nervous systems as well, as most aware parents could tell you. As the saying goes, you're only as happy as your least happy kid.

It's not just human parents and children who show such neural synchronicity. Many different species show it with other species members. If you inject a mouse's paw with an irritant, for example, the mouse will lick it as a way of alleviating some of its discomfort. The more potent the irritant, the more vigorous the licking. It's a simple transaction, right? It is, until you show the subject mouse a second mouse through plexiglass, also injected with an irritant in its paw. Invariably, the first mouse will synchronize its licking to that of the second mouse. If the second mouse licks less, the first mouse experiences less pain. If the second mouse is in a lot of distress, the first mouse will increase its licking. How much pain the first mouse is in is determined by how much pain she sees in her fellow creature.

Of note, this reaction works only if the two mice know each other. If they are not cage mates, all bets are off. Furthermore, the synchronistic licking is most predictable and most strongly mirrored if the two mice are a pair. It seems that *I feel your pain* is connected to *I feel you generally.* The closer the relationship, the stronger the mimicry. Could this be mouse empathy? Mouse love?

More and more literature has emerged on the interpersonal nature of our brains and nervous system. Are we individuals? Yes, in a way, but at the same time we are utterly interdependent, neurologically entwined. We are individuals, yes, but individuals whose lifeblood is connection. As the neurobiologist Dan Siegel puts it, "The brain is a social organ, and our relationships to one another are not a luxury but an essential nutrient for our survival." We are individuals whose very existence is predicated on belonging.

In the early 1950s, the psychiatrist René Spitz was asked to consult at a number of orphanages with unusually high death rates in the infants in their care. These babies were regularly fed, changed, swaddled, and burped. But Spitz found that the babies were never spoken to, jostled, or played with—in a word, they never emotionally synchronized with an adult. *Failure to thrive syndrome* was the official name for what happened. In plain English, these babies died from loneliness.

Our nervous systems were never designed to self-regulate. We all filter our sense of stability and well-being through our connection to others. And yet the culture of individualism saturates our society. The idea of a freestanding rugged individualist is a cultural story having little to do with the truth.

If you want to see what a person who is totally removed from relational interaction looks like, examine the brain of someone who endured prolonged solitary confinement in prison.

On June 19, 2012, Craig Haney, a professor of psychology at the University of California, Santa Cruz, told the Senate Judiciary Subcommittee on the Constitution, Civil Rights and Human Rights, "The conditions of confinement [for the eighty thousand U.S. inmates enduring often long periods of solitary imprisonment] are far too severe to serve any kind of penological purpose." They can precipitate for some prisoners a descent into madness. The *APA Monitor* went on to report:

> *Former inmate Anthony Graves, who spent 18 years on death row, including 10 in solitary confinement for a murder he didn't commit, drove home Hanley's points. "I would watch guys come to prison totally sane, and in three years they don't live in the real world anymore," he said. One fellow inmate, Graves said, "would go out into the recreation yard, get naked, lie down and urinate all over himself. He would take his feces and smear it all over his face."*

Behold a totally freestanding individual! Deprived of all social connection, we deteriorate, even unto madness.

All manner of new research is emerging that examines the borders between us, the ways one partner's emotional state, often inarticulate, even unconscious, will affect the other's. Of the many emerging descriptions of our social brain, for me the simplest and most elegant is the highly regarded Social Baseline Theory of Lane Beckes and James A. Coan, two researchers at the University of Virginia.

My understanding of Social Baseline Theory was foreshadowed years ago while I was on safari in the Serengeti Wildlife Preserve. My friend, the seasoned safari leader Rick Thomson, and I sneaked out at dawn to look for a potential kill. A tawny lioness was squatting low in the tall grass, all but hidden in the bush. A few yards beyond her stood potential breakfast, an insouciant warthog nuzzling the ground for a grub. As if in perfect unison, lion and warthog both looked up and then sprinted like mad, the lioness charging after the warthog. After an amazing burst lasting mere seconds, both animals—again in seeming unison—stopped dead in their tracks. The lion lay down and carelessly licked her paws. The saucy warthog swished his rump as if doing a little dance: *Ha, ha lion. Not your morning.*

I asked Rick about their synchronicity. What made both animals stop at the same exact second? "Conservation of energy," he explained. "It's the law of the land here. Exert as little as possible—preserve your energy—while still staying alive. That moment you watched," he explained, "was the line both lion and warthog passed through that told them further pursuit would be pointless—the lion would not catch up."

The term biologists use is *economy of action,* the calorie-saving principle that is rather ubiquitous in the animal kingdom. Food is not always so plentiful.

Our brains burn fuel—a fair amount, it turns out—and research shows us clearly that by far the largest energy draw in our brains is the prefrontal cortex, those higher-level functions that develop last in the brain and that emerged most recently in human evolution. The prefrontal cortex is a wise, highly adaptable, extraordinary calculating device made up of billions of neurons. It is the complex mainframe we need for thoughtful, deliberate, intentional action Wise Adult capacities. But it's energetically costly. Scientists have known for decades that the brain relegates more habitual jobs (like checking breathing and heart rate) to less thoughtful, more automatic, less energy-draining parts of the nervous system. But Beckes and Coan reviewed a vast array of studies and deduced that the energy-costly prefrontal cortex not only offloads, as it were, less demanding functions to other parts of our nervous system, it also does a fabulous job of conserving energy by offloading one person's brain functions onto other people's brains.

Previous research had shown how people seek others for co-regulation. Social Baseline Theory goes further, asserting that no matter the culture, "close proximity to social resources is the baseline assumption of the human brain." Our brains *assume* we are embedded in a familiar, rich, interdependent web in which a variety of what might have been individual neural tasks are spread out and appropriated by the group. Let's take an extraordinarily simple example. I tend the fire. You're on the lookout for attack.

Studies seem to indicate that multitasking is a yuppie invention. We don't, in fact, attend to two different tasks in the same instant, though we may tell ourselves we are. In fact, we switch our focus, toggling back and forth between the two tasks, doing neither as well as we might have done if we'd attended to each one singly.

So, back to the fire. If I am tending to the fire and watching out for a wild animal attack at the same time, my prefrontal cortex is working overtime. But if I tend to the fire and trust that my pal and cave mate, Ralph, will look after us both, my prefrontal cortex can relax and focus. And indeed, that was the finding that sparked Beckes and Coan's theory. Both men were researchers on neurological processes linked to self-regulation. They began their research assuming that when individuals enter a social space of interaction, their higher-functioning prefrontal cortex will fire up. There are a lot of subtle cues to read when we're with others. What they found instead, to their initial chagrin, was that our prefrontal cortices almost always slow down and grow quieter when we interact with others.

How could this be explained? New research showed how humans help regulate tough emotions like anger, fear, and pain in one another, but Beckes and Coan went further. Their revolutionary insight was that when people interact socially, it isn't so much that their prefrontal cortices work overtime to deal with negative feelings, or even that they supplement each other. It's that the emotional stress doesn't arise as much to begin with.

The emotional load sharing and efficiency of the "group mind" leaves each individual's prefrontal cortex with a lot less work to do than it would have on its own. Neither self-regulation, nor even human co-regulation, has as much reason to occur because the security of "group mind" (*I'll build a fire, while you look out for bears*) leaves us with less that needs to be regulated. Our brains assume a baseline of shared social competence. Here are the authors:

> *Social proximity can offset much of the costs associated with the [prefrontal cortex]. For example, individuals who have recently entered a romantic relationship may come to rely less on their own personal activity to regulate their behavior, because they will begin to perceive the environment as less threatening, dangerous, and difficult to cope with and because their partner will engage in behavior (e.g., supportive hand holding) that will help achieve regulatory effects without having to regulate themselves.*

And the more intimate the bond, the greater the relaxation. When someone is undergoing a difficult medical procedure, holding a stranger's hand increases their security and decreases their pain and anxiety. Holding a friend's hand is more potent, and holding a loved one's hand is the best analgesic of all. All this led Beckes and Coan, and many others since then, to question the wisdom of singling out the individual as the proper unit of study in human psychology. The labor-intensive processes of self-regulation seem rather muscular and inelegant in the light of the idea that social connection gives connected individuals less stress to need managing.

Those of us who are in long-term intimate relationships may instinctively understand this as a both/and situation. Yes, our rich social connections protect us from the savagery we would unleash on ourselves in, for example, solitary confinement. Yes, connection gives us a deep sense of ease. But we also know from experience that few things can trigger us or make us go crazy like our intimate relationships can. Love is like a Roto-Rooter—it will push every button you own; it will bring up to the surface every unhealed wound and fissure that has lodged inside your body. Nothing stimulates hurt quite the way love does. As we shall see, we all marry our unfinished business. And so, both negatively and positively, our neurologies intertwine.

The Wise Adult, the prefrontal cortex led by the right hemisphere of our brains, recognizes the whole and understands how interdependent we are. But when we are under stress—and for some of us, that is most of the time—the protective Adaptive Child muscles in and takes over. We shift to a left hemisphere orientation, which is singularly logical and instrumental (concerned with accomplishing the task at hand). And we lose the perspective of our prefrontal cortices, being led instead by our more emotional, more primitive limbic system. We no longer value the relational.

What really gets us into trouble is that the left-brain orientation of the Adaptive Child matches our society's culture of individualism. When we are "left shifted"—that is, led by our left hemisphere—logic and instrumentality reign. The task at hand is privileged over the relationships of the people performing the task. This is true both for the Adaptive Child in each of us and for society at large. Only recently has the corporate world awakened to a new kind of leadership, relational as opposed to hierarchical.

Summit, a young IT freelancer, was having a tough time with his business despite being enormously smart and talented. What particularly galled him was that he routinely gave on jobs more than what was asked of him, yet he'd lose bids or not be asked back. As we spoke together about his work, a pattern emerged. Summit began to realize what he thought of as his strength was, in fact, his great weakness. Burning the midnight oil, he would deliver a software program that was appreciably more elegant, complex, and multifaceted than what he'd been asked for. Instead of a Ford, he'd deliver a Lamborghini, but the Lamborghini was unwanted. So instead of his anticipated praise, Summit routinely heard, "Couldn't you make it simpler?" His left hemisphere led him to choose the thing over the people who would be using it. His Adaptive Child designed a near-perfect product without the guidance of his Wise Adult, which would have listened to his client's needs instead of his own.

Because I see mostly extreme cases, almost everyone I've met has lived much of their lives using the Adaptive Child parts of the brain. They think they're Wise Adults, but they're not. The world has mostly rewarded them handsomely. Because the Adaptive Child reflects the cultural values at large, people who primarily live from their Adaptive Child parts are generally great successes in the world financially and professionally. Meanwhile they make a hash of their personal lives.

A central tenet of individualism is that the self is distinct from nature—or to be precise, man is *above* nature. In the beginning, according to Genesis, God gave Adam *dominion* over everything that walked or swam or crept upon the earth (1:26–28). That was a bad idea. The ancient Greeks had more humility. For them, holding oneself above nature was hubris, overweening pride, and the source of every tragic hero's fall. Yet dominion—the deluded obligation and entitlement to control—is a central pillar of traditional masculinity and of patriarchal culture. Most of us don't spend much time taming the elements these days, but you may be applying the concept of dominion to your wife, your kids, your own body, a colleague at work, or the world at large.

This delusion of control will be the focus of any hospital-based stress management program you may wind up in after you have a heart attack. It is corrected by AA's twelve steps, the core tenet expressed in its Serenity Prayer. Our individualistic, linear, Newtonian worldview features man as above nature and capable of manipulating it, bending it to his will, the way a surgeon works medically on a body or a mechanic bends over a car. We are made in the image of God, the Great Watchmaker, as one Enlightenment trope had it. We live above the system and work upon it.

If managing the world is a central component of traditional masculinity, managing the manager is a central component of the traditional feminine role—"managing up," as is said. But as anyone who has worked with issues of so-called codependency knows, accommodation, while overtly self-denying, is in fact, also a form of control—trying to "not set him off." I define codependent behavior as occurring when you back away from perfectly reasonable behavior—like telling the truth—for fear of your partner's unreasonable response. Both traditional masculinity's manipulation of nature and traditional femininity's manipulation of men are attempts at control—as if one could assert one's will upon others or upon the world directly.

Relational consciousness, by contrast, is synonymous with ecological consciousness. It corrects the delusion of dominion and replaces it with the knowledge that we are not outside and above nature but rather live within it as parts. This is ecological humility. The only thing in nature that we can directly control is ourselves, and that's on a good day. I see the shift from hubris to humility as being on a par with placing the sun instead of Earth at the solar system's center.

As we as a species move from a nature-dominating model to a nature-cherishing one, we will realize that the water we keep pumping plastic into is the water we drink, and that the air we pollute is the air we breathe. If we survive at all. COVID-19 is our first experience of nature turning against us on a planetary scale. Will it serve as a wake-up call? I doubt it. This global outbreak will be followed by others. Today we wear face masks. Perhaps tomorrow it will be gas masks. Our actions are so self-destructive, they are borderline suicidal. Yet we persist.

As above, so below. The same drama of dominance that is now being played out with our planet erupts in our personal lives. We position ourselves as apart and above in many relationships. We attempt to control our partners, our kids, our bodies, and even the way we think ("I will not be so negative"). Take a step back, and you'll see that running your relationships from a place of power and control is lunacy. Even with that awareness, the minute the emotional temperature begins to rise, more reactive parts of the brain take over, and that is precisely the model we revert to: "I'm right, and you're wrong. You win, and I lose. I can let you in, or I can protect myself."

Collectively and personally, we stand in desperate need of a new paradigm. The relational answer to the question "Who's right and who's wrong?" is "Who cares?" The real question is "How are we as a team going to approach the issue at hand in a way that works for both of us?" The shift from individualistic to relational thinking may at first seem like pie-in-the-sky idealism, but I see its transformative potential day by day in my office.

Let me give a perfectly ordinary example.

Stan: You Can Be Right or Be Married

"He won't listen!" cries Lucy, who is white and in her mid-thirties. She flings open her arms as she sits on the edge of the couch, as if to implore me.

"I don't get her," says Stan, also white, and forty-three. He is sinking his face into his hands, beleaguered, exhausted, as if to say, "No matter what I do . . ."

And then there's me, watching, listening. Lucy and Stan's marriage is on the edge of dissolution—and over what? A misapprehension.

This past weekend was a disaster. "It was supposed to be a restorative time alone together in our house on the Cape," Lucy tells me. "We were both looking forward to it. We needed it." She looks down at her hands. "We almost didn't even make it there. I almost turned my car around and drove home."

So what happened?

"It's so trivial you could laugh," she says. "But nevertheless . . ."

Nevertheless, I think—that good old, familiar *nevertheless*. So trivial one could laugh, but nevertheless . . . worth falling on your sword over. Domestic life plays out on a small stage full of gigantic emotions.

"So what happened?"

"This whole thing is ridiculous," Stan declares, one leg pumping, impatient, annoyed.

"We took two cars," Lucy cuts him off, taking charge. "Both were loaded with groceries. So I couldn't see out the back. Already I'm nervous. I don't like driving at night. I ask Stan to stay by me, in case I—I don't know, I get lost, take a wrong turn, whatever."

"She wanted me to keep an eye on her," Stan tells me, to hurry the story along. "Which I did."

"Which you didn't," says Lucy.

"Which is *exactly* what I did. Look." Stan turns to me, the arbiter. "I was winding my way through the traffic—"

"Another issue," Lucy cuts in.

"Let's stay focused," I tell her.

"I'm about two cars ahead of her—"

"But I can't see him," Lucy interjects.

"I've got her square in my rearview mirror." Stan's expression is harried.

I'm already sensing where this is going.

"She calls me, panicked, out of her mind. 'You said you wouldn't leave me!' Already, she's like screaming at me."

"Oh, Stan," from Lucy, as if dismissing a child.

"Honey, I'm sorry you were out of it, you said—"

"But you left me! After you said—"

"You were right behind me. I told you the goddamn make of the car in front of you. I was there, honey. There was no need—"

"Why couldn't you just drop back so—"

"Okay," I interrupt, "I think I've got it."

Stan and Lucy are caught in a typical who's-right-who's-wrong battle, hinging on their slightly different definitions of what it means to "be there" for Lucy. And they are both right in saying the argument is trivial—but then there's that pesky *nevertheless*. *Nevertheless* can screw up a marriage. *Nevertheless* can lead to divorce.

To Lucy, "being there" means being right by her side. For Stan, it means keeping an eye on her. Who is objectively right? Well, to be fair, that's a trick question.

I ask the couples I work with to swallow a few important bitter pills. Here's the first: *There is no place for objective reality in personal relationships.* Objective reality is great for getting trains to run on time or for developing an important vaccine, but for ferreting out which point of view is "valid" in an interpersonal transaction, it is a loser. It leads to objectivity battles. Is Lucy overreacting, or is Stan neglecting her? These circular arguments go on forever, like a dog chasing its own tail; there's no way out because the assumption of objective facts is wrong to begin with.

In intimate relationships, it's never a matter of two people landing on the one true reality, but rather of negotiating differing subjective realities. Between the two, I side with Lucy— a difference between Relational Life Therapy and other therapies. We take sides. Stan is factually correct but relationally incorrect. Did Stan, as promised, look after Lucy to make sure she was all right? Yes, absolutely. And if he had been the one to make the request, he would have been fine. But Stan isn't married to Stan. Lucy wanted the comfort of Stan by her side, in sight of her. It wasn't his aid she was after, but the reassurance of his company. In this instance—as in so many others just like it, Lucy assures me—Stan didn't "get it." He missed the point because he wasn't thinking relationally. Like so many of the men I treat, Stan was being *instrumental.* His focus was on the task at hand, not on the subjective feelings of his partner. He was looking after her; he was not attending to her emotional needs.

The noted linguist Deborah Tannen addressed this point in her 1990 book *You Just Don't Understand,* in which she wrote of men's "report talk" versus women's "rapport talk." "Objectively" Stan was 100 percent right. At the same time, however, he was 100 percent tin-eared when it came to his wife's subjective experience. Worse, every time Lucy tried to tell him what bothered her, every time she tried to bridge the gap between them, Stan only retreated more staunchly into his precious rightness.

"Let me explain," I try helping Stan out. "Let's see if you can't change your reference point. When Lucy speaks, you, Stan, have two orientations, two reference points that you use as touchstones. The first is objective reality. Did you or did you not look after her as she wished? Is she or is she not valid in her assessment? To which I say, my friend, 'Good luck!' Was she, or wasn't she; did she, or didn't she—I'm sorry Stan.

I'm afraid no one cares. What you're doing is applying the scientific method to your relationship. It doesn't work.

"And your second point of reference, judging by the look on your face, has been, well . . . you. You tell yourself, 'Oh my god. Do I really need to listen to this?' "

Stan stirs on the couch, but he's not balking.

I go on. "What I want you to do is change your reference. Just try it. It's not about accuracy, I'm sorry to tell you, and it's certainly not about you or how put out you are by the whole thing. Stan, it's about Lucy, her feelings, her reality—her subjective experience. In this moment, right now, ask yourself, would you rather make the case that you're right, or would you rather make peace with your wife and help her feel better?"

"Meaning?" he says, tentative but listening.

"Here's the ten-thousand-dollar line, Stan. Ready?"

He nods.

I turn to Lucy, role-playing Stan. The first thing I do is soften my expression, my voice. "Honey," I say gently, "I'm sorry you felt bad. I didn't mean to make you feel that way. Is there anything I can say or do right now that would help you feel better?" Then I turn to Stan. " 'I'm sorry you feel bad,' " I repeat. " 'Is there anything I can say to help you feel better?' Stamp that on your forehead," I tell him. "Put it on your mirror when you shave in the morning."

Stan says nothing, sitting quietly, thinking it over.

Next to him, Lucy cries.

"If those tears could speak," I say, turning toward her, "what would they be saying?"

"It's just . . . ," she begins but falters. "It's just . . ." It doesn't matter if she's momentarily inarticulate; I know why she's crying. She dragged her husband to three therapists before me, and not one of them had taken him on. She's crying from relief.

Even though he is on the brink of divorce, Stan isn't a bad guy. What he argued so vehemently for, the point he got so defensive about, was, in fact, right—in the linear, individualistic, Newtonian world we all live in. But to be emotionally present to his wife, all he needs to do is trade in his usual worldview for a completely different paradigm. Listen, clients drag their partners in to see me not because they want better communication—although that's what many initially say—or to improve a few behavioral transactions. Women like Lucy bring in men like Stan so I can teach them how to be more relational.

What Lucy wants is nothing less than a whole different Stan. Most couples therapists back away from such bold aspirations, but in Relational Life Therapy we embrace it. "I'm in the personality transplant business," I tell Lucy, then turn to Stan. "Wanna try it?"

"Like?" Stan looks alarmed.

I smile. "Turn to your wife right now, and tell her something from the heart," I coach him, and bless him if, with a bit of encouragement, he doesn't comply.

"Lucy," he takes her hand. "I'm sorry, okay? I'm sorry you felt so abandoned that day."

"And you're sorry you didn't hear her," I add.

"I am," Stan says. "Really. No BS. I wish I could have listened better." He looks at his wife's tearful face.

"Wanna hug from the guy?" I ask her, and she lurches forward, reaching for him. "Take your time," I tell them, as Stan rocks her gently. "Take all the time you need."

Stan's well-meaning but misguided loyalty to "sorting things out," that is, to determining the one right reality about it (which was, of course, his), deprived them both of moments like the one they are having now in my office: moments of repair. Virtually all the couples I see in extremis, like Stan and Lucy, lack a mechanism of correction. They feel it important not to sweep things under the rug; rather, they are committed to trying to resolve things. The problem is that their model of resolution is to come to agreement—to figure out the one correct answer, to be on the same page together. It's a common, deep, and understandable wish. Unfortunately, for most partners, the one right version of the story is, well, mine—and my stubborn partner thinks the same of theirs. The paradox is that resolution comes only by giving up that dream and taking in that you and your partner are not, in fact, going to see all things the same way.

And you needn't. You can have different realities, which in turn may kick out a different set of emotions for each of you. When Stan stopped defending himself and instead tended to his wife's bruised feelings, she felt heard, the chasm between them was bridged, and everyone could breathe again. That moment brings up an important point. Relationality doesn't mean that you're both seeing with the same eyes, thinking the same thoughts, and feeling the same emotions; Relationality is not some boundaryless form of fusion. Quite the opposite — relationality demands an *I*. But it's an *I* embedded in a larger context. By recognizing that Lucy might have a legitimate vision of reality that differs from his, I am actually inviting Stan to be more differentiated from her, not less, but differentiated within that larger whole called his marriage.

What I'd like us to appreciate is that shifting from an individualistic, linear world to a relational one can be nothing short of transformative. As clients learn to think and act relationally, their character, their level of emotional development, evolves, often dramatically. They come to live for the most part in their Wise Adult self, led by the right hemisphere and governed by the prefrontal cortex. As we learn to think and act relationally, simply put, we grow up.

Steve: "Did I Get It, Doc?"

Steve, tall, Black, in his early forties, describes himself to me early on in our work as a type "triple A" personality. One A isn't good enough for him, he informs me. And indeed, he does seem to be one of those captains of the universe with the world in his palm. Handsome, smart, and athletic, he went to all the right schools, has a killer job in finance, is already rich by most people's standards, and in his early forties, is on his way to more.

He also has eight-year-old fraternal twins with fragile X syndrome, both severely developmentally delayed. These are big-hearted adorable kids, and everyone loves them to pieces—everyone except Steve. Embarrassed and stubborn, he confesses to me in one session that, while he'd never say it to anyone other than his therapist, his real relationship to these kids is that he hates them. They are a blot on his perfect résumé, a hostile visitation from God. Why does he deserve . . . ?

Hearing all this, it occurs to me that Steve and I might do well to work on his capacity for empathy. And we do. For weeks, I coach Steve to practice what I somewhat facetiously call *remedial empathy*.

"Before you open your mouth," I tell him, "I want you to stop and think. Ask yourself: 'What is the thing I'm about to say going to feel like to the person I'm speaking to?'"

About three weeks into this exercise, Steve bounces into my office all smiles. "Doc, the empathy thing"—he flashes a thumbs-up—"nailed it."

"Okay," I say. "There's a story here. Tell me."

"Last Saturday I took one of the boys to a baseball game. Now, I don't know about you, but when I take my kid to Fenway Park, I regale him with all the ice cream and hot dogs and candy he can cram in. It's a blast."

Having two sons of my own, I know the drill well and tell him so.

"Well, on the way home," Steve continues, "the little guy gets carsick." He turns to me, his voice urgent. "He had his hand up to his mouth, and Terry, goddamn it, he was holding in his own vomit because he was scared of me." Tears slick Steve's eyes. "I looked at my son, at the fear in his eyes. And I was appalled. I was appalled at *myself*, and I said, 'Honey, be sick, for god's sake, don't worry about the goddamned car, just—'" Steve straightens. "And I realized all at once. It's not about me. It's not about the damn car. It's *him*; it's about *him!*" He smiles, shaken, moved. "Got it?" he asks.

"Got it," I tell him.

What I'm telling you is that, as a therapist of thirty-plus years, I firmly believe Steve climbed up the developmental ladder that afternoon driving home from Fenway Park. By learning to think relationally, he became a different—and a better—man. Disconnection sickens us, while reconnection restores us.

Learning to think relationally means living each day with the realization that your relationship is your emotional biosphere, It's the environment we live in and depend upon. Sure, you can choose to pollute your biosphere over *here* with a flare-up of temper. But you'll breathe in that pollution over *there* in the form of your partner's withdrawal. I speak to clients not about altruism but rather about enlightened self-interest.

"It's in your interest," I tell them, "to keep your partner happy. You love them, for one thing. But closer in than that, you have to live with them, remember? Happy spouse, happy house."

You are connected, you and your partner; there is no escape. And delusions of being unaffected, above it all, are not merely insensitive but sometimes downright dangerous. The people we know and love are literally inside us. They watch for bears while I tend the fire, they set the table while I round up the kids. The people we know and love trigger the deepest wounds and insecurities in us, and at the same time they provide the greatest comfort and solace. Thinking of ourselves as individuals who are apart from or above all this is a delusion. And believing in that delusion can breed disastrous consequences. For good and ill, in how we are treated and how we treat others, in the very structures of our brains, we do not stand alone.

3

How *Us* Gets Lost
and *You and Me* Takes Over

When we get trauma-triggered in our close relationships, our Wise Adult shuts off, and we are seized by our Adaptive Child. We feel "taken over" and we want to push back. When people first learn about this Adaptive Child part of them, usually their initial instinct is to want to control it, to see it as bad.

"I hate the way I flame out at the kids!" Daniel, Asian and in his late twenties, tells me in an early session. "I keep a tight lid on it ninety percent of the time, but periodically it builds to the point where"—he puffs out his cheeks—"I just blow." The Adaptive Child is not some toxic force you must banish or destroy. It is a young part of you that learned to cope the best way she could at the time. What she needs is to be parented, and the only person who can reliably do that at this point is you. There's a spiritual principle at work here: to move beyond some part of you, you must first get to know it and ultimately befriend it.

When I first encounter someone's Adaptive Child, their particular version of *you and me* consciousness, I try to understand its origins. Daniel's Adaptive Child throws tantrums. Yes, he yells at his kids and his husband. But more than that, he's hurled plates, hit the wall, and broken a chair into pieces. Fury is Daniel's dysfunctional stance—his way of featuring himself in the world, the position he takes.

As I listen closely to his story, my articulation of his stance becomes more precise. He sees himself, in triggered moments, as an aggrieved party. He is a professional angry victim. The idiot at the checkout line, with his lackadaisical tempo, made him late. The moron who picked him up at the airport kept him waiting for fifteen minutes and barely spoke English. The lid on the mayonnaise jar thwarted him by not unscrewing. Daniel moves through an adversarial world out to get him. But man, he goes down swinging.

An avenging angel, Daniel has a Ph.D. in what one of my most important mentors, the great trauma and recovery pioneer Pia Mellody, called *offending from the victim position*. When we offend from the victim position, we feel like a victim while acting like an offender. "You hurt me, so I get to hurt you back twice as much. And I have no shame or compunction about what I'm dishing out because you victimized me." And so the chain goes. Each generation acts out of its wounds, parents passing down a version of their own hurt to their offspring. We can do better than this. But we must liberate ourselves from our reactive brain, our *you and me* consciousness, our Adaptive Children, the filter that shades so much of our world.

———

Take a moment to see if you can articulate *your* dysfunctional stance. Unless you're perfect, you probably have one. Of course, I assume that 364 days out of the year, you operate in your Wise Adult self, your prefrontal cortex. But on that one little day when you're off, just where would you tend to go? Your dysfunctional relational stance is what your Adaptive Child keeps repeating, unconstructively, in relationships — pursuing, withdrawing, pleasing, complaining, controlling.

If you are having difficulty articulating your particular relational stance, that shouldn't be a problem. Just ask for help from your partner! I'm pretty certain they'll be willing to lend a hand with this one. A dysfunctional stance will never get you what you want. Angry pursuit, for example, is a dysfunctional stance. You will rarely get closer to your partner by getting mad about how distant they are. Angry pursuit is an oxymoron. As I tell pursuing clients, "I have bad news for you. Angry pursuit is not seductive."

You can come up with dozens of dysfunctional stances if you just take a moment. Martyr is one, tyrant another, victim yet another. Once you have identified your particular stance, try describing it more precisely. Ask, "What kind of victim am I? Helpless? Furious? What kind of tyrant?" And so on.

Once a Relational Life therapist gets each partner's dysfunctional stance, the next question is, "Where did it come from?" Ask about yourself and your partner, what was that little boy or girl adapting to? After you have a fair idea what your repeated dysfunctional stance looks like, here are three questions to ask yourself:

- *Who did you see do this?*
- *Who did it to you?*
- *Who did you do it to and no one stopped you?*

That last question is often critical. Not one person in Daniel's family raged—except Daniel. He has been having temper tantrums as far back as he can remember.

"And how did your parents respond?"

He shrugs. "They didn't. They usually gave me what I wanted."

"Which is why you're still having tantrums at forty-three," I remark.

Someone once told me that kids are like gas; they will go to the perimeter of whatever contains them. When Daniel was young, he had no container, so he repeatedly spilled out into his environment. He was still doing it when we first met. No one on the street would tell you that Daniel's Adaptive Child was forged through trauma, but I would. That's because I likely have a more varied description of what constitutes trauma than the one you think of. Daniel, for example, was subject to *falsely empowering psychological neglect.*

You may recall that earlier I asked skeptical readers to wait until after a discussion on the nature of trauma to decide whether they'd been subject to any. Well, here is that promised discussion.

Relational Trauma

When we think of trauma, we tend to think of what the trauma recovery field often calls Big Trauma, capital T—circumscribed catastrophic events that endanger life and limb. A tsunami, a hurricane, combat. In Relational Life Therapy, we're sensitive to and work with Big Trauma, but we're just as much tuned into "little trauma" or relational trauma. Not the one time you pulled Mom off the ledge of her fourteenth-floor balcony, but the hundred thousand times she told you that you were too much of a burden for her to bear. Psychotherapists rarely encounter a one-time catastrophic event, like one incident of incest. Rather, it's most often smaller, but no less corrosive, transactions happening dozens of times a day—every day of your childhood.

Joey and Linda: No One to Tell

"It's like when Joey gets aggressive, I just—I just want to go away," Linda tells me.

We're sitting together, the three of us, in a one-session-only demonstration interview in front of a room filled with therapists. Linda has described herself to the group as Native American, Cherokee nation. She is thirty-three.

"Aggressive? What does that mean? What does he look like?"

"All Joey wants to do is talk about it," she goes on, ignoring my question. "But I'm like, 'Leave me alone!' I lock myself in the bedroom, and he's pounding away, yelling. But I am *gone*."

"You're behind a wall," I say.

"Big wall," she agrees.

"Like, 'You can pack your bags, get out, get hit by a car in the street. I don't give a good goddamn what you do!' Did I get it?"

"That's right."

"That's a pretty hefty wall you got there."

"Yes, it is," she says. Her back straight, her hands in her lap, she is looking at her husband, Joey, a big man with a large Afro squished down by a leather cap.

After a moment I ask her, "So how does it end? When does the wall come down?"

"When do we make up?"

"Yes."

"Well. When Joey softens up, when his tone changes, and his body language gets more gentle, then . . ."

I turn to Joey, who's Black and younger than his wife at twenty-seven. He affirms Linda's story. Yes, when he gets aggressive, she pulls away. But the thing she leaves out, according to Joey, is that often he gets aggressive *because* she's already pulled away.

"But what Linda says does work?" I ask, keeping him on track. "When you gentle up and soften up, she comes out from behind her wall?"

"Yes, that does work," he says. "When it works, it works."

"And how long until . . . ?"

"Couple, three days," he shares, as if that were normal.

We fall silent a long minute or so.

"I don't know, Joey," I say at last, "but I imagine—what I make up, as we say—is that on the other side of Linda's wall, there's a little boy inside you, and he feels quite alone and abandoned and overwhelmed."

Joey nods vigorously. "Bingo."

"Bingo," I say to his averted face. "Tell me—"

And then out of nowhere, he opens up about something he rarely thinks of, let alone speaks about. "You see," he interrupts me, "I was abused as a child."

"You mean—"

"Sexually." He looks down between his feet. "By my aunt."

"You were—"

"Seven," he says. "No one knew. I didn't tell nobody." And this big man begins to cry. He balls his hands into fists and cries into them.

"I'm sorry," I tell Joey. "I'm so sorry." After a time, I add, "So that little boy outside Linda's door . . ."

"It's like," Joey tells me, still tearful, "it's like no one's there. There's no one home, no one to tell, like no one cares about *my* story."

Listen to the way Joey describes his feelings when Linda shuts him out: "Like there's no one to tell, like no one cares about my story." His inner child feels the aloneness that that boy of seven must have felt in his family; if he hadn't felt so alone, he would have told someone about his aunt. And indeed, Joey later describes his mother as a prescription drug addict while his father was out with a succession of girlfriends. A therapist might, quite legitimately, focus on the one incident of sexual abuse—and that did need to be tended to. But what caught my interest was the aloneness of that little boy. His aunt abused him once; his parents abandoned him 365 days a year. This is *relational trauma*. Trauma meted out every day of your childhood. Notice that in his relationship with Linda, it isn't Joey's feelings of being used or suffocated—feelings he'd associate with his aunt's incest—that get activated. It's his far more damaging feelings of abandonment.

Relational trauma wounds.

And it wounds deeply and early in one's development. When Joey stood outside Linda's door, he was that seven-year-old again. He didn't recall his emotion; he became it.

Abandonment is a child ego state. "Adults don't get abandoned," I tell Joey. "Adults get left, or even, if you want, rejected. But they survive. Abandoned means, 'If you leave me, I die.' Children get abandoned. When you feel that petrified, desperate feeling, you are no longer in your adult self. You are in a child ego state."

Joey wants Linda to care for that hurt, angry seven-year-old. We all want that. We all want our partners to reach in and heal the young wounded parts of us with their love. And they always, to some degree, fail us. Because they are human and therefore imperfect. Because, on the day you most need them, they have a toothache and can't be bothered. Because in that perfect moment when you throb with desire, they ate and drank too much and just want to go to sleep. The tough news here is that the only person who can with absolute consistency be there for our inner children is us. And that's okay. That's enough. Once we learn how to do it.

By the end of our session, Joey, with my help, has met and conversed with that little boy living inside. He cries at not having been able to protect him at the time, and the little boy forgives him. He pledges to care for that vulnerable part of him from now on. "You don't ever have to be alone again," he says to the boy. And then this big, tough man, with eyes closed, scoops his young self onto his lap, puts his arms around him, and grieves. "Got ya," he murmurs through his tears. "I got ya."

Maturity comes when we tend to our inner children and don't inflict them on our partners to care for.

The Trauma Grid: *Four Types of Injury*

Joey's sexual abuse is what we normally think of as trauma — physical and emotional violation. But that is only one of four types of psychological trauma, and each type causes its own predictable damage and tends toward its own particular adaptation.

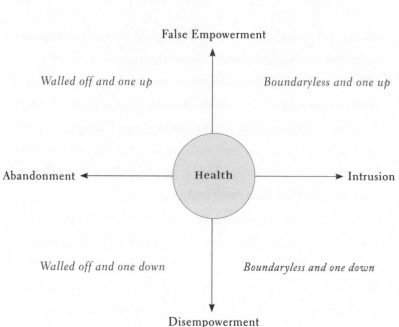

The Trauma Grid should be viewed as a cross. The vertical line represents self-esteem, from too high to too low, and the horizontal line represents boundaries, moving from too-strong boundaries on the left to nonexistent boundaries on the right. More on that in a moment.

The kind of trauma that little Joey suffered at his aunt's hands was the kind we all think of as abusive: boundary-violating intrusive behavior. That happens a fair amount, unfortunately, in harsh families. But you can also get hurt by the opposite of intrusion: by being left alone. As wounded as Joey was by his aunt, it was the day-in-day-out trauma of his every-day neglect that triggered Joey's aggression: "Like no one's home. Like no one cares about my story." In Joey's intimate relationship, abandonment trumped intrusion.

Here's how to tell if you were in an abandoning family. It's a little drill you can use. Good parenting consists of nurture, guidance, and limits, so ask yourself a few questions.

- *Were you intellectually nourished?*
- *Were there family discussions at the dinner table?*
- *Did you read with anyone?*
- *Were you physically nourished? Hugs? Cuddles? Did someone cook your favorite dish just because you like it?*
- *Were you sexually nurtured, meaning did your parents give you guidance? Limits? Was your budding adulthood enjoyed, even celebrated?*

And now the big set of questions in the emotional domain.

- *Did your family nurture your emotional life?*
- *Did they have one themselves?*
- *Could you turn to someone in a state of emotional vulnerability?*
- *Did a parent teach you about feelings—how to express them and how not to? Or were you on your own?*

Many people with this kind of passive trauma, or neglect, think they had swell childhoods, but then why are they having such a hard time expressing their feelings?

So, two points. One, relational trauma that's repeated or ongoing may be as damaging as circumscribed catastrophic trauma. It's like water on a rock. Two, passive trauma can do at least as much damage as intrusive violation.

If you look at the horizontal line on the Trauma Grid, you see that trauma can be intrusive, boundaryless, or it can be abandoning, walled off. If you look at the vertical line, you see the spectrum of power. Health is in the center. Healthy transactions leave the child feeling neither superior nor inferior to anyone else. That's healthy self-esteem. When we think of trauma in childhood, we mostly think of shaming transactions, of words or behaviors that leave the child feeling less than, impotent, and helpless. This *disempowering abuse* leaves those who experience it in a shame-based position their entire lives unless they do the work of transformation.

On the other hand, if you elevate your child into a state of superiority, we say you are *falsely empowering* them. If disempowering actions lead to later issues of shame, false empowerment leads to issues of grandiosity. How can you falsely empower a child? Make her the family hero, the star performer, or confide to her your complaints about your spouse. I ask clients, "What are the nine most harmful words in the English language?" The answer: *Honey, you understand me more than your father does.*

When a parent elevates a child and at the same time uses them, we call that *enmeshment*. The energy goes from the child into the parent, instead of the other way around, as should be the case. The child becomes the parent's caretaker, leaving her feeling both special and drained. Incest is the most extreme example: "You're so beautiful, I couldn't resist you." Icky, right? That icky feeling comes from the combination of sexual intrusion coupled with false empowerment: "You're so special I had to molest you."

You don't need to actively elevate a child in order to groom them for grandiosity. A child can be falsely empowered through neglect, as happens when kids are parented by gangs of peers in lieu of appropriate adults to guide them. Children need limits. Children's natural grandiose, selfish tendencies need to be ameliorated by an adult.

When my oldest son Justin was only four or five, he invited a school chum to our house for one of his very first playdates. Coming from Boston, land of the Bruins, my son started the playdate by asking the kid, "Hey, do you wanna play hockey? How 'bout some hockey? Wanna grab a stick? Go out in the street? Slap a puck around?" After his classmate left, young Justin bounded up to me, asking, "Do you think he had a good time?"

I looked into the upturned face of my child, took a breath, and told him no.

Justin was stunned.

"Listen, honey," I remember telling him. "If you want to do exactly what you want to do, be alone. The minute you let somebody into your world, you have to at least pay some attention to what they want to do."

And my darling boy looked up at me and said simply, "Too much hockey?"

Now fast-forward twenty years, and I'm sitting with my forty-year-old client, Chris, and his wife, Linda. Their marriage is on the brink. Chris took Linda to the Caribbean for four days for some much-needed R&R. According to Linda, the four days went like this: "Hey, do you wanna have sex? Wanna get physically close? How 'bout some intimacy?"

Did she have a good time? She says, "No."

And Chris, bless him, is stunned.

What do I, as his therapist, do with Chris? Easy. I tell him the Justin story. "There's a name for what I was doing with Justin that day," I tell Chris. "It's called parenting. It's what you deserved and did not get. That's neglect, Chris. Emotional neglect. Now you have to drag yourself to Boston and pay me a ton to download into you a sensitivity chip that should have been installed when you were three, four, five years old. I'm really sorry."

Some injurious transactions are clear examples of disempowerment (*You little shit!*) while others are clear examples of false empowerment (*You're the only good thing in my life!*). But most relational trauma empowers and disempowers at the same time.

Earl, a tightly wrapped gay man in his late twenties, had a temper, just like his old man before him. Earl's father often screamed at him and demeaned him as a child. The father's behavior disempowered young Earl, made him feel small and worthless. But Earl's father was simultaneously sending another message: "When you grow up and get angry, this is what an angry man looks like." Earl's father falsely empowered his son by modeling grandiose thinking and behavior.

So, now we have moved from thinking about one form of trauma to four. Trauma might be:

- *Intrusive and disempowering, e.g., being sworn at or beaten*
- *Intrusive and falsely empowering, e.g., incest, emotional caretaking (regulating a parent)*
- *Abandoning and disempowering, e.g., "you're unworthy," scapegoating*
- *Abandoning and falsely empowering, e.g., "you don't need us," hero*

Are you still thinking you dodged all trauma in your perfect family? Perhaps you did. Throughout every epoch, there have been loving families. Perhaps yours is an open, communicative family that shares vulnerabilities and emotions, rarely speaks or behaves disrespectfully, and apologizes in short order. Perhaps it is a family where issues are hashed out and, at the end of the day, parents hold compassionate hierarchical power. A family where repair is in good evidence, and everyone is welcome. Maybe you came from such a mature, emotionally intelligent family. If you did, count yourself lucky, because our society does not produce many such skilled family groups.

As Leo Tolstoy wrote, "All happy families are alike; each unhappy family is unhappy in its own way." The particularities of your parents' limitations and dysfunctions became the imperfect "holding environment" you adjusted to. That adjustment, that adaptation, becomes your particular version of *you and me* consciousness, the imprint on your limbic system of your unique Adaptive Child.

Your Adaptive Child almost always represents an amalgam, a mixture of the ways you reacted to the intrusion or neglect that came your way. It's typical to resist intrusion or neglect while simultaneously internalizing it: you take in the dysfunctional ways you and the world were seen. Those two forces—*reaction* and *modeling*—combine to forge your Adaptive Child.

Reaction

As the saying goes, in psychology no less than in physics, every action causes an equal and opposite reaction. Show me the thumbprint, and I'll tell you about the thumb. Tom's mom was intrusive. She disrespected his boundaries, his privacy, even the sanctity of his diary. Tom is now love avoidant. He lives behind walls. Janie's mom was abandoning. A tough single mom, she worked long hours and came home too tired to care much, leaving her daughter to her own emotional resources. Janie now clings to her new boyfriend like a life raft.

If you look again at the Trauma Grid, I want you to notice something:

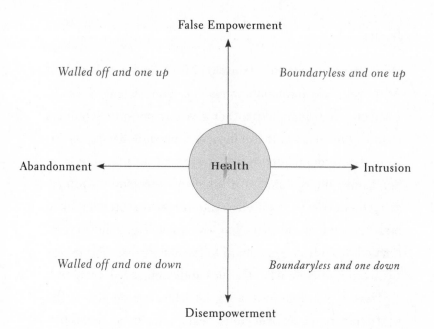

Notice the way each form of trauma tends to evoke an op-posite reaction from the Adaptive Child. Tom had an intru-sive (boundaryless) mother, and now Tom self-protects with thick walls. He isn't intrusive with his partner and kids; he's the opposite—abandoning. Similarly, Janie had abandoning (walled-off) parents, and she is now a needy, anxious young woman most likely to be not neglectful but its opposite: intru-sive and suffocating. *In reaction mode, our Adaptive Children tend to do the opposite of what we ourselves experienced.* Intru-sion breeds walls. Abandonment breeds intrusion. This is our resistance. It's that aspect of our Adaptive Child that is defiant and will not take in what was handed to us.

But reaction is only half the picture.

Modeling

While reaction to trauma tends to resist it, the second mode of Adaptive Child formation, *modeling*, tends to internalize it. Everyone does both. Whenever a young person encounters trauma, they react to it and they also repeat it. Modeling has elements of identifying with the aggressor. In modeling, you don't resist the dysfunctional mores of your family—you re-enact them. You see yourself as you were seen; you internalize bad behavior as normal. Thus shameless grandiosity gets handed down from generation to generation—until one person in one generation has the luck and courage to lay it to rest.

How do you transform a legacy? How do you give to the next generation a set of defaults, deal them a hand, that is better than the one you got growing up? The work is in this moment, now, here. Stop, breathe. The next time emotional temperatures rise, ask yourself, "Which part of me am I in now?" The Adaptive Child is who we revert to when we are triggered. It is an immature ego state, frozen at about the age of the (violating and/or neglectful) injury. Most of us flow into and out of these states fairly regularly. Most of the clients I work with have some experience of their Wise Adult self, the part of them that understands relationships, *us*. But some of the clients I encounter don't have much Wise Adult on board when we first meet. They often regard the extreme qualities of their Adaptive Child as virtues.

Take a moment to contemplate your own Adaptive Child. Think only about your current intimate relationship. Not your relations with colleagues or kids, and not how you were ten years ago, but how you are now, in this one relationship. Do you tend to ride in the one-up, grandiose, superior position or the one-down, shame-filled, inferior position? Is your Adaptive Child more of a pursuer or more avoidant? Can you articulate your go-to dysfunctional stance and your partner's?

In my book *The New Rules of Marriage*, I identified five losing strategies to which an Adaptive Child part will naturally turn. The five strategies are:

- *Being right*
- *Controlling your partner*
- *Practicing unbridled self-expression*
- *Retaliating against your partner*
- *Withdrawing from your partner*

Take a moment to articulate your own Adaptive Child's losing strategy profile. Then try your hand at your partner's. When you are in the right mood, this makes for a good parlor game. Share with each other what you think, then compare notes. How well did you get each other?

One thing that distinguishes Relational Life Therapy from other forms of therapy is the attention it pays to grandiosity in partners. For well over fifty years, psychotherapy has struggled mightily to help people rise above their feelings of inferiority and shame. But what about the other self-esteem disorder? So far, we've done a terrible job at helping people get over their sense of superiority and grandiosity. Superiority and inferiority are flip sides of the same coin; most people have both disorders. In our culture, we often tend to link the two, seeing grandiosity as a defense against shame. Every bully is really wounded inside. A common notion is that if someone were only able to love and heal the core of their insecurity, their grandiose thinking and behaviors would wither away on their own. Good luck with that. Two kinds of people hold a strong belief that loving the hurt child underneath will cure a person's grandiosity: they are codependent women and psychotherapists.

This vision, of curing grandiosity by going underneath it to the wounded child, reminds me of the thousands of alcoholics before AA who languished on psychoanalysts' couches getting to the root causes of why they drank. One of the gifts of AA is release from that myth: "Mr. Jones, you drink because you are an alcoholic. Period. So, before we look at your issues, let's deal with your drinking." Similarly, I don't want you to go under it or over it or around it: "Mr. Jones, you have issues with grandiosity. Let's deal with this by itself." Research shows that about half of all people classed as narcissistic are driven by inward shame. The other half simply think that they are better than everyone else. Grandiose traits of superiority may be an escape from feelings of inadequacy, but they may also simply be the legacy of false empowerment.

False Empowerment Is No Favor

When I was in first or second grade, I brought home a bad report card that I was petrified to give to my rageful, at times physically abusive father. I was already acting out my familial distress at school. You never knew how my dad was going to react. But this time, instead of getting furious, he laughed, threw the report onto the floor, and loftily opined, "It's just that you're so smart, those idiots don't know what to do with you!" I remember his words as if it were yesterday, because I lived my whole childhood based on them. Up through high school, I dropped into class every few days and was content to cruise with a grade of C or D. After high school, I wound up for a year in a local community college in order to get grades good enough for admission into the state university. And to this day, I deal with gaping holes in my education.

My father's words did me no favor, and in fact, this kind of *false empowerment is a form of abuse*. Yes, incest is a form of abuse. Confiding in your child about your disappointing marriage is also a form of abuse. And making a child into the family hero—the light all others depend upon—is a form of trauma.

If you are struggling with grandiosity issues, or if someone you love is, I'd ask you to take a moment now and open your heart a little. Think of yourself or your partner as the child they once were. No one asks to be groomed for grandiosity—it happens *to* them, through false empowerment, and they generally take it in by modeling a grandiose parent. Remember, through reaction, we resist the way our family viewed us; through modeling, we internalize it.

While I was training as a family therapist, I learned about mutigenerational legacies. The early pioneers of family therapy all observed the Faulknerian handing down of issues from one generation to the next. Great-grandfather was an alcoholic, grandmother was an alcoholic, mother married an alcoholic, and so on. Violence, phobias, and sex addiction all seem to run in families. Not until I encountered Pia Mellody's work, however, did I come to understand the actual mechanism of these transmissions: *Multigenerational legacies get passed down from one generation to the next through trauma.* When my father laughed and told me my teachers were idiots, he was passing his grandiosity on to me—whether I wanted it or not. When he strapped me as a young child, he was beating his own depression and shame into me, grooming me—unless I did the hard work of stopping it—to behave as he did. When he raged, he disempowered me as the recipient and, simultaneously, falsely empowered me through modeling.

Freud regarded all neurotic symptoms as compromises between the expression and repression of illicit impulses. I consider our Adaptive Children to be compromises between internalizing the family system we grew up in (modeling) and resisting it (reacting). The particularities of your Adaptive Child, your unique version of *you and me* consciousness, is largely a response to your particular trauma. Were you emotionally neglected because you were so heroic and wonderful that you didn't need help? (You were abandoned and falsely empowered.) Were you emotionally abandoned because you weren't worth your parents' time? "Honey, just let me mix this drink and I'll come listen." (You were abandoned and disempowered.) Did a parent use you and elevate you to be Daddy's little girl, or Mom's surrogate husband, and tell you that you were endlessly special? (They were intrusive and falsely empowering.) Or did they scold and control you? (They were intrusive and disempowering.) Were you, in fact, related to one way by one parent, and quite another way by the other? Were you Daddy's little princess (intrusive and falsely empowering) and Mommy's little rival (intrusive and disempowering)?

Reaction and Modeling:
How They Work Together

Many children face a different response from each parent. In those instances, the child chooses. Should I be a hammer like Dad or a long-suffering anvil like Mom? Most children will *model* themselves on the parent with whom they identify — the one they feel closest to (not necessarily the same-sex parent) — and *react* to the other parent in many of the same ways as does that parent's spouse.

As a boy, Ryan had an intrusive mother and a passive, withdrawn father. He learned to respond to his mother's attempts at control by exercising passive resistance, just like his dad did. He *reacted* to his mother's intrusions by *modeling* his behavior on his dad. Now, as a grown man, he instinctively "wards off" his partner's attempts at closeness, mistaking them for intrusion. He sees his partner through the spectacles of enmeshment with Mom and reacts with the tactics of his — often unconscious—model, Dad. This one-two punch generally forms the contours of the Adaptive Child—resistance through reaction, internalization through modeling.

If we lived consistently in *you and me* consciousness, we would do fine in the public domain but be miserable in our personal relationships. Fortunately, there is more to us than that. From the first moment of my encounter with a new client, my job is to reach through the defensiveness, the righteousness, the fears of their Adaptive Child, and connect with their Wise Adult, to awaken their *us*. The tough news here is that only the Wise Adult part of us wants to be intimate. Our Adaptive Children choose self-protection over the vulnerability of connection every time. So which part of you am I speaking to right now? Which part of you is reading these words?

I tell my clients that whenever one of their inner children kicks up, they should put the child on their lap, put their arms around them, listen compassionately to whatever they need to say, and *take their sticky hands off the steering wheel.* They are not driving the bus; you are, the prefrontal cortex, the Wise Adult.

When my wife, Belinda, comes at me with upset, I take my Adaptive Child, little eight-year-old Terry, and in my mind's eye, I put him behind me, physically, where he can hold on to my shirt. I make a deal with my younger self. I say to him, "You can stay back there, and I'll protect you. Like Superman taking the blast with his spread-out cape, I'll take the brunt of Belinda's upset." That way her hurt and anger would need to get through me, my strong back, to get to my Adaptive Child.

"So my part of the bargain is that I will protect you. Now, here's your part of the bargain. You let me deal with Belinda. Don't you try to do it, okay? You'll make a mess of it. I can deal with her better than you can."

In case you find the language and imaginative work with our inner children a bit treacly, please remember that an imagined, or even personified, inner child is nothing more than the traumatized, reactive ego state formed at about the age you were when the injury occurred. It is your personified point of arrested development. Trauma doesn't precisely get remembered; it gets relived. A grown man whose wife is yelling at him does not remember the eleven-year-old beaten boy he once was—instead, the yelling reactivates his trauma. Teaching someone how to work with their triggered inner child represents a helpful, easily grasped method for working with their activated trauma states. Cultivating an ongoing practice of recognizing these states (the children in us) and working with them has the power to transform individuals and their relationships.

In some moments, our partners are on board and doing reciprocal work on their side. In other moments, we feel quite alone in achieving our hard-won maturity. Our partner is off to the races, temporarily wholly taken over by their own Adaptive Child and exhibiting no interest in connecting with us. I'd love to be able to say that in those raw moments, turning to social support will offer wisdom and sustenance, as it might in

some traditional cultures. But I'm afraid that our highly individualistic society is more likely to support the Adaptive Child
than any wise impulse toward intimacy.

Western society has been individualistic for centuries,
starting with the early Renaissance. That intense bias toward
the individual and away from relationship has been rife in psychotherapy and, in fact, all the personal growth and development approaches. Since the dawn of the personal growth
movement in the 1970s, personal growth has meant *personal*
growth, not relational growth. In our discussion so far, we have
focused on the developmental and familial context of injury
and adaptation.

Let's pull back for a moment and consider our narcissistic,
individualistic society. When, where, and how did we all collectively turn our backs on relationality? When did we, as a
group, begin to privilege the individualistic abilities of our left
hemisphere over the intuitive, relational wisdom of our right?
The idea of the individual—just like any other idea—has a
place, a history. It offers many gifts—and also many problems.
The mythic image of the great American cowboy, riding off
into the sunset with nothing but his gun and his horse, might
be beautiful in its way, but it is utterly discordant, even atavis-
tic, in modern life.

Thus far in our discussion, we've looked at the familial and
developmental forces that forge *you and me* consciousness, our
Adaptive Child. Let's look now at the cultural piece to understand why it is so hard to maintain skilled relationality in a pug-
naciously individualistic, unskilled, antirelational world.

4

The Individualist at Home

"We're stuck," Brit tells me in the first moments of our opening session. White and in her early forties, she is built like a square, muscular tough, and her head is tilting slightly forward, as though she were bucking a headwind. "Three therapists, and we're as miserable as ever."

Her husband, Jim, also white, a tall drink of water, leans back in his chair. He crosses his long, elegantly clothed legs, looking every inch the privileged Carolinian gentleman that he is. "We get caught up in the same damn escalation every time," he says. "It's so annoying."

"It's a nightmare," Brit adds, upping the intensity.

"Okay," I say. "Tell me."

"How would you like it?" Brit asks with a broad inviting smile. "You want critical race theory, or would you rather talk diapers?"

"'Cause it's the same thing?" I guess.

"Everything is the same thing," she says, exasperated.

I glance over at Jim, who is listening intently.

"Okay," I tell Brit. "Let's start with diapers."

"He won't change them. He won't touch them," she says.

"Well, I—" Jim begins, glancing away.

"You—" I start.

"As in 'never,'" Brit answers for him. "Not once. Not even when his wife was sick with a damn *fever*."

"Look, honey—"

"Not when we thought I probably had COVID," she plows on, her voice rising.

Jim sits stony-faced.

"What's it like to hear this?" I ask him finally.

"Well, sir, I've heard it before," he replies, at once confiding and dismissive.

"That doesn't quite answer my question," I persist.

Now he turns on me, his eyes hard. "I've heard it before," he repeats, doubling down, "like, a *lot*."

And I start to get the feel of him, how he handles himself— the cut of his jib, as my father would say. I want to slap him. Get something different out of that stone-faced, vaguely pugnacious, vaguely long-suffering, utterly maligned poor-guy routine he appears to be so practiced at.

"May I?" he asks me, unnecessarily.

"Sure. Go on."

"Look," he explains. "Yes, we have little ones, two, and they can be taxing, no doubt about it. But we're not without resources. We live in a big house. Brit can have all the help a person could want. Just don't ask me—"

"This dear, sweet man," Brit confides, "says he's just not good with babies."

Jim smiles sheepishly. "I just can't relate," he tells me. "I will when they're older, but now . . . infants. I'm likely to drop one of those squirmy little buggers and mash it."

"Not likely at all, darling," she contradicts him, though halfheartedly, as if she no longer expects to be heard and is pretty much past being hurt by that. "Jim," she informs me, "is old school. He's a guy's guy, a good old boy, nothing woke about this man."

Jim snorts, amused.

"Checked into the dorms at Harvard University carrying tackle and a rifle," she goes on. "'Don't nobody fish nor hunt 'round here?'" she mocks.

"Why Harvard?" I ask Jim. "I would have figured Duke or—"

"Wanted to broaden my horizons." He too offers a wide smile, though his expression remains tighter and less inviting than Brit's. "See how the other half lives." He almost winks, gesturing upward with his thumb, as if to say, "You know, that other half—up north." Then he turns to his wife, drapes his hand on her leg, friendly, proprietary. "Instead, I brought a little of the North back home with me," he says, still smiling.

Brit takes her cue. "You might think this is tension between America Red and Blue," she tells me, smiling ruefully at her husband. "But oh my gosh, it's really still about the Blue and the Gray."

"As in critical race theory?" I guess.

"I just don't appreciate anyone running down America," Jim announces.

"Which is anyone," Brit interrupts, "who seems to remember that we enslaved millions of people for hundreds of years—"

"I don't deny history," Jim mildly bridles.

"—or that systemic racism still permeates virtually every—"

"Now, that's where we may see things a bit differently," he says.

And then, somewhat to my chagrin, both partners just stop, which is no doubt a re-creation of what they do on their own. We three sit together for a few uncomfortable moments in abrupt, heavy silence. I'm wondering where in the world to go and decide to ask, "Is this how it is at home?"

They look up.

"You fight like this and then just stop talking?" I ask.

"We each go to our separate corners," Jim says.

"And despise each other," Brit adds helpfully. Neither looks at the other. Or at me, for that matter.

"I have the right to be civilly treated," Jim mutters to no one in particular, some invisible jury somewhere, sullen and resentful.

"And I have the right to express myself. What good is it if we can't be honest with each other?" Brit returns.

Individualism: Rugged and Romantic

The force that so substantially deforms, even threatens, Jim and Brit's marriage is nothing less than the culture of individualism. And not just individualism per se, but two distinct and in some ways contradictory versions of individualism. Jim is what I call a *rugged individualist*. His brand of individualism comes straight out of the philosophy of the Enlightenment era, the writings of Thomas Hobbes and John Locke, the same philosophical roots as the American Revolution and soon after that the French Revolution. Gone forever was the doctrine of the divine right of kings. It got replaced with the idea of a social contract, in which government was to serve the people, not the other way around. And by *people*, these authors meant a unit that had not existed in previous epochs—the freestanding, self-determining individual.

A person. And not merely a person, but a person born with certain "unalienable rights." "Life, liberty, the pursuit of happiness," these and others as represented in the American Declaration of Independence and in the French Declaration of the Rights of Man and of Citizens. In earlier eras, these rights, indeed, one's very personhood, had not been givens.

According to one of the first and greatest observers of modern democracy, the French aristocrat Alexis de Tocqueville, "Aristocracy links everybody, from peasant to king, in one long chain. Democracy breaks the chain and frees each link." Once each link—meaning "each man," as women weren't included in these democracies—is free, what exactly are they free to do? Well, he becomes free to follow "his own good pursued in his own way." But guided by what principle? What morality?

The Age of Enlightenment swept away the received authority of faith and ushered in the new gods of reason, science, and empiricism—and created the individual as a political unit, the stand-alone rugged individualist. Soon after that, a second wave of individualism arose in Germany and swept over Europe. While most Enlightenment thinkers had stressed the abstract and general, this new movement stressed the particular and personal. The group known as the Weimar Classicists, led by the towering figure of Johann Wolfgang von Goethe, ushered in a new kind of individualism that was emotional rather than rational, artistic rather than scientific. The period of the Romantic individualist had begun. Here's Goethe: "All that is alive tends toward color, individuality, specificity, effectiveness and opacity. All that is done with life inclines toward knowledge, abstraction, generality."

The Romantic aesthetic rose up, like a challenge from the right hemisphere of the brain, against the inhumane, relentless logic of the left hemisphere. In glue factories across France, for example, horses about to be rendered were literally torn apart while still alive. The animals' screams were sloughed off as mere exhalations of air and gas inside their shredded bodies. Perhaps the most cerebral of all modern philosophers, René Descartes, had logically proved that humans were the only sentient beings, and so it was an impossibility that these animals were actually feeling anything.

If the Enlightenment individual *thought*, the Romantic individual *felt*. A new ideal type emerged in Goethe's 1774 novel *The Sorrows of Young Werther*: the man of deep feeling, of *sensibility*. Rugged individualists, like Jim, believe in the code of individualism, the assertion of one's unalienable rights. By contrast, Romantic individualists, like Brit, are moved not by individualism but by the unique expression of individuality, finding and manifesting one's singular individual "genius." In today's language, one would want to discover and express one's "voice."

What does all this have to do with Jim and Brit's dilemma over diapers?

As I listen to them, I think to myself that when men of my father's generation pulled the "I don't relate to babies" card, they largely got a pass. But I hadn't heard a man try to use that excuse for lack of involvement in years. In part, I muse, it might be regional: liberal Massachusetts may not churn out a ton of good old boys. But I was used to working with clients from all over. When Jim refused to help his beleaguered partner, he was, whether he articulated it this way or not, standing up for his rights as an individual, pushing back at what he experienced as an encroachment on his freedom to be left undisturbed — as if meeting the needs of his family was an imposition. In Jim's world, Brit had somehow taken the place of big government, while Jim held a tea party. But tea parties can be tough to live with.

And then there's the matter of the porch. Jim and Brit's house, in Charleston, stands on a hill near the port and takes a beating during hurricane season. There are lots of rips in their marine-grade screens. Brit has asked Jim to take care of it. Jim, who is handy, could mend the holes but chooses instead to wait for his order of high-grade marine steel to come in so he can rescreen the whole room in one go. Evidently, waiting doesn't bother Jim. Mosquitoes don't seem to bother him; nor, evidently, does the fact that his wife is covered in bites and red scratches. Because the screens on the porch offer no protection from bugs, Brit has asked Jim, until he fixes the porch, to enter and leave the house only through a side door, away from the porch. He promises to honor that request but then "just forgets"—over and over again.

I decide it's time to take a dive into Jim's childhood. And I have a suspicion. If I were directing a movie, I'd call this exploration "Jim does what he damn well likes."

"Jim, do you have a theory about why you tell your wife you're gonna do something—like take off your shoes, or only use the side door—and then it just goes plumb out of your head? You're a smart man. What happens to you?"

He shrugs, not that engaged. His nonchalance with me in the room echoes Brit's description of his style at home—a kind of benign fatherly neglect, an airy, good-hearted, warm dismissal.

At that moment, had I not been present, Brit would have gone after him, trying to wring a response out of him. She doesn't understand yet that you don't get someone to open up by attacking them. Brit is a poster child for angry pursuit in the form of complaint. She has fallen prey to the third losing strategy: unbridled self-expression. "You did this today. A week ago, you did the same damn thing. Last year you did a really bad one. I'm hurt. I'm devastated. You always. You never . . ."

I'm thinking that they're both grandiose in their own ways, he passively, she more overtly. My wife has a saying: "Beware of 'nice' men with 'bitchy' wives. They're killers." Yelling and screaming, name-calling, blaming, and shaming are all relational violations, but it is also violating to make contracts and break them over and over again, as Jim has. This is a common pattern for many hetero couples, in which the man is passive-aggressive while the woman is over-the-top explosive.

Generally speaking, grandiose women are even more difficult to treat than grandiose men. Not always, but quite often, grandiose women have advanced degrees in offending from the victim position: "You hurt me, so I have no shame or compunction about hurting you twice as hard back because, after all, I'm your victim." Grandiose women often inhabit the role of angry victim, a righteously indignant avenging angel. They are difficult for therapists to work with because, unless the therapist goes very carefully, confronting a grandiose woman may well cast him or her as the new victimizer.

I often confront grandiose men pretty directly. "You're a verbal abuser," I might say. "Yelling, screaming, shaming someone. Those are all forms of verbal abuse. What's it like to hear that?" But with a woman, I tend to be less direct. Remember, any fool can clobber their client with the truth. But a therapist who *joins through the truth* takes the client along, helps them see where they've veered off track. In order to accept the therapist's confrontation, the client must feel that they are on their side. That's what *joining with them* means. And the best way a therapist can help a grandiose woman client feel heard is to prove their usefulness by taking on her partner.

I turn my attention to Jim.

Jim Does What He Wants

"How was it for you, growing up?" I ask Jim. "Were you the star, the hero child?"

"I don't know about—"

"Or the rebel," I continue. "It could go either way."

"I never thought much—"

"The point is, Jim, did you do pretty much what you wanted?"

He looks at me.

"In your house," I add. "Growing up."

"Well . . . no," he stammers after thinking awhile. "My household was very strict, actually. My parents were very religious."

"Where was this?" I ask.

"In Charleston," Brit pipes in. "He took over his family business. He's been remarkably successful."

"Evangelicals?" I ask, staying with Jim.

Again, the look.

"Born again?"

"Yes," he says, "and strict."

"And prejudiced," says Brit.

Jim grimaces slightly. "Certainly, they were of their time and place, but they weren't bonkers like nowadays. You know, they didn't believe Democrats sell children."

"But they were restrictive as parents?"

"Yes."

"One more than the other?"

"My father was more in the background. My mother was more in your face."

"How so?"

"Oh, the usual, I suppose," he says loftily. "Yelling, throwing things, hitting—"

"She'd hit you?"

He nods.

"With?"

He regards me blankly for a second, then comes present. "Anything. Belt, stick, shoe." He's looking a little rattled.

"Are you feeling anything?"

He shakes his head. "Just go on," he directs me, fatigued, impatient.

"And where was your father? Why didn't he protect you?"

"He was out. Between work, church, and his pals. He was smart, he stayed away. We'd hunt together sometimes, fish."

"And when he was home?"

"He'd just tune her out," Jim tells me. "Just tune the whole thing out."

The whole thing, I think, *including that little boy.* "Did he drink?"

Not really.

Take drugs?

No.

I lean in toward Jim, and we hold each other's gaze for a moment. "He threw you under the bus," I tell him. "Left you to handle your mother on your own."

"Oh, he did a lot worse than that," he agrees, that tight smile.

"What do you mean?"

"Oh, come *on.*" He makes a face. "You're the therapist."

I wait.

"He left me to her, yes, but he also taught me, didn't he? He taught me how to handle her."

"Meaning?" I prompt.

"Give her a wide berth, lie whenever necessary, never really give in on the inside but slap on that smile on the outside." He looks at me, seeming equal parts condescending and desperate. "You catching on?" he adds gracelessly.

"The same strategies you employ currently in your marriage."

He nods. "And"—he begins to dig himself into a hole—"in reaction to the same kind of unreasonable, demanding—"

"Jim, hold up," I say, literally holding my hand up to gesture to him to stop.

To my left, Brit bristles, and then, after I stop him, tentatively settles down again.

"So, Jim," I say, "I'm gonna ask you a few questions that I imagine we both know the answers to. First, how do you respond when Brit complains about you?" More bristling from the corner. "When she tells you she's unhappy," I self-correct.

"Well." He stares down. "At first I try to be reasonable—"

Brit interrupts. "How 'bout this?" she says nastily. "How 'bout you get defensive, act like I'm a bad wife for bothering you, like I don't appreciate the great life you afford me and the kids, which you do, and yes, we all are grateful. But that's not the point."

"I'm not sure," Jim harrumphs, half mumbling, "if there *is* a point!"

"And *that*," cries Brit, "is exactly what I'm talking about! Superior, disqualifying, sarcastic." She gathers steam. "This—this passive-aggressive *bullshit!*"

"Okay, Brit." I try calming her down.

"No, it's actually not okay." She breaks free of constraint. "And you know what is really, really not okay?"

"Listening to your criticism night and day?" chimes in Jim.

"Jesus!" Brit looks apoplectic.

"You know, I can try to help her," I tell Jim. "But you have to stop poking her in the eye."

"Poking her in the—I am not—"

"You're arguing with her," I tell him. "Instead of listening, you're—"

"I'm not sure I'd—"

"And now you're going to argue with me about arguing?"

Jim literally sputters, but then relaxes, looks at me, and smiles.

"I can teach you how to disarm her and be the compassionate, kind guy I know you are all at the same time. Sound interesting?"

"Sure," he says, still with the same stretched smile.

But What About Me?

Jim and Brit are caught in an endless loop because they are thinking of themselves as individuals rather than as a team. Jim doesn't listen to Brit; he passive-aggressively refuses to do as she asks, because like his father before him, he's allergic to being controlled by her or by anyone else for that matter. Whether he admits it aloud, or even to himself, his motto could be "Don't tread on me." Or maybe "Live free or die." But it's hard to live with a man whose credo can be summed up in a license plate. He might have a hard time seeing it this way, but as for all such rugged individualists, Jim's principal concerns are his rights, his freedoms. He changes, or doesn't change, diapers as he pleases. He goes through whatever damn door he wants to. He is drenched in Enlightenment-era political rugged individualism. He doesn't like being told he needs to wear a mask, he hates big government spending his money, and he doesn't much like being coached by his wife on how to behave. What matters to Jim is fairness, and in his mind, he is being treated unfairly. Why can't Brit just kick back and enjoy the fruits of his labor? And his bank account?

"Are you aware," I ask him, "that you are arguing still? Can I show you another way?" I lean back and look at Brit. "Pick something to talk about, something you're unhappy about, something small," I say. "Bite sized."

"I want money," Brit says. "Lots."

Oh boy. This is going well, I think.

"I want my own money. And I want to build an art studio," she says.

To my surprise, Jim does not get defensive, dismissive, or argumentative. He looks at me and smiles. To beat me to the therapeutic punch, he asks her, "Tell me, what would having your own money mean to you? What would having your own studio do for you?"

Well done, Jim! I think. *Good to know you can show some curiosity.* "Look," she marches on, "I have to go to you for anything large or small. You go over my credit cards."

You're overselling, I think. "Brit, may I?" I cut in.

"Sure," she says.

"Okay, listen, may I coach you? He didn't invite you to complain about what *not* having your own money does to you. He asked what having it would *do*. See what I mean?"

She nods unconvincingly.

"Good," I say. "Try keeping it positive. Not what he's done wrong, but what right might look like."

She pauses, thinks, then looks up at me and smiles. "I just noticed how much easier it is to say what I don't want than what I do."

We laugh a little. "And hardest yet is to get it and allow yourself to receive it," I tell her. Because if Jim is a dyed-in-the-wool rugged individualist, Brit, as a passionate Romantic individualist, is equally drenched in the mandate to express her unique self. If the value that trumps relationship for Jim is the sainted freedom of the individual, the absolute value for Brit is the Romantic ideal of self-expression, of authenticity, of being "true to herself."

For rugged individualists like Jim, the great fear is constraint of their personal freedom. But Romantic individualists like Brit want more than simple freedom; they feel entitled to share themselves, manifest their full potential. What resonates for them isn't so much individualism as the notion of individuality—one's genius, one's unique stamp, spirit, personality. The rugged individualist's nightmare is being dominated; the Romantic individualist's great fear is of enforced conformity—of being shut down and stifled, of losing their voice.

As a rugged individualist, Jim asserts his fundamental right to be left unperturbed, to pursue his good in his own way—whether or not that includes diapers. As a Romantic individualist, Brit is committed to finding herself, as well as to exercising her fundamental right to let Jim know, in living color, just how she feels about pretty much everything. Both individuals stand up virtuously for their rights, neither thinking much of the whole. Which brings us to a fundamental historical fact: in earlier centuries, no matter what kind of individualist you were, rugged or Romantic, the ability to conceive of yourself as an individual to begin with meant you were white, male, and wealthy. Women and children were not individuals. Enslaved people, poor people, people of color—none of them were individuals. In the time of the idea's inception, the term *individual* was synonymous with *gentry*.

Privileged Obliviousness

Jim does not see himself as a member of an exclusive club. He believes with little hesitation that all Americans should have an even playing field. He also believes that, by and large, they do. Many men who share Jim's brand of rugged individualism are subject to what I call *privileged obliviousness*. Like most rugged individualists, he simply doesn't much register the existence of those who are excluded. Seeing himself as "autonomous," he doesn't note his reliance on the Latinx housekeeper who cooks his family's meals, the African-American gardener who grows their flowers, or the "immigrant" who sweeps their street. Jim appreciates the people who work for him; he treats them well, even thoughtfully. But they don't quite register as individuals to him. He doesn't let himself realize his dependence on them or the everyday forces of oppression with which they contend. When he jogs through his neighborhood with no thought of being detained or shot by the police, he doesn't register his exercise as an instance of white privilege.

As he makes clear in subsequent sessions, Jim sees society as a meritocracy. You can raise yourself up by your bootstraps. Cream rises to the top: if you are successful, it is because you have earned it. And conversely, if you are not successful, it is because of some internal flaw—a lack of drive, or intelligence, or some other capacity. Men like Jim believe in what he would call the American dream—the myth of the self-made man, as if all of us start off on a level playing field, as if issues of sexism, racism, classism could, and should, be overcome by one's will alone. No bleeding-heart liberal was he.

With all her emotionality, the Romantic individualist Brit does in fact possess a bleeding heart. The struggling, the disenfranchised—yes, she will empathize with them, will "feel their pain." But neurologically, as the biologist Robert Sapolsky has observed, the response of empathy and the response of action are two very different and distinct physiological circuits. Although Brit deeply resonates with the pain of those less privileged, unfortunately that does not necessarily mean she will be moved to do much about it. For years, progressives like Brit have been lulled into complacency. Most assumed that we were on the road to social equality—not perfect perhaps, but forward-moving enough to land a black man in the White House, to uphold women's rights, to recognize gay marriage. Then 2016 happened. And not just in the United States but as had been happening all over the world, strong man nationalism, racism, and xenophobia arrives—

Trump, of course, but no less Boris Johnson, Viktor Orbán, Recep Tayyip Erdoğan, a resurgent right in Germany, and white supremacism in America.

It might be appealing to say that the Enlightenment's political, rugged individualism has become the modern right, while expressive Romantic individualism has become the modern left. That would be half correct. Jim's hesitation in wearing a mask during the pandemic is an example of the confluence of his "rights" and the political "right." Lining up Romantic individualism with the political left is less clear, however. The celebration of individuality in, for example, the LGBTQ community and in women's empowerment is easy to see.

Other commonalities between the expressive Romantic individual and the political left are their shared disdain for conformity and their joy in rebellion. Fundamentally, however, the development of one's individuality is not a communal concern. Expressive Romantic individualism doesn't neatly line up with the political left because it concerns the self instead of the collective. Neither Jim nor Brit sees their fulfillment as coming from engagement with community beyond their privileged cohort. Neither turns outward to face and include the marginalized, the dispossessed.

The Triumph of the Therapeutic

In my lifetime, the 1960s saw an uprising of expressive Romantic individualism against the conformity and stultification of the rugged individualism of the preceding generation. For those who objected to the unpopular Vietnam War and the threat of universal draft, the quest to express themselves went hand in hand with a political critique of society. Then the war ended, and the volunteer army targeted the poor and minorities, leaving the privileged alone.

At that same time, my generation largely veered from collective to individual concerns. One's development, one's *Bildung*, as German Romantic individualists would call it, became the paramount value. Look at the rise of the self-help movement, the popularity of "motivational" leaders as distinct as Werner Erhard, Tony Robbins, and John Bradshaw, the advent of psychotherapy, the many twelve-step programs. My generation's focus shifted from social action to personal growth. And personal growth is personal growth, not relational growth. I've asked audiences around the world, "What is the one value shared by mainstream culture and by virtually all the so-called counterculture movements?" Answer: the primacy of the individual.

As several sociologists and cultural observers have noted, Enlightenment political individualism became the modern right, while Romantic expressive individualism became . . . the therapeutic. The left has always arisen from collective concerns, labor rights, civil rights, women's rights. By contrast, personal growth is personal growth, not collective growth—as if we could truly realize ourselves as individuals in a social context that denies that very right to so many. In these ways, individualistic narratives—of both types, rugged and Romantic—steer us away from collective concerns and collective action. As the sociologist Robert Bellah puts it:

> *In the absence of any objective criteria of right and wrong, good or evil, the self and its feelings become our moral guide . . . The right act is simply the one that yields the agent the most exciting challenge or the most good feeling about himself. . . . Utility replaces duty; self-expression unseats authority. "Being good" becomes "feeling good."*

In these ways, the culture of individualism minimizes social inequality and places one's central concern with oneself, thereby both justifying and serving the status quo. As it has for centuries.

Choosing the Common Good

How can we reconcile individualism with the collective good? Historians tell us that at least in early American democracy, people spent their lives neither selfishly nor nationalistically. Prior to industrialization, life was dominated by the mores of small towns, villages, and farms, what one historian calls "local communalism" or "collectivism in a smaller group." People living face-to-face with their neighbors might have more easily remembered that, as Thomas Paine put it, "public good is not a term opposed to the good of individuals. On the contrary, it is the good of every individual collected. It is the good of all."

Us consciousness might indeed have been easier to achieve in a local community where one interacted with neighbors daily. But the industrial revolution and the burgeoning urban centers fragmented that immediacy. It's hard to maintain the wisdom that one cannot fully realize oneself as an island now when so many are isolated. Today men like Jim, men of the old school, men who cleave both to the overt love of liberty and to the covert privileges of his caste, are being challenged as never before. Children now insist on their own paths, and women like Brit demand more—more say, more voice, more democracy. Moving beyond *you and me* consciousness, beyond the Adaptive Child, beyond individualism, means moving beyond centuries of patriarchy—male privilege, racism, white privilege, xenophobia, and homophobia.

Jim could have retrenched, played the power game, and maybe even steamrollered his free will. But in the end, he was smart enough to realize the cost and flexible enough to change. He realized that pleasing Brit did not make him less of a man. He began using the side door.

"Why?" I ask him in our final session. Why has he traded in his privilege to do as he pleased in favor of rendering himself more pleasing to his wife?

He looks me over, his hand draped on the back of Brit's chair. "Well, call it an exercise in the common good." And he smiles magnanimously, the tightness gone from his expression. "Who needs a constitutional crisis at home?"

"The people." Brit looks at her husband and smiles, shaking her head. "The people have been heard."

"You fix the porch?" I ask Jim.

"All in due time," he reassures me.

"It'll get done," Brit tells me, slipping her hand inside his.

Relational Life Therapy transforms patriarchy, transforms individualism, one couple at a time. I want you to move beyond patriarchy and the culture of individualism in your relationship, even in your own thinking. If Jim became a new kind of man, it was in deference to having married a new kind of woman, one he wouldn't be bored with, as he once told me. The preservation of individualism—of either type—has historically required the suppression of less privileged voices. The unacknowledged social underpinning of both forms of individualism is caste, privilege, and exclusivity. *You and me* consciousness is rooted in competition, as if resources were limited and only the strong survive. *Us* consciousness, by contrast, embraces the whole, acknowledges our relationship to the unseen, the orphaned, the exiled. Once we incorporate the perspective of the excluded—in this case, Brit—priorities reorder.

Unity or Tragedy

Today things are changing, painfully and rapidly. The force of *us* consciousness cannot be held back forever. It was not the culture of individualism that drove thousands of white demonstrators to join in protest, staring down armed police as well as a pandemic, to put their bodies on the side of black lives mattering. It wasn't individualism that accounts for the hundreds of men I saw at the Women's March on Washington, or the straight people who cheer gay pride.

Before he signed the Declaration of Independence, Benjamin Franklin famously quipped, "We must all hang together or most assuredly we will all hang separately." Bound by the limitations of his time, Franklin's *we* started and ended with an oligarchy of landed white male gentry. Today Franklin might say that *we* must include every man, woman, and nonbinary person, no matter their color, their faith, where they first hailed from, their gender identity, or their sexual orientation. Because *us* consciousness means embracing the unity, it also means realizing, centuries later, the inchoate dream of true democracy. Democracy among people in groups, democracy in our marriages, our families, and inside our own skulls. Democracy, not as an ideal but rather as a guiding principle, a personal practice, a map of how we should live our lives. Democracy is the cure for mankind's abiding illness—the Great Lie that one person or group is better than anyone else—and the illusion that anyone can win or lose with no connection to anyone else.

Once couples like Jim and Brit begin thinking relationally, they realize that if one partner wins while the other loses, they both lose. Once we move beyond individualistic myths like survival of the fittest, and wake up to our interdependence, it dawns on us that the willful denial of connection has consequences both to those who are denied and to the deniers. The cost of disconnection is disconnection. If *us* consciousness unifies, *you and me* consciousness fragments—our communities, our personal relationships, our very souls. As we will explore in some detail, the legacy of individualism is loneliness.

"I am not a mechanism," wrote the archetypal expressive Romantic individualist, D. H. Lawrence, in his poem "Healing": "And it is not because the mechanism is working wrongly, that I am ill. / I am ill because of wounds to the soul, to the deep emotional self." And what is that wound? It is a mistake "which mankind at large has chosen to sanctify."

And that essential mistake that mankind has enshrined is the fiction of an independent self—a self over all, over nature, over groups that we marginalize, over the partners and children we crazily try to control, over the neighbors with whom we compete, over the planet we disrespect. That is our potentially fatal error. We will awaken, or we will hand down misery for generations. We will learn, or we will destroy. This world does not belong to us. We belong to one another.

5

Start Thinking Like a Team

"I tell ya, doc," Rick begins, even though I've already told him over the phone that I'm not a doctor. In this, our first session, Rick is answering my usual opening question: "If you walk out of here at the end of the session, and you say, 'That was a stunning success,' what would a great success look like?"

"Terry, I'm a simple man," Rick confides. White, close-cropped gray-blond hair, jeans, a sweatshirt, around fifty, a little paunchy, he looks pretty much like the successful builder that he is. "I'd say we hit it outta the park if somehow, somewhere, between the two of us, we managed to get me laid." I pause and consider the speaker of this sentiment.

"You're not having the sex life you'd like," I deduce brilliantly.

"Oh no," he tells me, "I have a great sex life on my own. And once in a blue moon my wife joins me." *Bada boom*, I think, but before I speak, he leans forward slightly and adds, "A very blue moon, if you know what I mean."

I ask him why he thinks his wife, Joanna, over the years,

has turned away from sex with him. "'Turning away,'" he muses. "That would be like, she was into it once, right?" He shrugs. "I'm not sure she was ever . . . you know," he says, arms outstretched a bit, palms up.

"I mean, in the very beginning, yeah, sure, we were like two rabbits," he continues. "But it quickly went to shit, like years ago. You know that thing where you're supposed to put a jellybean in a jar every time you have sex the first year you're together? And then you take out a bean every time you have sex after that. How you never empty—"

"Yes, I've heard it," I stop him. "So listen, Rick, you're a thoughtful man. Why do you think Joanna has retreated from your sex life?"

"Oh," he says, "the million-dollar question. Why is she off sex? So like I've been trying to say, I don't think she was all that into it to begin with really. I just don't think she has much drive that way, you know, in that arena."

"She's just cold," I reflect back to him.

"Well . . ."

"Sexually," I clarify.

"Well, her whole family, her mother. You know, I come from a big Italian family. Lots of yelling and fighting but it all blows over in minutes, and then there's hugs and kisses, you know? I-love-yous. But Joanna, she's got that WASP business down to the bone. Mainline Philly. What do they call 'em? The 'frozen chosen'? Not much hugging and kissing. Cold, like I said. Her whole family."

Sitting with Rick, it doesn't take me long to suspect that he has a bad case of CID—chronic individualism disorder. As I listen, I think that he, like many of the men and women who come to me, is an essentialist. He thinks his wife simply *is* a cold person; it's her essential nature. I suspect, when I meet her, it will be a very different story.

"Screw him," Joanna begins.

"Excuse me?" I ask. With her expensive dress, coiffed hair, and nails, she looks the part of a Mainline lady. But that mouth . . .

"Fuck him," she clarifies. "He was in here bitching about our sex life, right? I know him. He'll piss and moan to anyone who'll listen."

"Well, he—"

"And I'm just a frigid bitch, right?"

I back off, letting her have her steam.

"I mean who says stuff like that anymore? Frigid." She snorts. "Who says—when was the last time you heard—"

"I don't recall actually," I try lamely.

"Oh please," she dismisses me. "I know the drill. Like he's got nothing to do with it. Shithead."

Inwardly, I smile at her directness, so like her husband's. They are from different worlds maybe, but they're not unlike each other. *Like he's got nothing to do with it,* I reflect.

Now her snort becomes a laugh. "Terry," she starts.

Oh my god, I think, *she's going to call me doc.*

"Listen," she says, as if to say, *Here's the deal.* "Rick is a terrible lover. First of all, he's a big man, if you know what I mean. I have to relax, I have to feel calm, a little warming up. His idea of foreplay is a public service announcement that he's horny. Like, 'That's nice. What am I supposed to do about it?'"

"Have you ever tried—"

"What? Talking to him about it? Sure. A dozen times. He just gets mad or defensive. Or he attacks me. It's my fault. I'm so uptight. Maybe I have vaginismus. Fuck me! Vaginismus. He can shove his vaginismus—"

"Okay, I got it," I stop her.

"Such a child," she mutters.

"Excuse me?"

"He's such a *child*," she says, her voice rising.

And now, I think, we've arrived at her essentialist image of her husband, of who he is as an individual. If she's "just" frigid, he's "just" a child. It's their natures, their personalities, who they'd be with anyone. Neither of them knows it, but they're both wrong.

"If I could turn Rick into a better lover," I ask, "would you—"

"Hey, I'm human. I'm a woman. He may not think so, but I have . . ." She trails off, too enervated to talk further.

I bring Rick back in for our last individual talk before beginning couples work together. I tell him, smiling, "I have great news for you!"

My great news—the thing I know but neither of them does—is simply that they are connected. They are on opposite ends of a seesaw. Rick is the big heavy guy on one end screaming at his wife on the opposite to please descend from her perch; he's reasoned, cajoled, begged. What I see that neither Rick nor Joanna sees is the seesaw. They are linked. The big guy who wants his wife to come down has tried everything under the sun—except getting up and changing his own position.

When you see yourselves as two distinct individuals, when you are in *you and me* consciousness, you are pulled into a linear control model. Either Rick controls Joanna, or she controls him. When you shift into *us* consciousness, you become aware of another level: the ecological whole of the relationship itself. It's like a fourth dimension. Instead of trying to convince her to come down, the big guy pushes up.

In the linear, individualistic model that most of us live with, our relationship to relationships tends to be passive. You get what you get, and then you react to it. It's a game-changing revolution when we realize that we need not be passive passengers in our own lives, in our relationships. It turns out that we have something to say about what we get. We can shift into us-awareness, then use the relational tools we've learned and developed.

Rick cannot "get" Joanna to have sex with him. Short of a gun to the head, outright coercion, I don't believe anyone "gets" anyone else to do anything. Except in extreme cases, the idea of unilateral control is an illusion. And even in extreme cases, if coercion fails, control of one person by another is impossible. Gandhi taught us that, and Martin Luther King, Jr., honed that strategy to an art. Civil disobedience can bring down an empire. If you are willing to die, no one can control you. The idea of unilateral control is, for the most part, a delusion, just as the idea of a freestanding individual is a delusion. But belief in either of these twin delusions has very real consequences.

The Wisdom Sitting Next to You

Rick, it turns out, has a rich, detailed, precise manual of Joanna operating instructions. He wakes up with it in the morning and goes to bed with it each night. That manual sits beside him, fidgeting, in my office for a couples session.

"Jeez," Joanna offers, looking around my office as if she were scanning for something tasteful to look at and is having a hard time with it. "I guess after this it's a root canal."

I smile. "Nice to see you again too."

"Oh, jeez. No offense," she adds quickly.

"None taken." I cast a cool eye on them both. "Look, you have both indicated that you'd like to be closer."

"I have?" says Joanna.

"What I said was—" says Rick.

I hold up my hand to interrupt him. "Closer physically, for sure. But I'm imagining you'd both feel better if you were closer in all sorts of ways."

"I'm not all that convinced—" Joanna says.

But again I stop her. "What if I could give you a playbook of how to win Joanna back, resurrect your sex life?" I ask Rick.

"Sure," he says, glancing at his wife out of the corner of his eye. "What mountain do I have to climb?"

"Fuck you, too," Joanna begins.

"Please?" I ask her, and she settles back down. Then I turn to Rick. "She's right, you know."

"Excuse me?" he says.

"Was that crack just now supposed to help matters?"

"Well, I—"

"I have good news and bad news, Rick. Which would you like first?"

"I don't care," he replies.

"Fine. First the good. I think I can help you."

"Nice," he says. "And the bad?"

"Angry complaint is not seductive."

Rick is a master in what I inelegantly call *Henny Young-man-ing*. You've all no doubt heard the classic borscht belt comic's dictum: "Take my wife. *Please!*" Rick has positioned himself as his wife's long-suffering victim, a common male stance. Listening to him, it's all about the unfair deal he's stuck with. In other words, it's all about him. Not them. Listen for a moment to the difference between the following two statements: "I won't live without sex for the rest of my life!" And: "We both deserve a good sex life. I miss you. What do we need to do as a team to set this to rights?"

What do we need to do as a team?

Boy, that's a rare question for a couples therapist to hear. Like a good old Enlightenment-era, rugged individualist, Rick isn't thinking of Joanna. He isn't thinking of the two of them together. He is asserting his *rights*, goddamn it. And he's proud to stand up for himself, even though he's cutting his own throat.

How different are the assertions "I need more sex" and "We need a healthy sex life." From ego to eco, from *me* to *we*. No matter the particular school or technique, what all good couples therapists have up their sleeves is the wisdom of *we*.

"So Rick," I say, "you'd like to have more of an erotic life together, yes?"

"Sure," he answers wearily.

"All this time you've been trying to change Joanna," I go on. "What if I gave you some new moves on your end that might get you more of what you want?"

"Well . . . like?"

"Like being nice, for starters," I tell him. "Like, stop complaining and start being curious."

"Curious about what?"

"The woman you live with," I tell him.

He looks confused, as if he's deciding whether to be offended.

"What *she* wants, what turns *her* on, what it would look like to warm *her* up."

"Warm her up? You're joking, right? Her idea of warming up is a quart of toenail polish and *People* magazine."

I pause and consider him. "I think it may be time to retire that," I say quietly.

"Retire *what?*" he says, his tone challenging, as if he's leaning toward being offended.

"Making her the butt of your jokes."

"What?" He tries to make light. "What will I do for material?"

But neither Joanna nor I is amused.

"If you want her," I tell him, as I must say to a dozen men each week, "if you want her, court her."

He looks puzzled, although I don't think what I'm saying is all that complicated.

"When was the last time you did anything romantic?" I ask him. "What do you do to warm her up?" Joanna laughs. I doubt that's helping, but I ignore it and go on. "I'm sorry, Rick. But you're not the first guy I've had in here who wanted more sex."

"Well, sure, I—"

"Listen, I had one guy, a nice guy, but oh my god. I asked him what he did to warm up his wife sexually, and he told me, 'Nothing.' 'Well,' I said, 'do you kiss her, touch her, tell her you desire her?' Nothing. 'Well, you must do something,' I tell him. 'I mean, how do you let her know you want to make love?' 'Oh, that's simple,' he tells me. 'Every night when I go to bed, I wear my underpants. And those nights when I'm horny, I just take them off.' 'Wow,' I told him, 'that must sweep her right off her feet!'"

Without waiting for more, Rick turns to Joanna. "You'd like something more from me?" he asks her.

"Oh my god, Rick," she says, mock breathless. "Where have you been for fifteen years?"

"He's being nice, Joanna," I stop her. "It's a straight question."

She sighs, no stranger to a long-suffering stance herself. "Okay." She turns to Rick. "Yes, Rick. Yes, I would like more."

"Tell him," I urge softly. " 'I want more . . .' "

"More joy," Joanna says. "More . . . more love, for fuck's sake. More, I don't know, like you *care*." And now some tears come, not a lot, and she's angry at herself for crying, I can tell. But they're there.

"What are you feeling?" I ask her.

"Jeezus," she exclaims, "I don't know. I don't know what I'm feeling half the time."

"But now," I press. "What are you feeling right now?"

"It's just . . ." she begins. "I've been so fucking lonely! We've both been lonely, baby."

And bless him, sitting next to his undone wife, Rick stops thinking about himself for a minute and opens his heart. He reaches out and takes her hands, which are clenched in her lap. "You're right," he says softly, gently. "It's been a fucking desert between us." He is gazing at her.

"Would you like to set this to rights?" I ask him.

"Sure," he answers gruffly, then catches himself. He looks at Joanna's streaked face. "Yes," he says quietly, holding her gaze. "Yes, I would."

"All of it, Rick," I say. "Not just the sex."

"All of it," he repeats. "Sure." Holding both of her locked

hands in his, he looks up at me. For that moment, he strikes me as guileless. No attitude, no routine. "How do I start?"

"That's the wisest thing I've heard you say," I tell him. I point to their hands, hers in his, holding tight. "Start there. If those hands could speak, what would they be saying?"

Rick regards her for a moment. "I do want you. Not just sex, either. You, Joanna. We used to have fun; you know?"

She nods, not speaking. But when Rick starts to peel his hands away from hers, she clutches them and pulls him back.

"Okay," I say, looking at the two of them as they gaze at each other, hanging on. "So we begin."

You may not be able to directly control your partner, but as Rick learned, you may be able to influence your interaction with your partner by changing your own behavior. This is called *working on your relationship*. You can come home after a long day at work and rail at your partner for the chaos in the house. Or you can walk in with a thoughtful little present, a babysitter in tow, and tickets to a show. Which of those two evenings would you rather inhabit? Well, okay then, get to it. Stop thinking like an individual and start thinking like a team. *Us* consciousness says, "We're in this together." *You and me* consciousness says, "Every man for himself."

Am I safe? Am I safe? Am I safe? Am I safe?

What determines when we stay wise rather than lurch into reactivity? Current research shows clearly that it's determined by our subjective sense of safety or its lack. Remember, far below your conscious awareness, your autonomic nervous system is scanning your body, asking, "Am I safe? Am I safe? Am I safe?" four times a second. And the answer to that question determines which part of your brain and nervous system gets activated—the one we use every day or the one we use in extremis. The problem is that one partner's extremis may not strike the other as all that alarming. Danger is in the eye of the beholder—or more accurately, in the body of your partner. We are rarely haunted by tigers any longer. But an insult, stonewalling, an unkind word may be enough to tell your body that you're not safe.

I do not believe partners can provide a "holding environment" for each other that is exquisitely and always safe. Relationships are to some degree dangerous. Otherwise, there would be no place for vulnerability. Where's the courage in jumping if you already know you'll be caught? We are mortal, as I tell my clients. Life is full of risk. If you want to stay utterly safe, don't get out of bed in the morning.

I think it's a huge mistake when therapists urge partners to be each other's safe harbors at all times. As if we human beings could really promise that to one another! We all long for it, of course. We all long to be perfectly held, perfectly met, perfectly understood. In our deepest hearts, we all long for the Divine, an impeccable God or Goddess who will complete us and never fail. But precisely the collision of your imperfections with mine, and how we manage that collision, comprises the stuff, the guts of intimacy. "Between the ideal and the reality," wrote T. S. Eliot in *The Hollow Men*, ". . . Falls the Shadow." That's where skills come in. I talk to clients about learning to work with the partner you're with instead of "the one you deserve."

Seeing each other as separate individuals, rather than as parts of a whole, an organism, sets you up to blame each other and give your power away. Rick believes he has nothing to do with Joanna's sexual distance. It's all her fault, he thinks, who she is as an individual. Poor guy. He can either leave her, I guess, or suffer through it. But learning to think relationally opens up new avenues of action, new possibilities. Instead of endlessly trying to get your partner to be different, you can try to change things by experimenting with new moves on your end of the interaction.

I hand Rick a dog-eared copy of the sex therapist Ian Kerner's 2009 classic *She Comes First*. This book, I tell him, believes the tongue is mightier than the sword. With their agreement, and with explicit permission for each to say no at any point, I set up a his-and-hers night for them, in which, with as few words as is possible, each partner shows the other what they like in bed. It's not a command performance but simply information about what pleases each of them. His willingness to learn to please her and her willingness to teach him counter their essentialist negative imagery about each other.

When you see yourself and your partner as two individuals, it's like viewing your partner through the wrong end of a telescope—they seem far away, squeaky, and pathetic, or conversely, they seem looming, in your face, and overwhelming. In triggered moments, our partners become caricatures of themselves, and the relationship suddenly seems impossible, hopeless.

Core Negative Image

There's an old saying in family therapy that most couples have the same fight over forty years. Why? Because the same parts of each of them are fighting the same caricatures of their partners. I call these caricatures each partner's *core negative image* of the other. Thankfully, these core negative images tend not to mutate. They remain steady throughout the life of the relationship. When we're looking through that inverted telescope, when we are in our Adaptive Children, our *you and me* consciousness, when our partners seem to us utterly unbearable, we will see them as insufferable in pretty much the same way that they always seem insufferable. We may torture one another, but at least we're consistent. That consistency can be put to good use—once you learn how.

Your partner's core negative image of you is a cartoon version of you at your worst. It's not you at your best or at baseline. It's not even an accurate portrait of you at your most immature, but a colorful exaggeration. Having said that, with rare exception, it is nevertheless . . . you. Not the person standing next to you.

Let me illustrate. Belinda's core negative image of me is that I am an undependable, self-centered, charming, narcissistic boy. My core negative image of her is that she is a controlling, insatiable, complaining witch. I share these descriptions with some ease, knowing that this heterosexual pairing is by no means rare. I tell Belinda it's a sign of how disturbed she is that she would even see me this way. She is rarely amused.

When we find ourselves facing a partner who is core-negative-image-triggered, we usually fight them. We almost universally react to the exaggeration. Hurt or indignant that our partner would even think such a thing of us, we ignore the grain of truth inside. It is, after all, me that Belinda is talking about. No one would describe me as insatiable and demanding. No one would describe Belinda as a self-centered charmer. We have each other's number, in a bloated, unforgiving way.

When Rick describes Joanna as sexually cold and uninterested, he's right. But when he sees her as *essentially* frigid as an individual, he's utterly wrong. He leaves himself out of the equation, blaming her and rendering himself helpless. Like most partners, she rejects his description of her out of hand. "Fuck you, I'm not a cold person." "It isn't that I don't want sex," she clarifies in a later session. "I just don't want to have sex *with you!*" The insidious problem here is that a wholesale rejection of your partner's caricature of you most often reads to them as unaccountability, which reinforces the bad imagery they had to begin with.

Let's say I'm late picking up one of our children. Belinda couldn't care less that workers unearthed a giant boulder in the middle of the road, snarling traffic, or that aliens in a spaceship zapped both front tires. She knows why I'm late before I open my mouth. I'm late because I am a selfish, undependable, charming boy. Now, notice what happens to me once her core negative image of me is triggered. Rather than reacting to the reality that I was, in fact, late, I am incensed at her exaggerated description. "Jeez, Belinda. I wasn't *that* late, and you have to understand . . ."

But the more I react, the more convinced she is of my undependable boyishness—which in turn quickly triggers my core negative image of her. If she is speaking to an irresponsible child, I now regard her as an insatiable complainer. We are both deeply embedded in *you and me* consciousness, our Adaptive Children pulling at each other.

"I was just fifteen minutes late, Belinda. I'm not Jack the Ripper!"

"Just once it would be nice to get a simple apology out of you! Why can't you ever be accountable?"

And there we are—off to the races. Our core negative images are fruitlessly duking it out. She and I could sit down and have a beer while they fight.

Don't Fight It, Relax

Like a Chinese finger puzzle that tightens as you try to pull it apart, you'll never get out of this mess by contesting your partner's core negative image. You have to lean into it instead. "Yes," I could have said, "I was late." Period. End of story. "And yes, it was irresponsible of me, as I can tend to be." Now that's an apology. So, here's the first tip for working on your partner's core negative image of you: the more you refute it, the more you'll reinforce it. But the more you admit to the kernel of truth within your partner's exaggeration, the greater the odds that the exaggeration will relax. Try it. Don't defend yourself—yield. Yielding can work as a core negative image buster.

Once a couple has taken on board a modicum of self-esteem and internal boundaries, I encourage them to put their core negative images of each other on the table. Note: this is a high-impact and potentially high-risk maneuver. Do *not* attempt it without supervision from a coach or a therapist if either you or your partner will be reactive, defensive, or volatile. Be clear that what you're sharing is how you see the person when you portray them as impossible, their all-time worst. Own your exaggeration; it might take the bite out of the description. If each of you can hear what the other thinks without storming off or collapsing, a lot of good can come of it. For one thing, knowing your partner's core negative image of you can take the sting out of it. It helps you not personalize and have better boundaries. *Oh, there goes Belinda again,* I think on a good day. *She's not talking to me. She thinks she's talking to that utterly irresponsible boy.* I've got nothing to be high and mighty about because I know I'm capable of being triggered myself in the next ten seconds.

Awareness of your partner's core negative image of you can serve as operating instructions—a compass reliably pointing in the opposite direction of where you want to go. Knowing how Belinda views me, I know that anything I do that comes close to looking irresponsible will likely upset her, and conversely anything I do that's remarkably responsible ("Hey, I noticed we're low on detergent so I stopped off to get some") is most likely to thrill. You can tailor your behavior to respond to your partner's specific desires for you. This is not an edict, but it can sure be useful information. Joanna's willingness to teach Rick how to love her and her capacity to respond as he learns run directly counter to Rick's core negative image of her as frigid. And conversely, Rick's willingness to learn and to please her broke up Joanna's conviction that he was "just a child."

It's easy to see how couples who think of themselves as two individuals can end up in escalating conflicts. Thinking that your partner simply *is* a certain way conveniently removes you from the picture and leaves little room for you to change or repair the relationship. The usual escalation goes from some particular incident to trend thinking (she *always*, he *never*) and from there to essential character (she just *is* cold, he just *is* a child). Once you're convinced you're dealing with a character issue, you can do little but plead with your partner to change who they are. Good luck with that.

What's missing here is the simple but demanding skill of learning to stay particular. If my conflict with Belinda is about this one time I failed to pick up a child, I have a shot at making a repair. I can apologize and make it up to her as best I can. But if our conflict is about all the irresponsible things I do all the time, there's a lot less I can do about it. And if the conflict is about my fundamental character as an irresponsible boy, what can I say? Give me your number, and I'll call you after ten years of psychoanalysis? Every jump from the particular to the general leaves me feeling increasingly helpless. And that makes me angry, which leads to more escalation.

Here's something to remember: *Functional actions in a relationship are moves that empower your partner to come through for you. Dysfunctional actions are those that render your partner paralyzed.* In a conflict, the farther your accusations stray from the particular, the more impotent your partner will feel, and the dirtier the move. It's fine to cast a cool eye over your whole relationship and deal with patterns you see, like "we're drifting apart," or "you're too angry at me too much of the time." These macro-level analyses are fine — if you are in your Wise Adult self, your prefrontal cortex. Remember this: *Don't jump from a microlevel upset to a macrolevel analysis when you're triggered.* Just as you shouldn't try to process deep issues when you've been drinking or you're stoned, you shouldn't do so when you're hurt and angry.

Remember your first skill, the *ur*-skill, the one from which all other skills follow: *relational mindfulness*. Take a break, throw some water on your face, take cleansing breaths with long exhalations, go for a walk. But don't try to grapple with relational issues from your Adaptive Child. Get yourself re-seated in your Wise Adult before attempting repair. Ask yourself which part of you is talking right now, and what that part's real agenda is. If your agenda in that moment is to be right, to gain control, to vent, retaliate, or withdraw—then stop, call a formal time-out if need be, and get yourself recentered. The only agenda that will work is the one about finding a solution. Only then will you have any luck using your newly cultivated skills.

I can almost hear you objecting to this plan of action: "What if I do all that and my partner stays a jerk? Why should I have to work so hard if he . . . ?" I'm telling you, that's your Adaptive Child speaking. "But it's not fair," you might say. Please. Fairness is a trap. Stop being centrally concerned with your rights for a moment. Stop acting like a rugged individualist, and re-member the wisdom of ecology, remember your biosphere.

Most of us have had the experience of watching our part-ners stubbornly double down on immature behaviors while we remain relatively sane by comparison. Good for you. Here's my advice. Stay that way. Don't jump into the mud pit with them.

Everyone gets to go crazy in long-term relationships, but you have to take turns. I call this *relational integrity*. It means that you hold the (Wise Adult) fort while your partner goes off their (Adaptive Child) rails. It's not an easy practice, but it builds strong relational muscles. If you behave well, and your partner responds in kind, that's a good day for everyone. If you behave well, and they don't—and you manage to stay in your Wise Adult self despite your partner's provocations—that's a bad day for your partner, a mixed day for the relationship, and a stellar day for you. You may not have achieved the result you wished for but you remained steadily in the you that you wish for.

Darlene and William: Learning Relational Integrity

"I can't help myself," Darlene tells me. "Son of a bitch, I take the bait every time."

"There's a sucker born every minute," I muse aloud.

Darlene chuckles, a warm, full-throated giggle that's hard to resist. Except that, sitting next to her on my couch, William seems immune to her charms. Both are in their late thirties, African American, vibrant, and quick. They're fun to work with, but less fun, I imagine, to live with.

"William pokes, and Darlene explodes," she observes.

"I don't have to poke very hard," he says.

"Well, that's a poke right there if you ask me," she says, crossing her legs and smoothing out the lines of her stylish silver skirt.

William contracts. With hunched-over shoulders, he seems congealed, hurt, and angry but is not saying anything about it.

"What are you feeling right now?" I ask him.

"I'm okay," he replies.

"That was never in doubt, but you do look a little upset." Actually, he looks a lot upset, but I thought "a little" might go down better.

He shrugs and glances at Darlene out of the corner of his eye.

"You're nervous about her," I try, noting his glance. "You're concerned about what she's feeling?"

"It's just that—" William sighs and stretches out his long legs. He touches together the toes of his wing-tip shoes.

"William?" I venture.

"You know," he tells me, "she says she explodes like it's not that big of a thing. But"—again that nervous glance—"maybe you should ask our daughter that."

"Say what?" Darlene rounds on him.

"That's right," William says, shrinking deeper into himself. "Ask Serene if it's no big deal."

"She's *five!*" Darlene is heating up.

"Old enough." He doesn't budge.

I'm starting to get how it goes between them, each partner's essentialist image of the other. *"William pokes and Darlene explodes,"* she had said, and she was right. As they describe their life at home, it becomes clear to me that Darlene is a handful and William is no help. Together they are caught in a loop that determines their actions without either's conscious awareness.

Remember, to live relationally, ecologically, you must first learn to identify your repeating pattern, your choreography, which you can describe simply in terms of *the more . . . the more*. The more Darlene rails, the more William's anger leaks out sideways. And conversely, the more William "lobs his grenades," as Darlene puts it, the more she rails. Darlene, of course, is the one who gets everyone's attention. But listening to them both, it doesn't seem to me that she is a lot meaner than her husband, just louder. In their marriage, and indeed, to their friends and family, Darlene is the problem: her anger is over the top. It is, and I am not condoning it, but I do put it in context.

Back in the early 1960s, one of the great pioneers of family therapy, Carl Whitaker, was doing rounds with young residents in a psych ward in Cincinnati. He was interviewing a suicidal, depressed woman who could barely speak through her tears. Beside her, her worried husband endeavored valiantly to cheer her up. He showed her pictures of their grandkids, smiling at the snapshots fondly. Despite her husband's perky reassurances, she only turned her head and gave in to another spasm of tears. "Everyone notices the wife's too-much crying," Whitaker famously observed. "Who sees the husband's too-much smiling?"

William is angry at Darlene. He is angry that she is so angry at him. He is angry that she "lost it on me" in front of their daughter. He is angry that he can't talk about any of these things without her blowing up even more. But the feelings he thinks he can't say straight out often manage to express themselves indirectly. The psychological term is *passive-aggression*, and William is a classic case; he acts out the feelings he doesn't address, through subtle putdowns and nonverbal complaints. He sighs, makes faces, rolls his eyes, and hunches up his shoulders like they carry the weight of the world. His relational stance is clear to me: he is the long-suffering aggrieved party.

Instead of seeing them as two individuals, I attend to the pattern linking them: William acting the vexed father to Darlene's wild, angry child. That means I can do things with their relationship they can't from inside it. I can, for example, try to pry Darlene out of her position as the bad one. In family therapy we call this *redistribution*. You take a quality that is supposedly lodged in one person—like badness—and you move it around.

"So William does it smooth," I reflect to Darlene.

"So smooth," she answers immediately. "So calm, so reasonable . . . and so mean."

"Tell me a mean thing he's said."

"He told me I didn't deserve my own child," she says, folding her arms across her chest.

"What I said," William starts—but one look from Darlene, and he backs down.

As a couples therapist, I keep my eye on the pattern. But change does not happen in the abstract, at a remove from the people in the relationship; rather, it comes from one or both partners. Keeping the dynamic in mind, my work is with each of the two individuals.

I start with William. As gently as I can, I tell him that he's passive-aggressive. I explain what that means and give him a few specific examples of the covert hostility that I've observed from him in the session. He's not happy hearing this from me.

"I have a belief," I tell him, "about passive-aggressive people in general and men in particular. Personally, I've never met a passive-aggressive person who didn't grow up in an environment in which being openly aggressive would have gotten the snot kicked out of him, if not physically then psychologically."

"That would be his father," Darlene says, shaking her head. "Kick out your snot and a whole lot besides."

William shoots her a look.

She's not looking back. "Meanest dude on the block. Just *mean.*"

"You felt free to express yourself?" I ask William.

"Not then and not now." He looks down at the floor.

"William, look at me, please," I say.

He looks up.

"You've got to stand up to her," I tell him. "You've got to be direct. I'll help you if you want. I'll walk you through every step. You didn't see this growing up, standing up for yourself respectfully."

He shakes his head.

"It's what you need now to get out of the cycle. I want you to be brave. Don't avoid. Steer into the storm. Will you do it? Will you learn?"

Without a cue, William turns to Darlene. "Listen, I'll be direct, okay? I don't like it when we fight in front of Serene. It's bad for her. You need to stop—stop yelling."

It's not easy to face down our fears, our negative expectations, and try something new and unshielded. I admire his courage and tell him so. "And Darlene—" I begin.

"I know," she says. "He's right."

I take a moment to explain the concept of witness abuse. "Children have no boundaries," I tell Darlene. "They're wide-open systems. When she hears you scream at William, it goes into her as if you were screaming at her. I'd do the same trauma work with her as with a kid who'd been sworn at."

Darlene looks at me.

"We have a lot of options. You can take a time-out. You can do an anger management course. You can try a little medication, you can—"

"How 'bout I keep just my mouth shut?" she says.

"You may need to take a physical break in the moment to do that," I caution.

"Okay, I'm on it."

"Thirty days," I tell her. "You have thirty days to stop this, or one of you has to move out for a while." She looks as if she's about to speak, but I keep going. "As we speak, you are traumatizing Serene. She's my priority, to be honest." That stops her. "Okay, you got it?"

"Moving out won't be necessary," she promises. And it wasn't.

By focusing on a couple's pattern, I hold no one at fault, yet have the freedom to call things as I see them. "Joining through the truth" is the Relational Life therapist's art of loving confrontation: we hold up the mirror of difficult truths and do not shrink from our role as mentor and coach. We confront difficult traits and behaviors while being loving so clients feel closer to us and trusting rather than resistant. Through confrontation, we join with clients and form alliances with them. Partners may say they want better communication or some other mechanical skill, but in almost all cases what they really want is major change in their spouse's brain; they want a more relational person.

Relational Life Therapy delivers on its promise of rendering each partner more relationally capable. I often see cases where someone gets up off the couch and swears off a behavior they've engaged in their whole lives — and with support, it's gone, permanently. My job as a therapist is to slip past the Adaptive Child and call out the Wise Adult self. That's the part I need to join with. I see things that you, the client, don't see yet. But you can borrow my prefrontal cortex until you grow your own new neural pathways. Together we will awaken the observer in you, the one with the reins, the one whose sight is undistorted: the one who can think, decide to act, and change.

And you may get surprisingly far on your own, dear reader, without a therapist. A part of you may wake up simply by resonating with these words.

Think for a moment about an important current relationship you feel stuck in—your intimate partner, of course, but also perhaps men or women in general, or your relationship to a child, friend, family member, or colleague at work. What is your core negative image of that person? Do you see them as overbearing or absent? Bullying? Controlling? Or shut down and ungiving? And when you see them that way, how do you characteristically respond? Do you plead, reason, cajole, and try to fix? Or do you withdraw, shut it down, escape? What do you imagine that person's core negative image of you might be, and can you acknowledge the grain of truth in it? What is your reciprocal role on the seesaw? Your dynamic? The more, the more? The more Belinda complains that I am irresponsible, the more I want to retreat into my work. What is your pattern? And how might you break free of it and be creative, fun, and even playful?

A friend of mine is married to an American Zen master. "What is it like," I ask her, "to live with a Zen teacher?"

"Well, it's really hard to stay mad at the son of a gun," she tells me. "We were in the supermarket just the other day and I started squabbling about God knows what. I turned to look, and he wasn't there. He had fallen to the floor and was kissing my feet. 'The problem here,' he said, 'is that these feet don't get enough attention!' How are you going to stay angry at that?"

I'd like everyone reading this chapter to commit to changing one relationally habitual behavior—complaining, controlling, shutting down. Hold a moratorium on your vain attempts to get the other person to change, and try something that will surprise yourself. In Relational Life Therapy, we say we want the weak to rise and the mighty to melt. If you are used to taking big, puffed-up positions—anger, indignation, control—lighten up, go soft, reach for vulnerability, and try leading with that instead. "I'm angry" becomes "I'm hurt." And conversely, if you've been frightened, try to find your voice, speak up, assert yourself with love toward your partner and care for the relationship. I call this *soft power*, and I'll have a lot more to say about how to exercise it in Chapter 8.

Finally, if you want to break up your pattern and get more of something in your relationship, try giving it. Instead of complaining that you no longer have fun, arrange a night out. Don't whine about your pathetic sex life—find out what turns your partner on, and try giving it to them. I was driving once and almost got into an auto accident because I was so taken with the bumper sticker on the car ahead of me: WE MUST BE THE CHANGE WE WISH FOR. And it was a quote from Gandhi. If you want more kindness, be kind. More laughter, be funny. Experiment with new moves and see what they bring you.

But if you cannot dislodge your stuck pattern no matter what you do, then you need help. You will know you need help, simply, when you cannot effect change between the two of you. But you may find yourself pleasantly surprised. When you stop railing at your partner to change and instead make sincere attempts to be more pleasing—or more forceful, or less aggressive, or whatever your change may be—you may find that a radical shift on your side actually elicits a different response on theirs. Don't fall into the trap of assuming the other person simply "is" this way or that. Put yourself in the picture.

Ask your partner what you might do differently to evoke a different response from them. And then when they make a suggestion or two, short of jumping off a local bridge, give it to them. Why? Because it works, silly. It delivers the nourishing closeness you seek, down through the shadowed trees that confuse you to the sustaining river of life, relationship, connection. You can use the relationships in which you find yourself as crucibles for your own change and transformation, and as sources of support and deep healing. Because love does heal us; love transforms—if we are willing to move past our own egos and show up for the occasion.

6

You Cannot Love
from Above or Below

Thinking of oneself as an individual, separate and apart from nature, breeds loneliness. But the difficulty doesn't end there. From its inception, the culture of individualism blended seamlessly with a much older cultural tradition: patriarchy. If you think of yourself as an individual, the world you inhabit is probably patriarchal, and patriarchy teaches us that not only are we separated from nature, we are also nature's masters. Individualism celebrates separateness. Patriarchy celebrates dominance. God gave Adam *dominion* over all the beasts that flew or swam or crawled upon this earth. That was a really bad idea.

Bruce and Leah: Toxic Domination

"I can't do it anymore," Leah tells me. White and in her early forties, with thick black hair and blue eyes, Leah looks more miserable than glamorous at the moment. Her marriage is coming unglued, and she is the one pulling the plug.

Beside her, Bruce sits expressionless. Wearing a suit, no tie, a starched shirt, and expensive shoes, he leans his athletic body toward me as if he were somehow coiled in his seat. His face is a mask, but his posture says *Bring it on!*

I instantly dislike him, though I can't say why. Are you shocked to hear a therapist confess to antipathy toward a client? One he's just met, no less? Let me be transparent and show you some of the backstage machinery. As a therapist, I deliberately allow myself to be swept up in whatever feelings I have toward my clients, which I believe is often useful information. It's like I have an antechamber in my mind, like an airlock in a submarine. I allow part of me to bathe in whatever the emotion is—annoyance, helplessness, repulsion—but the emotion stays contained in the antechamber while the rest of me, the observing me, decides how best to use that emotion.

Unless the client walks in with a placard saying I REMIND YOU OF YOUR MOTHER, I assume that what I feel is pretty much what everyone else feels. Minimally, I can use my reaction as data to help me arrive at a diagnosis—a relational diagnosis, not a psychiatric one. And at times I might choose to share my feelings as part of a therapeutic intervention. For the moment, though, I internally note my reaction to Bruce and attend to Leah, who has finished speaking and now waits for me.

"May I stay with this for a bit?" I ask Bruce, who nods his permission. Then I turn to Leah. "You're contemplating leaving the marriage?"

"I've already left. We're separated. Bruce lives on his own now."

I nod. "But you're here to . . ."

"Give it one last chance."

"Because?"

"Because," she muses, then ticks off the list, "three kids, almost twenty years together, I loved him once."

"You did?" I perk up.

"Yes," she says, not looking at her husband. "Very much."

I turn to Bruce. "How are you doing?"

"I'm okay," he says, though his tone is at odds with his claim.

"Is this a surprise? That she wants to leave?"

"No." He shakes his head. "No surprises."

"If this doesn't work . . ."

"I know," he says. "This is it."

"Do you want to lose her?"

"No," he answers. "But look, I'm not certain I want the marriage either."

Great, I think. *They each have a foot out the door.*

"Why would you want to leave?" I ask him.

Again, the head shake, but this time accompanied by a coy little smile, as if he's just told himself something amusing.

"Is this funny?" I ask him. "I wonder what you'd—"

And then Bruce makes his move. "You two were doing just fine when you were talking to *her*," he interrupts, gesturing toward Leah, managing somehow to direct me and utterly dismiss me all in one gesture. "You two go ahead," he tells us. "I'll wait my turn."

So, I think, *he's already bidding to take over the session.* I have him pegged as grandiose, superior, and controlling. A working hypothesis.

In his imperiousness, Bruce reminds me of a Parisian client I once had. At the first appointment, before saying hello, he'd handed me a list of his issues. "If you don't mind, I'd like you to Xerox two copies of this now and get them back to me before we begin," he said. Topping his list of issues, he'd typed *Narcissism.* "Well," I said, "you got the first one right!"

Rather than take Bruce on, I turn to Leah. "Why are you thinking about leaving?" I ask her.

She sits erect, showing little emotion, but she's quick. "I think you just saw a piece of it."

Bruce sits next to her, still, yet somehow quietly steaming.

"He's difficult to live with." She peeks at her husband, anxious about his reaction.

I pick her up on the glance. "You look at him," I say. "You're worried—"

"Concerned."

"About?"

"How he'll be when we're out of here."

I wonder what kind of reaction she's afraid of. And given what she's just said, I'm wondering if it's emotionally safe for her to say more.

At this point, I might have asked Bruce to wait in the waiting room while I investigated the potential for domestic violence. I don't ask women to speak truth to power if it's

physically dangerous. Relational Life Therapy holds that couples counseling is not the right course of action if there's a
threat of physical harm. But I'd already broached the subject
with Leah in her intake call. Bruce has never been physically
violent with her. His anger can be frightening, to be sure. He's
punched walls and shattered glass. These physical manifesta-
tions don't happen often, although, Leah tells me, they are
terrifying. Still, Bruce's violence has never been corporal,
nothing directed toward people, thankfully.*

And so I feel free to ask her in his presence, "What are you
afraid he'll be like?"

Leah leans in close to me, as if confiding a secret. "He'll
punish me!" is all she says.

"How? What will he actually do?"

She thinks about it a minute, still straining forward, her
hair fallen over half her face. "Hot or cold," she finally replies.
"Hot is yelling, screaming at me"—Bruce shifts on the couch,
as if to speak, but Leah plows on—"swearing—"

"Does he call you names?" I say, then turn to Bruce. "This
is her reality. It may or may not jibe with yours. We'll get there
I promise." Then, back to Leah: "Does he call you names?" I
repeat, adding, "Any sentence that begins with 'You are a—'"

Leah snorts. "Bitch. That's the biggie, with descriptors:
fucking bitch, cold bitch, nasty bitch . . ."

Bruce has had enough. "Now, just a minute—"

---

* If you are currently in a physically abusive or threatening relationship, please
read about resources in this chapter's endnotes.

"You haven't said these things to her?" I ask him.

"Hey look," he beseeches. "Couples fight, right? I mean, have I ever said such things during the course of twenty-plus years? Maybe. I could give you her list of—"

"You're mean." Leah looks her husband square in the face. "Couples fight, but not like you. You're cruel."

"You know, you're not always so nice either," he tries.

"That's not the truth, and you know it," she says. "Last Saturday?"

"I—well, I—"

"I slept in the den?" Leah says, turning to me. "Bruce wanted sex, but we were fighting." To her husband, she says, "You remember this?" No response. "So I begged off. Not in the mood for it."

Now she turns on her husband and looks at him, not with anxiety as before, but with a potent mix of fury, pity, and disgust. "So here's what my husband does. Without so much as a word, Bruce calmly folds my bathrobe, slippers, nightgown, and hairbrush into a neat pile. He places them all very carefully on the floor just outside our bedroom, then locks the bedroom door for the night, leaving me to explain to our two teenage daughters what the hell just happened."

I turn to Bruce. "Did this happen?"

"Well," he begins.

"Did you do this?"

"I'm not just going to lie next to my wife when she's cold," he protests.

"Were you cold?" I ask Leah.

"Like I said," she answers. "We'd been fighting all day. I wasn't—"

"This was retaliation," I tell Bruce.

"Excuse me?"

"This was payback," I tell him, "pure and simple."

"For Bruce, any 'no' is cold," Leah adds.

Bruce crosses and uncrosses his legs. His whole body seems to crackle with indignation. He looks at us both, his tormentors. "I'm not going to sit here and get ganged up on."

"No one's ganging up on you, Bruce. I'm trying to save your marriage." More physical sputtering. For the third time, I decide to turn to his wife instead of taking him on. "Is this how he gets back home?" I ask her.

"Every time I have an issue," she tells me. "I'm the bitch, and he's the injured party." She tells me stories of Bruce stumbling home around four in the morning, drunk and horny. Or Bruce dropping significant money entertaining his high-powered clients in strip clubs. Or Bruce, enraged, throwing their youngest out of the house for, as he put it, "insubordination." "Are you kidding?" she asked him, rhetorically. "That's your *daughter*."

"Okay," I say. "I have enough." I have seen and heard enough to know that Leah is right about her husband. I believe her because Bruce behaves in front of me exactly as she describes him at home, and also because of the way I feel sitting with him. As a therapist, I have three sources of information: each client's report, what happens in front of me in the room, and how I feel sitting with the client.

Bruce, throughout this exchange, has been staring out my window, managing somehow to be both emotionally removed and furious at the same time.

I turn to him. "So Bruce, you've done these things?"

"Well, out of context, I suppose I—"

"I have a seventy-thirty no-quibble rule," I say. "If what's said is seventy percent accurate, it's good enough for our purposes."

"Sure," he allows, magnanimous. "Seventy percent."

I look at him for a while, and he looks right back. "So this is a make-it-or-break-it moment in the therapy," I say.

"Meaning?" he challenges.

"You're on or off the bus."

He waits.

I go for it. "Bruce, I have good news and bad news. Which would you like first?"

He thinks for a nanosecond. "The good."

"I'd be surprised if we can't save your marriage."

He nods.

"Want the bad?"

He nods a second time.

"You're a bully," I say. "You're entitled, selfish, and punishing when you don't get your way."

"All this you arrive at in thirty minutes?" he asks, amused, smirking.

Part of me wants to wipe that smirk right off his face. "It's enough," I say, undeterred. "You want to know why?"

"Sure," he says, generous, nothing to lose.

"First, you don't deny it," I begin. "But more than that, you've been, if I may say this, dumb enough to act the same way in front of my face."

"Now?" he asks, disbelieving.

"In the session."

Finally, his fury erupts. "This is *bullshit*," he hurls at me. "Where did you study?" And then, turning to her, "Where did you dig up this quack?"

"Like now," I offer quietly. "You're bullying right now."

"There's a difference," he says through clenched teeth, "between being a bully and just—"

"Hey Bruce, watch this." I turn to Leah. "On a scale of one to ten, how accurate am I being now in describing your husband?"

"Ten," Leah says without a pause.

"And on a scale of one to ten, how important would you say the issue of his bullying is to you?"

"Fifteen," she says. "A hundred."

I turn back to Bruce. "If you want to keep her, which I get that you may not, but if you do, Bruce, I'd take this seriously."

He leans back on the couch and contemplates me for a long minute, deciding, I imagine, if he's in or out of our therapy.

"Okay," he says at last. "So she says I'm a brute. What about my complaints?"

"That she's cold, unavailable, not sexual, not affectionate?" I'm guessing. I've heard the list many times before from many Bruces. He's like the big guy on the seesaw complaining of his wife's uppitiness with no idea that his behavior has anything to do with it.

"Yes," he says, his chin jutting out, like a boy with a dare. "That, exactly."

"All that is real, Bruce. I want to deal with all of it. It all has to change."

"But?" he supplies.

"You have to go first," I tell him. "She won't come forward until you bring yourself down."

"Down?" Again the smirk. "From?"

I take a breath. "Bruce, let's talk a little bit about grandiosity."

The Seductive Poison of Grandiosity

For half a century, psychology has labored to teach us how to raise ourselves up from the inferiority of shame. But we've done a terrible job of helping people come down from the superiority of grandiosity—the sense of being above other people, contemptuous of the rules. Healthy self-esteem is a stance of *same-as*, regarding oneself as neither better nor worse than anyone else. Unhealthy self-esteem can look like shame—feeling inferior, *less-than*, defective. Unhealthy self-esteem can also look like grandiosity—feeling superior, *better-than*, entitled.

Here's a few things to know about grandiosity and, in particular, about the difference between grandiosity and shame. First of all, they are both lies; they are purely delusional. One human being simply cannot be fundamentally superior or inferior to another. Not fundamentally. Whether you're a serial killer or a saint, Mahatma Gandhi or a homeless alcoholic, all people have equal essential value, worth, and dignity. Your essential worth comes from the inside out; it can't be earned or unearned. It is yours at birth, and it's yours unto death.

This principle is, of course, the bulwark of democracy. Our society is built on the idea that we are all created equal, with each person afforded one vote, and one rule of law for everyone. At least that's how it goes in theory. We all know that equality doesn't play out anywhere close to perfectly in any human society. And therein lies the rub. Because while we all possess equal and irreducible value, it's hard to see that equality in everyday life. Whether we allow ourselves to acknowledge it or not, most of us have an exquisite sense, in any setting, of just where we are in the pecking order. And where everyone else is as well. The only problem with that type of judgment is that it's one hundred percent nonsense.

You may be a so-so tennis player who gets routinely beaten. You pay for lessons, you practice and practice, and six months go by. One day you beat the pants off the guy who had previously been beating you. Do you feel fantastic? I hope so. You earned it. You are now a better tennis player than your nemesis. Congratulations! You are not, however, a better person. You can be smarter, you can be richer, you can be short or tall—all that matters to a degree but none of it matters essentially. Essential worth comes from the inside.

The world of *us*, of interdependence, rests on a foundation of collaboration—collaboration with nature, with one another, with the inspiration that sometimes passes through us. The world of *us* is a realm of innovation and abundance. The world of *win-win*. But individualism rests on a foundation of competition—competition with nature, with one another. It bestows a lordly sense that you are your own source of inspiration. It's the world of *win-lose*. In our daily lives, the world we inhabit at any given moment depends on which part of our neurocircuitry we're in—left or right hemisphere, cortical or subcortical parts of the brain, sympathetic approach or parasympathetic avoidance.

Like many of the successful men I treat, Bruce has lived most of his life in *you and me* consciousness, and he's been well rewarded for it by the world. At the same time, it's made a disaster of his personal life. Our culture rewards Adaptive Children because the values and mores of that less mature, individualistic, nonrelational part of ourselves mirrors the values and mores of our culture's individualism. We live in an antirelational, narcissistic society whose essence for centuries has been the one-up, one-down world of capitalist competition.

Back when my kids were little, I attended a PTA dinner. As we sat together, a youngish parent I hadn't seen for a while struck up a conversation. Right away I noticed that the guy had lost some weight and looked fit. I became acutely aware of my own not-so-young belly and spun into a vortex of shame. I felt fat and old. Then suddenly I recalled that this man was a trust fund kid—he never worked a day in his life. *Sure,* I thought, *he can afford to be a gym rat if he likes, with family money paying the bills.* Zip! I was one up. Every penny I had had been earned. And while I was up there, looking down, I noticed that I still had more hair than he did. Ha!

But then I thought, *Wait a minute, he comes from money. The guy is rich. I'm not rich. Why aren't I rich? What did I do wrong?* And then—zip—I was one down. I went up and down, back and forth, until I snapped out of it and told myself, *Hey, why not listen to what the guy standing in front of you is trying to say?!*

Bruce rides in the one-up, grandiose position. He is hubris's poster boy: controlling, demeaning, and punishing when he doesn't get his way. Though married with kids, he feels entitled to drink like a frat boy and blow thousands in strip clubs. And he's cruel to his wife. "All this," I consider, "and *he's* thinking about leaving *her.*" He's contemptuous of his wife, and he's contemptuous of the rules. He's already setting himself up to experience his divorce with as little pain as possible. And he's right, by the way. Leah has become cold and less sexually acquiescent. She's less acquiescent in all sorts of ways these days. By finding her voice, Leah is changing the rules. That has to be acknowledged. But the individualistic, chauvinistic rules need to be broken for both of their sakes. Remember, I want the mighty to melt and the weak to stand up. For centuries, women have been taught to sacrifice their needs, "for the sake of the relationship." Let me be crystal clear. That is not what I'm talking about. Stepping into full voice and declaring their needs, for many women, is stepping into a relationship. Us-consciousness demands authentic assertion, not acquiesce. Leah's newfound assurance is good for their marriage. Although I suspect I'll have a hard sell in Bruce.

"Tell me about your childhood," I ask him.

"What do you want to know?"

"About your parents."

"I didn't have any."

"Excuse me?" I say.

"My mom took off when I was about three, never to be heard from again."

"That's tough," I offer.

He just nods.

"And dad was a big-time gambler and a drunk."

"Oh," I say, "I'm sorry."

"I spent my childhood in Vegas eating dinner with cheesy second-rate stars 'cause my dad was a high roller—when he was."

"Did he do well?"

"He was a compulsive gambler," he answers. "Are you kidding? We took off for Alaska for a year once because loan sharks were out to get him."

"How old were you," I hazard a guess, "when you started taking care of him emotionally?"

At first Bruce doesn't quite get the question, then it comes to him. "I didn't just take care of him feeling-wise. I'd try dragging his sorry ass into bed when he passed out. He was a big man."

"How old would you have been, at the youngest?" I ask.

"Oh my god, at the youngest? Four, five."

"You didn't get very far."

"No. I remember we were in this sketchy motel room, and I wanted him in bed with me, I kept pulling and tugging at him, but he wouldn't wake up, and I just . . . I couldn't drag him. He was too big."

"And you were too little," I add.

"Yes."

"You were just a little boy."

"Yes." He is looking inward.

"What are you feeling?"

"What?"

"Right now as we talk about it. I'm wondering what you're feeling toward your dad."

"Why?" His chin is out, challenging me.

"Why do I want to know how you felt toward your father?"

"Yes," he says guardedly. "Why?"

"As your therapist, it's important for me to understand how you felt, maybe still feel, toward your father."

"Because?"

"Because," I tell Bruce, looking him squarely in the face, "you have become him."

The Curse of False Empowerment

We all marry our unfinished business. We all marry our mothers and fathers. And in our closest relationships, we become our mothers and fathers. That little boy helplessly trying to drag his inert father off the floor is an archetype of disempowerment. He was five years old! And yet, insidiously, Bruce was also being spoon-fed a message: "When you grow up and become a man, you get to indulge yourself the way I do." Bruce was simultaneously overtly disempowered, which led to his underlying issues of great shame, and covertly falsely empowered, which led to his grandiosity, his sexual entitlement, cruelty, and attacks. Bruce's shame was hidden, tucked inside his drinking and acting out. His father was almost an alcoholic, almost a sex addict, and certainly a rager. Bruce had pulled his father off a barstool, and now Leah waits for her husband to come home after hours at strip clubs.

Here's the problem. Bruce loved his father. He was the only attachment figure and role model Bruce had. Consciously, Bruce despised his wretched father, but unconsciously he joined him, lived in the same world his father had inhabited. I call this *keeping a parent spiritual company*. Bruce had traveled from casinos to gentlemen's clubs, from craps tables to speculative investing. He was the success to his father's failure. While alive, his father had worshipped the holy buck, and Bruce had made enough money to roll in it for the rest of his life.

"I guess I showed him," Bruce announces to me as we discuss his wealth.

"Showed him?" I agree. "You completed him. You righted the wrong. You fulfilled the legacy."

Bruce looks up at me, and his eyes are slick with tears.

"You've been a loyal son," I tell him.

When I'm dealing with someone in their *you and me*, Adaptive Child consciousness—say rage, or quiet resentment, or angry pursuit—I always think of them relationally. What was this Adaptive Child adapting to? Remember, two paths of internalization form the Adaptive Child. One of them, reacting, tends toward resistance. Bruce's drive to succeed where his father had so spectacularly failed—his drive to resist his father's fate—fueled his workaholism. But the other pathway is modeling, and often, unconsciously, we model ways of being in the world that we consciously despise.

"Listen, Bruce," I begin. "Your father sounds like an alcoholic, a compulsive gambler, and he raged?"

"Oh yeah."

"At you?"

"Oh yeah."

"But you loved him," I say. "For all that, you loved him."

"It was the two of us against the world," he tells me.

I lean back in my chair and look at him, his face open to me for a moment. "It still is. Bruce, your poor father was a wreck. He was an addict, an alcoholic—"

"Yes," Bruce agrees.

"He was, in truth, utterly unavailable to you as a father."

"Yes."

I lean in close to him, speaking softly. "So I can teach you a way to be close to a parent who has zero capacity to be close to you. You can get nothing from them, yet you can still feel close to them."

"How do you do that?" he asks.

"*Be* like them," I tell him. "Live in their world with them. Live, in this case, in an angry, grandiose, self-indulgent world where ego is king."

Bruce sits back, hands folded, uncharacteristically quiet.

"I think you love your father," I say softly.

And now tears come. Not a lot; Bruce is hardly sobbing, but he is grieving and softening nonetheless.

"You cannot save him," I speak to the man, but more to the little boy inside him. "You cannot restore him."

"He's dead."

"Doesn't matter." We sit together in silence a long while.

"So, what now?" he finally asks.

"That's up to you," I tell him. "You have to decide who you belong to—your wild, grandiose father or your wife and kids. What kind of man do you want to be—an indulger, like your dad, or a real family man?"

"I love my family," Bruce says very faintly.

"Which family? The one you grew up with or the one you'll grow old with?"

Bruce looks timidly at Leah. "I don't want to be like my father." He reaches for Leah's hand and she gives it to him.

"You grew up near feral," I tell Bruce. "But you have a

family now. You chose well, Bruce. You have a nice family. The only thing missing in it has been you."

Clutching a used wad of tissues, Leah doubles over slightly and cries.

Bruce strokes her hand.

"Those tears are for you," I tell Bruce. "She wants you. She wants you home and normal."

"Normal is news to me," he tells me.

"I know. I'll help you. Every step of the way if you choose it."

Bruce stares hard at Leah, her crumpled face. "I choose it."

"Okay," I reply. "Then it's time to say hello to your wife and kids,"

"All right," he says.

"And goodbye to your father," I tell him.

His eyes fill with unacknowledged tears. "Maybe it's time, I guess," he tells me.

"Yes," I agree with him. "Maybe it's time."

Grandiosity Works in the Dark

The dysfunctional stance that we repeat endlessly in our relationships is driven by our Adaptive Child, which adapted to— with a mix of resistance and modeling—the treatment we received as kids. Most of us are painfully aware of the disempowering aspects of our childhoods, but we're fairly blind to false empowerment—our grandiosity—either directly, through a parent's pumping us up, or indirectly, through their modeling grandiose thinking and behaviors. Leaving the grandiose relational stance behind often means separating from the early relationship in which the stance was embedded.

Bruce was enmeshed with his father. As a child, he emotionally and physically took care of his dad, not the other way around, as it should have been. You can always tell if a client is enmeshed with a parent because they report that, as a child, they felt sorry for the parent. "Children aren't supposed to feel sorry for their parents," I tell Bruce. "Parents are supposed to be big enough to take care of themselves."

Why do we tend to be aware of a history of disempowerment and unaware of false empowerment? Because grandiosity works in the dark. When you're in a shame state, it feels bad. You know you're in it, and you want to get out of it. The open secret among therapists is that when you're in a grandiose state, half the time you don't realize it, and even when you do, it doesn't feel bad. In fact, in the moment, it feels pretty good. It feels good to let go of constraint and let your boss have it, or scream at your kids, or make out with a colleague. It feels good, but it just may ruin your life.

You have to think yourself down from grandiosity. Like when you resist that third glass or second serving, you have to let go of immediate gratification for the sake of a larger good — your body or your peace of mind or the emotional well-being of your children. You have to reach past the short-term hit of pleasure, for the sake of that longer-term, deeper pleasure called your family, or connection, or health. For your sake.

Coming down from the one-up of grandiosity is a capital investment in your own long-term happiness. Do it for your family certainly. But even more, do it for you. I tell grandiose men like Bruce that entitled privilege is like a knife that's all blade—it cuts the hand that wields it. Come down. Come back from cold outer space to the warmth of human connection. Come home.

The field of psychotherapy has been understandably obsessed with helping clients come up from one-down of shame. But in order to help people move into true intimacy, they must be *same-as*. You cannot love from above or below. Love demands democracy. More important, at the most fundamental level, there is no such thing as above and below. To think of oneself as better than or less than is a delusion. But it's a delusion with teeth.

Contempt-Free Living

Here's an insight that revealed itself to me one day as I was walking to my car. It suddenly came to me that the emotion, the psychological energy, of grandiosity and the emotion, the psychological energy, of shame were in fact not two separate feelings *but the same feeling going in two different directions*. The emotion driving both shame and grandiosity is contempt.

Think of it like a flashlight. When the beam of contempt swings out toward you, we call that *grandiosity*: "I can't believe what an idiot that guy was!" When the beam of contempt swings back in toward me, we call that *shame*. "I can't believe what an idiot I am!" It's the same feeling, sometimes expressed in the same words. As I've said throughout my career, contempt is emotional violence. Shaming someone, treating them as if they were inferior, is psychologically traumatizing. Psychologists writing on race have coined the term *microaggression* to describe the everyday, often unintended, slights and insults people of color routinely endure. Microaggression is an example of the emotional violence of contempt.

Contempt does not lie at the root of emotional violence; contempt *is* emotional violence, whether it's leveled toward others or toward yourself. I invite you, right now as you contemplate these words, to make a commitment that very well might have the power to change your life. A commitment to nonviolent living. Nonviolent between you and others, and nonviolent between your ears.

You can operationalize a nonviolent, contempt-free existence by committing to what in *The New Rules of Marriage* I called *full-respect living.* Full-respect living is a practice. Like most of the practices you'll be introduced to in this book, it is a minute-to-minute attentional discipline. Before words leave your mouth, you pause and ask yourself: "Does what I'm about to say fall below the level of basic respect?" If you judge what you're about to say as disrespectful, I have great advice for you. Shut up. And pledge, sincerely, from this moment forward, to do your best to curb actions and words that shame another.

And similarly, if someone is disrespectful to you, you will not stand still and do nothing. You may not be able to control them, but, whenever you judge it to be in your best interest, you can in most instances either speak up or, if need be, leave. Neither dishing it out nor taking it, you are finished with contempt and disrespect. You do this for your sake. That's important to remember. Because grandiosity often feels good, and because it often comes wrapped in self-righteousness, you have to think your way down from it. That son of a gun who just cut you off on the highway may deserve your rage, but *you* deserve to live a rage-free life. Someone else will have to confront his bad driving today. Not you.

Here's an exercise I'd like you to try. For about ten days to two weeks, keep a self-esteem journal. Take a few minutes at the end of the day and jot down, in your phone, in your computer, or on a piece of paper, moments when you were one-down that day and moments when you were one-up. What was the trigger? What occurred just before you went down or up? What were the thoughts, the feelings? Finally, what was the physical sensation? We carry shame and grandiosity in our bodies. How do you hold yourself when you're feeling inferior, and how when you're feeling superior? Get to know those physical postures. You can start to use them, once you're familiar with them, as markers—tip-offs that you're up or down.

Once you've done this observation exercise for a week or two, I recommend that you start the practice of intervening. Hard to accomplish, intervening is nevertheless quite simple to learn. If you're down, in your mind's eye you literally reach down with your arms and scoop yourself back up into *same-as*, neither better nor worse, looking levelly out of your eye sockets. If you're up, reach up and pull yourself down. Pia Mellody gave us a mantra to use for this moment: "Each person has inherent worth. No one more than. No one less than." Democracy in action, I say. Democracy in our skulls.

Our Relationship to Ourselves

We tend to hold ourselves the way we were held. If you were treated harshly, odds are your self-talk will be harsh. If you were indulged . . . and so on. Coming out from under the Great Lie of individualism, superiority, and inferiority means coming into healthy self-esteem. To me, healthy self-esteem means exactly what it says: it is our capacity to esteem ourselves—to hold ourselves warmly, tenderly—in the face of our screw-ups and imperfections. You are perfectly imperfect, as Pia Mellody would say.

In Relational Life Therapy, we make the distinction that the great American pediatrician Benjamin Spock taught a generation to appreciate: the difference between the behavior and the person. Before Dr. Spock, we commonly disciplined a child for who they were: "Don't be a naughty girl! Don't be a bad boy!" It was Dr. Spock who taught us to say, "Now, Dick, you're a good boy. Please get that two-by-four away from your little brother." You zero in on someone's behavior, not on their character. Feeling bad about bad behavior is good for us. It keeps us accountable and connected. Not feeling bad about bad behavior is shameless, grandiose, one-up. But feeling bad about who you are as human being moves you from remorse to an ad hominem attack; it is shameful. The bad feelings you have about your behavior should be proportionate to the severity of the behavior. You shouldn't feel horrible about running over a child's toy, nor casual about running over a child. But no matter how slight or serious the offense, you stop short of that internal habit I call *taking yourself apart*.

After our session, Bruce went home and fell into a deep depression. At first, I thought it was a good thing, a thawing out of his defenses. But he kept going. He had a hard time getting out of bed and dragging himself through his day. He had fallen into what every partner of a grandiose person and what many therapists fear. Faced with confronting his defensive thinking and offensive behaviors, he moved from inflation to deflation. From grandiosity to shame. He was appalled and repelled at the way he had been.

Actually, that's what I look for. Remember, to unlock a frozen neural pathway, the client and I need, first, to make explicit what was implicit—in Bruce's case, grandiosity that he'd never acknowledged, grandiosity so like his father's. And once we made it explicit, Bruce needed to feel the discrepancy between how he was living compared to how he wanted to live. He should feel some recoil, he should respond no! The great feminist family therapist Olga Silverstein, of the Ackerman Institute for the Family in New York, taught me how to arrange such collisions between how the client sees themselves and how they actually operate.

Like a lot of people in general and men in particular, Bruce deflated. When a client shifts from shamelessness to toxic shame, they move from one form of self-preoccupation to another. You're still preoccupied with yourself, even if you're telling yourself that you're a terrible person. While shame is all about you, guilt focuses your energy on the person you hurt. To repair a relationship, it doesn't help to keep berating yourself. You need to shift your attention to the person you hurt. It's not about you one way or another. Accountability to the person you hurt sounds like *I'm sorry I hurt you. What can I do to help you feel better?*

In a later session, as Bruce drones on about what a bad person he is, I stop and explain to him the difference between shame and guilt. "It takes some effort to pull yourself out of the poor me's into 'What can I do for you?' Shame isn't easy to get over," I tell him. "I'll give you sixty seconds."

Bruce visibly softens.

"Great," I say. "Now, from this place, turn to your wife and tell her from the heart something that you think she needs to hear from you right now."

He turns and, under my direction, takes his wife's hands in his own. He inhales deeply and lets out a long, shuddering breath. "Well," he begins haltingly, "I've been a . . . I've *behaved* like a fool. I've been selfish. I've been insistent."

Leah lifts an eyebrow, waiting.

"Okay," he tells her, "okay, straight up. I've been mean."

She begins to cry.

"I will never lock you out," he begins.

"That's a low bar," I say, pushing him a little.

"Look," he says to Leah, ignoring me, "I've been a shit, and I've treated you like shit."

"I'm not your employee," she tells him.

"I know," he says meekly.

"And I'm not some girl in a club," she adds, crying a little and annoyed at herself for her tears.

"I'm sorry." He reaches over to push the hair from her eyes, wiping away her tears. "You're right."

"I'm afraid those club dates are over," I tell Bruce. "You're just gonna have to tell your eager clients you got married."

Bruce shakes his head. "So are they!" he informs us, but he understands.

"It's time to remember that you've got a family," I tell him.

"Yeah, okay," he says, looking at Leah. "I get it."

And he did. I continued to see them for another few months, but our heavy lifting was behind us.

I often talk to the men I work with about learning to become true family men, men who stretch themselves and give more. I tell Bruce toward the end of our work together, "A boy's question to the world is: 'What do you have for me?' A man's question is: 'What does this moment demand of me? What do I need to give?'" If having an intimate partner doesn't grow you up, having kids will stretch you like nothing else — assuming you let it.

Belinda and I will sometimes listen to a friend say something that strikes us as precious, like "I have to nap by three each afternoon or I'm just useless." We'll look at each other with a look that says, *This guy never had kids!*

One night when our children were babies. Belinda, who has a full-time clinical practice of her own, had been up three nights running. This night, at about two a.m., I awoke to the sounds of our youngest wailing and the feel of an elbow in my ribs. "Your turn, sweetie," she mumbled.

"But Belinda," I told her. "I've got a massive lecture tomorrow. I'll be out in front of over a thousand therapists!"

At which point, my dear wife said something quite simple that changed my life forever. She told me, "Give the lecture tired."

That's a family man. You are not the top priority.

Research shows us that giving brings much longer-lasting happiness than receiving does. Once we trade in the Great Lie of superiority and inferiority, we can step into the humility of knowing we are not above but a part of our marriages, our families, our society, our planet. Many of my dissatisfied clients wish their partners could do a better job of showing up, of enriching the relationship with their presence. But you can't be present to your partner unless you are in the present with them. And often our troubled past overtakes our present. We are no longer "here and now." We are distinctly "there and then."

Coming out of trauma means moving into the now, into connection with whatever is happening—in you or between you and others—without feeling the need to control or shape it. Moving beyond our trauma means opening up to the natural process of our own lives, working with our lives by accepting what is. Once you let go of hubris, you can relax. You'll find you're more able to let things emerge, hear other voices, listen for the unsaid. You'll begin to develop, at any age, the basic trust that psychologists would wish you to have in your twos and threes, the simple trust that things will work out on their own without the stamp of your will.

What Bruce mostly does, in the weeks after he realized the grandiosity he'd lived with, is sleep. "I didn't realize I was so utterly bone weary, just exhausted," he tells me in our final session.

"It takes a lot of energy," I reply, "to hold yourself up with each step, propel yourself through the universe."

"An uncaring universe," Bruce agrees, looking at Leah.

"All the while," I say, "it turns out it was you who was uncaring."

Bruce looks deeply into his wife's eyes. "Will you be here for me?" he asks with heartrending vulnerability. "Despite how I've pushed you away?"

She lets her tears answer for her.

"I've been such a fool," he tells her. "Can you forgive an ex-asshole?"

She laughs out loud, and then they both laugh. "That's a big word, ex."

"It's not a word, actually," he corrects her. "It's a prefix."

"That's not convincing 'ex' behavior," Leah declares.

"Just kidding." He takes her hand. "Honest, just messing with you." He grins. "Not great timing I guess, huh?"

"You know, Bruce —" Leah begins.

But I cut her off. "Let's just call your husband a diamond in the rough."

"Sparkle, sparkle," Bruce tries. She does not seem amused.

"This is the part where I say that you need to work with the man you've got instead of the one you deserve," I tell her.

"Some discrepancy," she tells me.

"Sparkle, sparkle."

"Oh god." She groans as she regards the spectacle of her husband. "Some people get themselves unrepressed, and you kind of wish they hadn't."

"Be careful what you ask for," I agree.

And that was the last I saw of them.

What I'd like to leave you with is simply this. Even something that sounds as individualistic as working on one's self-esteem turns out to be social. You are neither better than nor less than other people. Those countless others who we carry in our heads, judging us and being judged. Who's up, who's down, who's right, who's wrong. Wake up. None of that matters. As I think about Leah and her new "ex," I am reminded of a line from Rumi, the ancient Persian poet, who once wrote simply:

There is a field
Beyond right
or wrong . . .

I will meet you there.

Chapter 7

Your Fantasies Have Shattered, Your Real Relationship Can Begin

"I can't breathe! Oh, my god, I can't breathe!" Angela, a petite, dark-haired white woman, wearing a purple velvet frock with a lacy white neck, twirls her hands in desperation as she gulps air.

"Okay," I say, hoping to reassure her. "Slow down."

"I can't." She clutches at her chest. "My heart—"

"I think you may be having a panic attack," I tell her.

Next to her, her husband, Mike, shifts in his chair. A big, square man, he rests his forearms on his spread knees and leans in, all concern.

"Angela," I say, "I want you to take deep, slow breaths, long exhale, like this." I show her. "Put your feet flat on the floor. Feel your feet on the floor."

With her eyes locked on mine, her black hair pinned back, Angela places each of her sensible black shoes flat on the floor and starts to breathe slowly and deeply. Her thin body shudders a little as she calms.

"That's it," I tell her. "Nice and slow. Doing fine."

She breathes, hands clenching and unclenching in her lap. She closes her eyes to concentrate, then opens them again seconds later, terrified.

"Take your time," I tell her. "Just breathe. You're doing fine."

Slowly, painfully, Angela brings herself back. "Wow!" she says at long last, looking up at me and smiling. "That was really something." And then she bursts into tears. "Shit!" She slaps herself in the leg, hard. "Shit!" She collapses into a sob and rocks. "I can't stand this," she mutters as she cries, "I can't take this."

"I know," I soothe, "I know." Inside I think: *Welcome, my dear. Come on in. You have crossed over into the realm called adultery, infidelity, betrayal. A hot knife in your gut. A two-by-four to your skull. Enter here, and let me do what I can to ease your utterly miserable human torment.*

Angela no longer lives in the world she inhabited three weeks ago. In that old world, the one no longer available to her, she led a stable, happy life. She had three kids, age fourteen on down, a solid career, and a great husband. Then one morning, while he was in the shower, seized by impulse or by intuition, she took a good look at her husband's phone. She found, buried in obscure accounts, emails. Lots and lots of emails. Hot, salacious emails. From Loreen, or sometimes just Lor. Lor, who couldn't wait to taste him again, feel him against the back of her throat, inside her body.

My heart bleeds for Angela. It used to be that a woman would smell someone's perfume or notice lipstick on a shirt.

Nowadays, with the internet, she may well have a front-row seat to every graphic detail. Death by a thousand cuts—and not all of them shallow. "Did I really need to know about her smooth, creamy thighs? Fuck you!" She suddenly turns to her husband like she's going to hit him. Instead, she collapses into more tears. "Fuck you," she repeats with less conviction.

Shattered

Infidelity, being cheated on, lied to, betrayed: that indescribable rip that starts in your heart and goes on to decimate reality itself. Are you not who you've pretended to be all these years? Who I believed you to be? I don't know you. Who are you? Who have I been living with this whole time?

In 2002 Ronnie Janoff-Bulman wrote an influential book on trauma entitled *Shattered Assumptions*. That title captures a lot about the nature of trauma. Trauma shatters you, but not in the places you'd expect. It rips the rug out from beneath you; it rips out the very floor beneath your feet. It takes aim at your assumptions, the things you trust every day in your life without thinking about it—like that your spouse is at the conference he said he was at and not in some lover's arms. Trauma means you lean against the kitchen wall and somehow sink right through it. The world no longer behaves in a reliable way. There's more than a tinge of horror to it. Well, if you can sink right through a wall, what else can happen?

And here's the realization that can really turn your bowels to ice: if your spouse can do *that*, well, what else can he do?

Everything you believed has been shaken. You ask, "How long did this go on? How many lies did you tell? Was this your first affair? The only one? Have you, in fact, been cheating throughout the whole relationship?" This flood of emotion is vast, insanely intense, profoundly confusing. The one person you'd most likely turn to for comfort is now the cause of your anguish. Love, hate, desperation, repulsion, lust, disgust, blind need—all rotate in wild succession. In your whole life, you have never withstood such an emotional storm.

Now, here's the radical claim I'd like to make. Does everything I've just described indicate that Angela and Mike are in a bad marriage? It does not. They are in a horrible moment in what might, in the long run, prove to be a superlative marriage. It's too early to tell. In Relational Life Therapy, we're distinctly uninterested in helping a couple who have been devastated by betrayal get back to the old equilibrium. Our aim is higher than that. I'm not interested in merely helping Mike and Angela survive the crisis. I want to use this crisis as a springboard for fundamental transformation—in each of the two partners and in the marriage itself. As a family therapist, trained in general systems theory, I know that in crisis lies opportunity. Both transformation and dissolution begin with crisis, with disequilibrium. Enough disequilibrium spells death to the system as it is. But even that might not be the end of the story.

"The marriage you once had is gone," I tell Angela and Mike. "The only question is, can you forge a new one?"

My colleague Esther Perel has quipped, "I expect to have six marriages in my lifetime, and I hope they are all to the same man!" Some infidelities do end in divorce, to be sure, but, statistically, most don't. Two-thirds of marriages survive the hit. And that doesn't factor in going to therapy to get help. Angela and Mike are riding out the maelstrom. This is the dark night of the soul of their marriage.

What has been yours? Most of us have had one, whether it's as big and wrenching as infidelity, or more a case of everyday wear and tear, drifting apart, death through attrition. Whether it's large or small, most of us face a shakeup, a wound, a disillusionment so profound that it opens up the unthinkable possibility that you might not make it after all. Let me remind you, we are mortal. Death is baked into our human condition, along with limitation, imperfection, and imbalance. Our imperfections collide in ways that disappoint, that hurt, and that even, yes, betray one another.

James Framo, the father of couples therapy, once said that the day you turn to the person sleeping next to you and realize that you have been had, that this is not the person you fell in love with, and that this is all some dreadful mistake—that, Framo claims, is the first day of your real marriage. Welcome to humanity. No gods or goddesses here. And what a great thing that turns out to be. While we may long to be married to perfection, it turns out it is precisely the collision of your particular imperfections with mine—and how we as a couple handle that collision—that is the guts, the actual stuff of intimacy.

Harmony, then disharmony, then repair is the essential rhythm of all close relationships. It's like walking. You have your balance, then you stumble. You catch yourself and rebalance.

This cycle of harmony, disharmony, and repair begins when you are a baby. At the start of one of Dr. Ed Tronick's famous film clips, a baby is molded into her mother's arms, no bones, a noodle, perfect contentment. Then something happens: gas, or a noise, or hunger. The infant starts to freak out, thrashing and crying, and refuses to settle. The mother freaks out as well, her face tense, her jostling more frantic. Her angry look of frustration bores down on the child. The baby instinctively crosses her tiny forearms to cover and protect her face, blocking mother out. And then, miraculously, the pacifier is accepted, or the gas passes, or the noise quiets, and then—ah—molded again. All this occurs within forty seconds.

Freud described the early relationship of mother and infant as one of "uninterrupted oceanic bliss." But it took researchers like Ed Tronick and T. Berry Brazelton to actually stick a video in front of mothers and their babies and observe the real story of finding connection, losing it, and finding again. The endless round of peek-a-boo is many an infant's first mesmerizing game: here, gone, here again.

We all know about the harmony phase, the honeymoon, that marvelous heart-swelling time of being in love when a heady chemical brew hits the brain. One of the main chemicals in the brew is dopamine, the reward chemical and the same chemical cocaine releases to cause addiction. Another is norephedrine, an arousing chemical central to fight-or-flight vigilance, leading to an enlivening feeling akin to a runner's high. Levels of testosterone and estrogen also increase, two hormones that create the quickened pulse of lust. What goes on in the brains of young lovers is so like an addictive process — even including physiological signs of withdrawal when the love object is absent — that psychologists have long noted the phenomenon of romance or love addiction. I have personally encountered troubled souls who were addicted to this mix of endogenous "drugs" as surely as any drug addict.

Her name is Pam, a pale Southern beauty with that flirty, solicitous charm characteristic of privileged Savannah women. I was "on the other side of the desk," as we say — a participant myself in a deep healing weekend group. Pam is telling us about her bottoming out, the moment that catalyzed her recovery from a long-standing pattern of love addiction — erotomania, as her psychiatrist called it. Pam had fallen obsessively in love with a famous writer who'd recently moved next to her on their rural lane.

One summer evening, Pam tells us, the object of her adoration drove off with a weekender luggage bag, his two Doberman Pinschers tied on long leashes in the yard. The thrill of opportunity rippled through her body. On automatic, she found herself rifling through her refrigerator. Ah, there it was, hamburger. She spread out the ground meat on a plate and then kneaded into it the spilled contents of eight tranquilizer capsules. She then took herself over to her neighbor's yard and fed the sedative to his dogs who, in less than thirty minutes, knelt over in a dead sleep, snoring. Satisfied with her handiwork, she jumped up onto his trellis and inched all the way up to his second-floor bedroom. Angling herself from the trellis, she stretched toward the bedroom windowsill. She gazed, as if at a shrine, into her neighbor's bedroom, his clothes strewn about, books everywhere.

"I could just about smell him," Pam tells us. "I felt so at peace. Close to him, this glorious man. And *that* was when the dogs woke up."

We listeners in the group are unsure how to respond. Should we laugh? Commiserate? Blake, a long skinny bean of a guy, just says, "Aw shit," and scrunches his face as if he'd licked something sour.

"So, there I was," Pam tells us, "tippy toes on the trellis, literally hanging by my fingernails, with two growling Dobermans beneath me." She scans our faces. "That's when I said the words that changed my life. I looked at my own wretched face in the window glass and distinctly said, out loud, 'Girl, you need help!'"

Pam somehow got herself down in one piece and off to her first Codependents Anonymous meeting. Life has been better for her ever since.

Untreated, many love addicts simply move from one honeymoon phase to another, often leaving a trail of destruction behind them. Russel, in his mid-seventies, had been financially successful enough to pull off such a tragedy in style. He would fall madly in love and quickly marry. Things would be great for a few years, and then "by year three or four, the real people would show up. What a pain in the ass!" The more his wives complained, the more Russel withdrew until he landed in his next affair. A few years would go by, and he'd ditch wife one for his mistress, now turned into wife two—only to rinse and repeat. By the time I met him, he was on what he described as "wife five-B." As he put it, "I proposed to potential five-A, but she was perspicacious enough to turn me down, so I wound up married to the next one." With five wives, seven children, and a bushel of grandkids, Russel described his life as "utterly and chronically vacuous."

Like a car that can't slip into second gear, Pam and Russel were stuck in the first phase of a relationship. Neither had grappled with much of anything in their relationships, trading in reality for fantasy, gratification for intimacy. I call this first relationship phase *love without knowledge.* You may have a deep intuition that this person is the one for you, a soul recognition. But you have no idea how they pay their bills, or handle their family, or the condition of their bathroom floor.

Sooner or later, reality begins to intrude, and harmony is replaced by disharmony, the second stage of relationship. The idealization characteristic of the first stage yields to an at times overwhelming disillusionment: "You're not at all who I thought you were." For many, disillusionment comes when the extraordinary joy of the harmony phase yields to the disappointment of boring, mundane life. But for others, like Angela, disillusionment comes all of a sudden, punching us in the gut. Everyday familiarity eases us into disillusionment. A betrayal like infidelity rips the curtain away from our illusions in one bloody tear.

Wiry and fragile-looking, Angela grapples with such a flood of disenchantment that it's hard for her to get through the next five minutes; she's in an acute state of shock. She turns to Mike and utters the same question that she has endlessly repeated since discovering his affair: "How could you?" That is one of two questions virtually every hurt partner is haunted by. "Literally what were you thinking, when you left her bed to have a cozy dinner with your family? How could you do that?"

Since disillusionment through infidelity almost always brings shock, the other question common to all hurt partners is "How can I know you won't do it again?" Reality has been ripped apart. Hurt partners, like all trauma survivors, are driven to put reality back together again. Angela has a hundred unanswered questions. "When you said you were in Chicago last Christmas, you were really . . ." She needs to know the size and model of the truck that just ran her over. But infidelity is just the most dramatic form of a process common to all relationships—the sinking feeling that this is not what it was supposed to be.

———

In family therapy, we are taught to think of couples as having a "marital contract," usually unspoken. Maybe it's *I will protect you and see that you never come to harm*. Or *I will always see you and be on your side, the way no one has been before*. Or *You will be my stability, and I will bring passion into our lives*. These unspoken contracts work great—until they don't. *You will be my rock* morphs into *I don't need a daddy*. *I will bring passion to our lives* becomes *And to Harry's and Bill's as well*. Sooner or later—and to a degree, almost inevitably with the arrival of kids—the dream cracks open, and the very thing your partner helped you escape gets served to you on a platter.

Falling in love means that whether you acknowledge it or not, you think, *With this person I will be healed, or at the very least I will avoid and compensate for my earliest lacks and injuries*. Disillusionment comes with the cold realization that not only will your partner not directly heal you, but they are also exquisitely designed to stick the burning spear right into your eyeball.

Here's the thing about the disharmony phase—it hurts. I mean, it really hurts. For more than twenty years, I've spoken to audiences about what I call *normal marital hatred*. And not once has someone come backstage after and asked, "Terry, what did you mean by that?"

My first concerns for Angela, given the state she's in, are concrete. Is she eating? Sleeping? Is she plagued by intrusive thoughts? (*Her creamy thighs.*) Could she use a little medication to sleep, or to feel less depressed, less blasted? Should we do some frank trauma recovery work, some EMDR perhaps, to help with those torturous sexual replays that loop in her head?

Then I turn to Mike. Why did he cheat? The sheer wall of that question for the unfaithful one: why?

Generally, in response, I hear two types of reasons. The first is simple selfishness. "I don't know. I was traveling on business. We'd all been drinking, It just . . ." Right. And the second is "Gosh, it just happened somehow. I don't know. I didn't actually make it happen. I was hardly there." Sure. The problem with these lines of defense is their utter lack of responsibility. It was irresponsible to cheat to begin with, and now you compound that with your lame attempts at accountability. And what does that mean, *It just kind of happened*?

"Mike," I say, "we don't ask someone why they cheat— that's obvious. Affairs are flattering, new, exciting, sexually pleasurable. We ask someone why they don't cheat. What makes someone say no?"

Mike shifts in his chair, about to speak.

But I keep going. "I'm saying no these days and have for quite some time. Can I tell you why?"

Mike nods.

"Because I don't want to hurt my partner. I don't want to look into my kids' eyes and explain why Daddy screwed around on Mom. I don't want my reputation ruined. And

believe it or not, I'd rather live in a state of integrity. Those are
my reasons. But something in you overrode your no. It's our
job to figure out what that was."

Over the years, I've found two general factors that override
the no. Affairs happen when either:

1. The unfaithful partner has insufficient constraints in
    themselves. In other words, their selfishness trumps
    their relationality. Sooner or later they'd cheat on
    anyone. The issue in these cases is narcissism and
    entitlement. *Life is short. I deserve it.*
2. The relationship has become so unsatisfying—so
    contentious, or distant, or dead—that the cheater feels
    there isn't enough worth protecting. *If I'm found out,
    well, it's not so great in this marriage anyway.*

As the therapist charged to help the pair move back into closeness, I usually make a determination whether the primary
problem is the character of the cheater or the state of their
union or both. It turns out Mike's case is relatively simple.
Even though he has been married for sixteen years, he's never
fully left high school. He's routinely gone off with his pals for
weekends, drinks like a fish, and parties like a nineteen-year-
old. Utterly entitled, he rarely helps with the house or the
kids. He works long hours, makes a steady living, and once
home, generally prefers to be left alone. His hard work as an

electrician and his paycheck are enough of a contribution to family life, as far as he has been concerned.

When Mike first met Angela, back in high school, he had been *wild,* and she had been *good.* Such was their unspoken marital contract. He provoked her to loosen up, dance, and have great sex. She was his stability and moral compass. Mike's dad was a drinker and a womanizer; his home life was full of strife and chaos. Angela's nice family seemed blessedly normal. He was to teach her how to play; she would teach him responsibility. The only problem was that Angela, true to form, turned out to be the better student. She had little difficulty in the bedroom, trading in her velour shifts for racy lingerie and velvet restraints, while Mike had little difficulty trading in Angela for, well, just about anyone willing to take him.

Mike had had a series of frat boy affairs: he went out with the same "kids," as he called them. Drank with them, fished with them, hunted sometimes, "picked up girls sometimes." He had never quite digested that he was no longer single. With his despised father as his unconscious model, and with his South Boston boy pals egging him on, he saw family as the home base from which to launch his adventures. It simply never occurred to him to sit still in his own home with his wife and kids and have fun. Family, to Mike, was obligation—fun was in the back alley. Mike was living out what some therapists call a *love-lust split.* Home was stable, good, responsible, and dead. Outside, the street was adventurous, bad, selfish, and alive.

"You know," Mike tells me after I explain this to him, "I've got a big heart." Which he does, I note. "I'm not one of these shut-down characters who don't feel nothing. Right?" He turns to Angela, who barely nods. "And I'm in my body. I mean, I can move—like, sexually."

"Uh-huh," I say.

"I just can't seem to do both with the same woman."

"Okay," I say, and pause. "Hey Mike, tell me about your mother."

His mother, I'm not surprised to hear, was a living saint, a long-suffering martyr cut straight from Boston Irish Catholic cloth. While Dad scorched the earth, Mom kept the home fires burning.

"Okay," I tell him. "Now I get it. Where your entitlement came from."

"Entitlement? What do you mean?"

"Your expectation, Mike, that Angela will put up with your bullshit."

He lowers his head, angry.

"Like your mother has," I go on. "You've re-created your parents' marriage."

Mike is shocked, but I'm cautiously optimistic. At least he was in couples therapy and trying. I can't tell you how many overly accommodating women I've seen over decades who put up with their husband's bad behavior for years, afraid to rock the boat, only to be left for another woman anyway. I talk to the couples I work with about *fierce intimacy*, the courage to skill-fully take one another on when they are in a state of disharmony. (For more on fierce intimacy, see my online course "Staying in Love: The Art of Fierce Intimacy," at Terryreal .com.)

Angela and Mike met in high school. They were both "from the neighborhood," meaning South Boston Irish, and Mike wasn't completely crazy to imagine that his wife would somehow tough out the hurt that streamed from his various antics. His mother had. But as I tell him, times have changed.

"I hated your drinking, and leaving me, and partying with your friends," Angela tells us. "I just thought you'd grow out of it. You'd figure it out. But this"—she spreads her hands and stares between them, as if she's just uncurled a map—"I never thought this. I trusted you, Michael. I thought we had a bond."

"We do, Ange," he whines.

"We did, Michael. You broke it." She looks away. "I don't know where we are now."

Where they are now, I think, *is the threshing floor, the slaughterhouse.* They are inside the alchemical crucible that dissolves and only then might transform. Pain had melted Angela down to her essence. But can I help them cross over to safety? Is there a possibility of repair?

"Do you still want him?" I ask Angela.

"Not as currently configured," she answers with admirable directness and force.

"What needs to change?"

"*He* does!" she exclaims. "Every goddamn cell in him." She wheels on her husband. "It's simple, Mike. Grow up or pack up."

Why, Angela, I think, *you have a spine after all.*

"Now," she adds. "Change now. Or don't. I'm not waiting much longer."

"Aw, Ange," he pleads. "Baby, don't—"

"Don't you 'baby' me!" she snaps. "Save your 'babys' for your girlfriends."

He looks up at me, helpless. *Do something,* his look says.

"Mike, do you want to hear from me?"

He nods vigorously, as if to say, *Help! Throw me a lifeline.*

"Okay, I'll tell you what I think." A pause. "She's right. You've been a wrecking ball." I talk to him about the particular form of grandiose entitlement called *being a bad boy.* "You're a thirty-six-year-old high school greaser."

"Hey," he says, "I was never—"

"You know what I mean," I push back. "You might as well have a cigarette tucked behind your ear and a rubber in your back pocket."

He cracks up, laughing at me. "I think you may be in the wrong era." He smiles.

But I'm not laughing. "Why'd you get married? Why'd you have kids?"

"I love my wife," he says, stung. "I love my kids."

I lean in to face him. "Then pull yourself together and protect them. Every time you step outside your marriage, you put them in harm's way."

He doesn't look happy hearing me say this.

"Mike," I conclude, "I have great news for you that I don't think you've ever really fully digested."

"What's that?" he asks.

"You have a family."

Coming back. Repairing. How do you put back the pieces? Why even try? I call the harmony phase of a relationship *love without knowledge*; I call the disharmony phase *knowledge without love*. Now you know exactly and precisely all your partner's flaws and blemishes. You see them all. But you don't love your partner very much. You are utterly in *you and me* consciousness, facing an adversary, fighting for your psychological survival.

How Angela copes with Mike will have everything to do with the particularities of her Adaptive Child. Except that her usual adaptation—to be accommodating, to be good—just split open and spit in her eye. Maybe it is time for a change. And this is the painfully hard-won gift of disharmony.

Remember, to unlock a neural pathway the implicit must become explicit. For Mike, it's *I've been an overgrown teenager.* For Angela, it's *I've been a pacifying doormat.* And the old habit must no longer appeal. *I'd rather learn to show up for my family.* And *I'm learning to speak my mind and put my foot down.* In other words, by touching the hot wire of Mike's infidelities, both partners, with my help, might just possibly blast their way into the more mature traits and behaviors characteristic of their Wise Adult selves. *My family needs me to show up for them,* thinks the new Mike. *I better speak up and stand up,* thinks the new Angela. In this way, both partners dramatically transform their character, and their marriage enters a fresh new stage of development—one that can regularly incorporate the skills of repair.

Making a permanent shift in the stance of the Adaptive Child involves what neurobiologists call *memory reconsolidation*, as does shifting the automatic expectations of the core negative image.

Angela's previous emotional knowing was "If I stay passive and accommodating, I will keep myself safe." But that was shattered by the affair, which made her for the moment extraordinarily pliable. The gift of discord is the opportunity for memory reconsolidation. Angela's new knowing is: "Standing up for myself will keep me safe. I will not depend on Mike to keep me safe." Because it cannot be true that accommodation and standing up for herself will both keep her safe at the same moment, the disconfirm is achieved and she has a new emotionally known truth in the implicit neural network.

Memory reconsolidation is a change to the Adaptive Child directly (subcortical, implicit emotional knowing) rather than a change to the Wise Adult (prefrontal cortex connected and responsive to the subcortical). It makes it much easier for the Wise Adult to run the show because it has less to regulate in the subcortical system. Repeated experiences of real-life encounters disconfirming our negative expectations have the power to heal close intimate relationships and even, in some instances, if the conditions are right, severe trauma. Kindness can heal. Empathy can heal, if indirectly. The best way to open another's heart, it turns out, is to open your own.

The Blessing of Repair

Repair is the final third of the cycle of harmony, disharmony, and repair. I call the stage of repair *knowing love*. Here you are utterly aware of your partner's failings and shortfalls—the temper that's too big, the affection that's too small, the sloppiness, or stinginess, or impulse to control—and yet you choose to love them anyway. What the relationship gives you far out-weighs what it lacks. And so you embrace those parts of your partner that, left on your own, you might avoid.

Mike is toxically selfish and painfully immature. He also adores his wife and kids—though you'd never know it by the way he's been behaving. Does Angela want him still? Yes, if he can grow up and stay faithful. She loves her big hulk of a guy. Is he the world's most sensitive husband? Hell no. But he lights her up with his stupid grin, and when the five of them are together, what can she say? It's home.

"You have a choice," I tell Mike. "You can submit to being married, or you can be free and go back to being single. You just can't do both at the same time."

Mike looks long and sorrowfully at his wife. He's so completely awkward with his feelings, so inarticulate, that I almost feel sorry for him, until I recall all the damage he's done.

"I'm sorry, Ange," he says. "I don't know what else . . . I'm so sorry, sweetheart."

Sitting next to him, she bristles.

I intervene. "Listen," I tell her. "Just listen to the guy."

Mike stares down at the floor.

"Look at her," I tell him. "Tell her."

"It's just . . ." he begins, frustrated that he can't find better words. "Angela, it's just—you're the best thing that ever happened to me. You and the kids, I mean. You're *everything.*"

"Then act like it," she answers coldly.

"I know, I know. I've been a total shit, I get it." She looks up at him. "I'm an asshole. I know it. I don't deserve it. But if you did, Ange. If you could somehow forgive me. I would never . . ."

"Yeah?" she says, waiting, unimpressed.

"I'd never hurt you again. Not like that. Not ever, Ange. Or put my family at risk. If you could . . . I know. I know. I don't know why you would. But if you ever *could* forgive me, learn to trust me again." He pauses, looks at her.

She raises her face toward him.

"Never again, sweetheart. I can't begin to tell you."

Soft, undefended, Mike pleads his case. "I will never hurt you like that again. I'll do anything," he says.

"Good," I tell him. "I'm going to hold you to that."

I send Mike away. Under my direction, he takes himself off to a week of intensive treatment in Arizona. During that week, my big Boston lug does talk therapy, bodywork, psychodrama,

EMDR, equine therapy—you name it. He returns, as I'd hoped, a softer, more connected man. In our first session back, he cries his remorse—and Angela is gracious enough to believe him. In subsequent months, I stagger their sessions. One week with the two of them, one week with Mike alone—sideline coaching sessions in relational skill, in stepping into the role of husband and father. I become not only Mike's therapist but also his mentor.

And this is another key difference between Relational Life Therapy and conventional therapy. Relational Life therapists, male or female, explicitly step into a mentoring relationship. We speak with the authority of our training and clinical experience, to be sure, but we're grounded more deeply in our own relational recovery. We're more like twelve-step sponsors than blank-screen traditional therapists. Look at the power we give away when we therapists hide behind the wall of "professionalism" and "neutrality."

"If you come from a dysfunctional individualistic, patriarchal culture, Mike," I say, "so do I. If you grew up in a dysfunctional family, so did I. I used to be my version of you, Mike. Hurt, hurting, entitled, clueless. But with the right help, I grew up. And you know what, dear man? If I can do it, you can do it."

Mike isn't looking at me. As I speak, he gazes at his wife.

"That's a nice look you just gave her," I note. "Can you put that look into words?"

"It's just that I—"

"Say it to her," I tell him.

He swivels, so that his whole body faces her. "I don't know, I mean, I can understand why you don't trust me, Ange." He bends his head down.

"Look at her," I instruct, and when he lifts up his face, silent tears stream from his eyes.

"I mean, I don't know why, I mean, where you'd ever get the—you know, to trust me again." He reaches out to her, and she takes his hand. "But you can trust me. You don't have to believe it yet. I mean, I know I have to prove it to you." He sighs. "But *I* know. You may not know yet, but I do. I've learned." And now his tears flow in earnest. "You're the best thing that ever happened, ya know? To me, anyway." He pauses to take a long, ragged breath. "I gotta treat ya like I feel about ya. Really."

She turns to him.

He takes her small hand and presses it into his chest, his heart. "From here," he says, pressing his chest. "From in here."

Angela strains toward him.

"You want a hug from him?" I ask, and she nods. "Go ahead," I say as they yield into one another. "Hold tight. Hold tight."

Harmony, disharmony, repair.

Our culture is infatuated with the harmony phase of relationships. A great relationship has no real discord, just like a great body has no belly fat, and a great sex life is like that of a twenty-year-old. Nowadays, in my field at least, the buzzword du jour is *attunement*. Parents are admonished to be endlessly attuned to their offspring; marital partners are taught to be exquisite "holding environments" for each other. If you ask me, though, I'm with Ed Tronick. It isn't unbroken harmony that makes for trust in relationships, whether parental or marital. Rather, it is precisely countless repetitions of surviving the mess. Here's Tronick:

> *Rather than a sense of helplessness, an infant who has moved through countless moments of error to reconnect develops a hopeful way of interacting with her world. She has made a specific meaning of her experience, one of optimistic expectation, which gives her a sense of resiliency.*

Listen, all ye anxious helicopter parents: resilience originates not in the absence of disharmony and discord but in its survival in you *as a pair*. Life is messy, but you're in this together. You experience disharmony, mismatch, and failures in attunement as disruptions in the relational field but not as unbreachable ruptures.

Further, whether it's your relationship or your parenting, let me share something most of my clients, like myself, find reassuring. While some level of disharmony may be good for the relationship, how much is too much? How much grist breaks the mill? Well, it turns out that Tronick, and the generation of child development specialists who have followed him, have a formula. What proportion of attunement and mis-match breeds a healthy child? How much disharmony can a relationship bear and still be a "good enough" holding envi-ronment? Seventy-thirty is the principle that researchers use. Seventy percent misalignment to thirty percent alignment—as long as the misalignment gets repaired. It's like a baseball hitter. If three out of ten times you're on a base, you're great—as long as your teammates give you a hug during those times when you've fouled out.

So, how do we make repair exactly? How do we reconnect once a disruption occurs? For parents and infants, it's simple; they just have to find each other again. For luggage-carrying grown-ups, it is more complex. We get triggered. New wounds evoke old ones. Present conflicts are encrusted with scar tissue from injuries long past. We people our present with expecta-tions from our past. You will treat me as they did.

Neurobiologists speak of such negative expectations as part of our implicit memory, the projected assumptions about our-selves in the world and how the world will react to us. Our negative expectations in the present are carryovers, a type of learning if you will, from our pasts—from discord that was too much or too intense—that is, traumatic—or from discord that was left routinely unrepaired, as in *Well, you made me do it, after all! It hurts me more than it hurts you.*

The key lies in the felt experience of safety, and safety, from my family therapy perspective, is a boundary issue—an issue of distance regulation. You will not wall off and abandon me; nor will you intrude and try to control me. The neuro-scientist Stephen Porges posits that feeling safety in another person with whom we interact consists of two important qualities—the absence of an agenda, and the absence of judgment. *I will neither intrude nor disappear.* What needs to be added to Porges's insight is that the situation is neither static nor individual. Partners in couples routinely co-regulate each other. If you feel intruded upon, you might say, *Hey, could you please remove your foot from my neck? I don't like it.* Or if your partner disappears, you might say, *Hey you, please come back from the wild blue yonder. I miss you.* Partners in healthy relationships push each other back or pull each other in. They regulate each other's distance. And this is the other great gift of discord; it's the chance to speak up and reshape elements of the relationship.

Don't Be a Passenger in Your Own Life

In mainstream individualist culture, our relationship to relationships is passive. We get what we get and react. But learning to live relationally, artfully, and skillfully opens up the possibility that we will have a say in our relationships. You are more than a helpless passenger, saturated with negative expectations, driven by your Adaptive Child's losing strategies. Even while you are triggered, you can take a moment, or twenty, and access your Wise Adult self, the part of you that can stop, think, observe, and choose. Disharmony is to your relationship as pain is to your physical body. It's a signal that something is wrong, that someone needs to get their hand off the stove. Our prefrontal cortex can process that signal and choose what to do about it. On the other hand, *you and me* consciousness knows just what to do in times of disharmony: (1) wrap yourself in rightness, (2) attempt to control your partner, (3) give vent to every emotion and infraction, (4) retaliate, (5) shut down—or some combination of all five of these losing strategies.

When we are triggered, injuries from the past get activated. Our neuroceptive body scan (*Am I safe? Am I safe? Am I safe?*) says no! Our automatic response pulls us into *you and me* consciousness. Injuries in the present evoke injuries from the past, and we tend to pick partners who, no matter how great they looked at the start, are devilishly designed to throw us right back into our childhood muck. This not a bad marriage; for most, this *is* marriage. What renders a relationship bad or good is not the depths of disharmony, but the presence or absence of repair.

Like virtually all my clients, Mike and Angela were clueless about what repair looks like. He had certainly never seen it growing up, and neither had Angela. Conflict and its resolution were not big items in Angela's family, where nothing was ever explicitly addressed or processed. Everyone stoically— and if you asked them, they'd say happily enough—just got on with things. That had been Angela's strategy in the marriage: not to acknowledge, not to even quite let herself see. The cost of her ever-good Adaptive Child stance was not acknowledging the shadow. And that was perhaps exactly why she had chosen this bad boy for marriage. The cost of her adaptation was her substance, her authenticity, and her guts—all qualities that the current crisis now pushes her to reclaim.

We all marry our unfinished business. Most of us wind up partnered with an all-too-familiar failure, limitation, or offense. We are thrown back in the soup of our relational traumas from childhood. What makes a great relationship is not avoiding that retraumatization but handling it. And—if we are fortunate, like Angela—we also marry the next step of our own development. Angela chose Mike to break her open. And in a deep unacknowledged way, Mike knew that Angela, sooner or later, would hold his feet to the fire.

To use the crisis rather than be buried by it, however, you have to keep yourself above the flood of reactivity that threatens to sweep you away. You have to have a skill that can be cultivated and made stronger—the skill of self-regulation. But as Tronick, and all the interpersonal neurobiologists, show us, the skill of self-regulation emerges from successful experiences of repair. It's hard to be optimistic about the possibility of repair if you've never experienced it.

I tease Belinda that someday I'll write a memoir of our marriage (heaven forbid!). I even have a working title: *A Fight Worth Having*. And that's how it is, being human. A hurt worth bearing. We stand grounded in the humility of our own imperfections. Who are we to get high and mighty? The poet

W. H. Auden wrote in his beautiful poem, "As I Walked Out
One Evening": "You shall love your crooked neighbor / With
your crooked heart."

You might want to ask yourself: What is the dark night of
the soul of my current relationship? What do I miss? What
keeps going awry? And then you might ask: How do I usually
deal with these issues? Do I charge in, complaining? Do I "set
the record straight," in no uncertain terms, demonstrating my
rightness? Do I vent? Retaliate? Shut down and avoid? And,
finally, if I were on my game, if I could stay seated just a few
minutes longer in my Wise Adult, how might I handle things
differently? What would it sound like if I met my partner with
compassion rather than judgment or control? What changes
would I need to make inside myself to evoke and stay grounded
in my own maturity, no matter how they might respond?

In Chapter 8, I will go over the practical tools and steps of
repair. But the critical first step is remembering love, getting
seated in a part of you that wants to repair to begin with. As
hurt, disillusioned, and angry as you may be, nevertheless you
say to your woebegone partner: "Why, yes, you can be a real
jerk sometimes. Oh my God, there are times I'm not sure I
even love you anymore or you, me. But, for goodness' sake,
don't just stand there in the doorway sopping wet and cold.
You know you can be such a disappointing, hurtful, imperfect,
mess sometimes. But hey, it's okay. I'm almost as imperfect as
you are. What are you waiting for? Door's open. Why don't
you just come on in?"

8

Fierce Intimacy, Soft Power

No one bothered to tell her it was over. Not her professor husband, or their friends, or her family, and certainly not the children they were raising together. There had been signs, of course, red flags, indications to which a wiser woman might have attended: his not coming home until late, his not fully explained sudden business trips, his surly evasiveness, his rise in irritability—particularly if closely questioned. Her friends all told her to drop the creep, but she didn't really blame him.

Not in hindsight. She knew better. If their marriage was dead, they had killed it together. Now, as the vast plateau of loneliness stretched before her, she blamed herself as much as him. They'd let go a long time ago, years ago. She had told herself all this time that it was just a tough patch in the long story of their lives. He was crazy busy with his work, and three kids were so demanding. She knew they'd suffered as a pair, but this, she'd figured, just wasn't their time. Let the kids get a little older. Let him make his mark in his career. They'd been a twosome before. Their time would come again. So she had thought. So, she'd assumed, they had both been thinking. But she was wrong.

"I told you," Phil proclaims in our first—and possibly last—session. "Honey, I sat at the bottom of our stairs crying like a baby, telling you you were losing me. Don't you even remember?"

Sitting next to her husband on the couch, Liz unconsciously strokes her long brown hair. With round rimless glasses and a simple taupe dress, she looks like she might break into a protest song any minute, join a rally, march for a cause—anything but be there with her husband. Her earnestness is matched by her sheer bewilderment. She spreads her hands, beseeching him. "But," she says, for what he calls her four-hundredth time, "I thought you were happy."

"Yes, I know you did," he rounds on her. "And can I tell you why?"

I sit up, ready to intervene if need be.

"Can I tell you why you thought we were both so happy?"

Liz palpably shrinks in her chair.

"Because," he says, "because you've been fucking clueless, that's why!"

"Well, maybe, yes," she tries.

Phil turns to me. "There's nothing wrong, except that if Liz woke up in the morning and found me sprawled on the stairs with my throat cut, she'd step over me, say, 'Good morning, hon,' and fix me a cup of coffee."

"That is so unfair," she says, stung.

"Liz," he continues, White, tall, rail thin, and imperious, "I said it. I screamed it. I left her goddamn emails right on my computer—"

"Oh Phil," she says, "I thought it was nonsense. A school-girl crush. Look, you're charismatic. I thought—"

"Except it's not a crush. She's not a girl, and she's not one of my students."

"I know all that now," Liz allows, chastened.

"What did you need?" Phil continues, furious. "An arrow painted in lipstick?"

"Okay," I cut in, "that's enough."

He sits back on the sofa, collecting himself. "We let go, Lizzie," he says, quietly. I can feel worlds of pent-up hurt beneath his anger.

"I think if you were really honest, Phil, you'd be saying that she let go of you," I say softly.

"No"—he shakes his head—"no, it was a team effort. Team neglect," he adds bitterly.

"What does that mean?"

"You know how they say 'We drifted apart'?"

I nod.

"Well, we didn't drift. We steamed, we rocketed. She poured it all into the kids. I went to work and"—he turns to his wife—"before you knew it, there was so little left. We were used up. Gave at the office."

Next to him, Liz quietly cries.

"You didn't know?" I ask her. "You didn't know how un-happy he was?"

She shakes her head, wiping away tears. "I just . . ."

"We don't talk," Phil answers for her. "Liz and me, see? We're doers, not talkers. Got a project, someone in need? Meet us for doubles, a hike? We do that part really well."

"Jesus," Liz swears, pale, hurt, and devastated. "I thought it was all great fun."

"It was, sweetheart," he tells her. "And you did all that. You were the hearth. You were the playdates, the skiing, the chil-dren's operas. I'm so grateful—"

"Well, then, for crying out—"

"There just wasn't anything left over for me, for us."

"But that's all us," she protests. "Everything you just said—"

"For the unit, Elizabeth. For the five of us." He leans in close, tight, angry. "But not *me*. Not for years."

Liz sighs, ragged and undefended. She turns to her hus-band and asks with heartbreaking vulnerability, "So now what?"

The very question I, too, had in mind.

They Had Everything but Each Other

Liz and Phil remind me of a bumper sticker from the 1980s that read MY LIFESTYLE ATE MY LIFE. On paper, they were golden; they had it all. They were handsome, professed the right values, and stood up for those in need. A luxury SUV stood by in the garage ready to transport the kids to their liberal, sheltered schools. They'd barely had sex for the last four years, but where did that come in with kids barreling into bed with you at all hours and so much going on?

They rarely fought; they rarely overtly disagreed—and that was actually part of the problem. They never went from harmony through disharmony to repair. Instead, they went from harmony to each his own corner. One could say that, in their marriage, both Liz and Phil were individualists to the extreme. They both buried themselves in their work—he in his teaching and research, she in the kids and the family. Their couple's relationship stood dead last in the time-energy credit line—until there simply wasn't much left. Their marriage was on the brink not because of the acute crisis of Phil's infidelity but rather a lifetime of disrepair. Their garden had gone to seed through years of inattention—not from implosion so much as simple rot.

Liz was an expressive Romantic individualist focused, as such romantics are, on development, on unfolding each person's unique journey toward evolution, their *Bildung*, as the German Romantics put it. But she wasn't running off to meditation classes or Pilates. It wasn't her own development upon which she was focused, but rather the unique, not-to-be-neglected inner growth of their three children. A liberal mom, she lived as a Romantic individualist by proxy, ushering her kids through their various sports practices and art lessons. It was the kids' development, their *Bildung*, that preoccupied her and gave her meaning.

Phil was just as involved. Voicing ineffective protest from time to time, he nevertheless went along with America's traditional program. He went to work and was a hands-on dad once he got home. But he'd pretty much abdicated all else concerning the family and their couple's romance.

We've heard a lot over the years about how women like Liz have no voice in their relationships. How women give their own needs away to accommodate. In the traditional playbook of patriarchy, a good woman, like Liz, has no needs of her own; that would be selfish. A good woman lives to serve others. But a man, like Phil, has no voice either. With the exception of a supposedly ever-ready lust, a strong man should have no emotional needs, certainly nothing vulnerable. A strong man should be as needless as his wife, her goodness to his steel. Silenced "good woman" meets silent "strong man"—neither very capable of anything as simple as *Hey, I could use a hug.*

Liz and Phil are cut from good old New England Yankee cloth. They were born for those holiday newsletters detailing each family member's most recent success—Phil's promotion, Olivia's school play, Brian ripping it up on the tennis court, and little Amy lisping in French. And Liz presiding— Mom, the all-nurturing, sexless goddess. Phil and Liz had it all—except each other.

"We don't talk," Phil said. "We *do*." Which might have been fine if they had both been in on the contract. It worked great until Phil wanted more. Trying to pry Liz away from the kids was virtually impossible.

"So," I say, cutting in, "who's the other woman?" Phil shrinks, while Liz bridles. Neither speaks.

"Other *girl*, one might say," Liz finally tells me.

"She's gone. She's inconsequential," Phil broadly dismisses.

"Why?" asks Liz. "Did someone lose her teething ring?"

Phil shakes his head, brushing off an annoyance. "It isn't whatever I had with her," he pronounces. "It's what I didn't have with you, Liz. What we stopped having with each other."

"You blame me?" she says, finally angry. "I made you cheat on me? That's it now?"

"We just got lost," he says, deflated.

"Then say something!" she wails. "Grab me by the throat and make me take notice."

"I tried!" he exclaims.

"What, that once?" says Liz, incredulous, building steam. "One damn time, and I didn't even know what the hell you were talking about. 'You're losing me,'" she quotes in disgust. "Really, Phillip? Great. Why? How? What the hell I was supposed to do about it?"

"Did you ask?" he says lamely.

"Did you offer?" she pushes back.

And there we are, I think. *Check and mate. Don't ask, and don't volunteer.*

Liz and Phil, well trained by their families, were too polite to deal with each other. Both were raised by ever-harmonious, walled-off parents. They were like ghosts, swirling, circling each other—not quite touching. They were both type-one love avoidants—people raised in walled-off families where the raw eruption of conflict, hurt, and need all seemed rather gauche.

"We're doers, not talkers," Phil had informed me.

Well, I think, *that's grand. And now, here you are.*

Here's how the journalist John Taylor described the demise of his own union: "Our marriage wasn't hellish," he wrote, "it was simply dispiriting, a mechanism so encrusted with small disappointments and petty grudges that its parts no longer fit together." Taylor's "small disappointments and petty grudges" were, like Liz and Phil's, most certainly left unrepaired.

Like virtually all the couples I encounter, Liz and Phil simply did not possess, in their relationship, a *mechanism of correction*. Good couples regulate each other—conflict erupts, or distance feels oppressive, but they talk things out, and things get better. But for a couple like Liz and Phil, nothing erupts, distance is normalized, and nothing gets better. Then someone finally does something to foment a crisis—someone gets ill, or a child becomes symptomatic, or one of them reaches for something or someone beyond each other. Most men, as Thoreau wrote in *Walden*, lead lives of quiet desperation. Others, not so quiet. Liz had settled, but Phil needed more. While I in no way condoned how he did it, and said so, someone needed to shake up their marriage before it slipped off the face of the earth altogether.

As my colleague Esther Perel has trenchantly observed, you don't go off in an affair looking for a different person. You go off looking for a different you. And as a therapist working with infidelity, I want to know what avenues of vitality opened up in the illicit relationship in order to bring some of that juice back home. But when most people, like Phil and Liz, think about keeping their relationship juicy, they no doubt refer to the harmony phase. Juicy, in our culture, means hot. But in a real marriage, heat comes from heat. Real passion comes right out of real conflict, full engagement, taking each other on. If you want the high notes, embrace the lows. If nothing else, I needed Liz and Phil to hear this—smooth-functioning avoidance is romantic death. Partners need to rough it up now and then, to go deeper.

Fierce Intimacy

Fierce intimacy is the essential capacity to confront issues, to take each other on. It's what neither Phil nor Liz practiced in their marriage. Liz ran her family like a well-oiled machine, with nary a bump or wrinkle. But when you start thinking relationally, ecologically, you realize that it's navigating the bumps that makes for true intimacy, the fertile gift of disharmony. "Love," wrote Yeats, "has pitched his mansion / In the place of excrement." Liz's "USS Family," as Phil once called it, mock saluting, was sucking the life out of her husband.

But did Phil say so? Did he, as Liz asked, "grab her by the throat and shake her"? Did Liz even notice that his engagement grew more and more anemic? Did she miss him? She hadn't seemed to. She'd appeared to be just fine. Phil looks at her now with something like despair. "Underneath our surface of bland pleasantness," he pronounces, "lies a molten core of more bland pleasantness."

"Jesus, Phil," says Liz, hurt and angry, "that's so mean."

It is mean, I think. *And unfortunate. But that's not to say it isn't true.*

Working in Boston, I've seen many families like the ones both Liz and Phil hailed from. Whole systems stuck in the harmony phase—or more accurately, a kind of pseudo-harmony driven not by romance but by denial. I once saw a cartoon in which a woman scrawls in red lipstick across her living room wall: *Nothing ever happens here!* Some families are so civilized, so restrained, that nothing as indecorous as emotion—hurt, anger, or panic—dares to make an unwelcome appearance. Crying children are sent to their rooms to "collect themselves." No one learns how to navigate from disharmony back into repair, because disharmony itself is exiled, or at least unacknowledged.

For Liz, the oldest—a hero child, a good girl—this culture full of appearances, rectitude, and denial worked well enough. But Phil, while hardly a rebel, did have a streak in him, some passion. That's what had drawn her to him, that glimmer of aliveness. And there had been spark between them at the start. But once three kids entered the picture, their world filled up with activities, responsibilities, piano lessons, school conferences, skiing weekends, and hockey games. Liz felt fulfilled. But Phil felt lonely. "Family A plus, couple D minus," he'd told me. He'd tried to get through to Liz a couple of times. "Let's give the kids to your parents and slip off for a weekend!" But something always held them back. With apparent good humor, he submitted to his family's demands, tabling his longing. You see, he was no more willing to encounter his own unruly feelings than he was anyone else's.

Then one afternoon he found himself walking by the river with a young colleague he had no business opening up to. But somehow he had. Diana had pulled it out of him, even sought out, all the feelings inside he thought he'd turned away from. Like most affair partners, sex was not the real driver, but eroticism in its broadest sense. More than sex, what Diana offered to Phil was simply the thrill of kind attention — contact. When men fall for younger women, claiming it reawakens their youth, what they most often mean is that it awakens their lost vitality. The universal refrain of virtually all cheaters is "It made me feel alive."

In Chapter 7, I described two domains I look at when encountering infidelity — the entitled character of the unfaithful one and the health of the relationship. In this case, I did not see Phil as a thoroughgoing narcissist. Someone needed to break open a window and let fresh air into their house. We therapists encounter basically two kinds of couples — those who fight and those who distance. With fighters, I often find myself reaching through their many complaints to recall the good, what holds them together—their us. With distant couples, it's most often the opposite. Instead of pulling for elements of repair, I must first help them surface all the issues of disrepair they have refused to look at very closely. Before there can be an us, there must be two *I*'s.

As a therapist, I help empower each partner to speak up, surfacing their unvoiced needs and their anguish. In distant couples, you don't create intimacy by handing them a bouquet and helping them skip off into the sunset. You first hand them a mallet to demolish the stultifying edifice they've constructed. Then you teach them what grappling with each other actually looks like.

Which kind of couple are you on those rare occasions when you find yourself in trouble with one another? Do you tend toward fighting or towards distance? Do you need to find more constructive ways to talk to one another—less blaming and criticizing and more humble sharing of your own experience along with real curiosity about the experience of your partner? Or would a good fight, like a summer storm, shake a few leaves and clear the air?

Remember, generally speaking I invite the weak to stand up and the mighty to melt. If you are used to big, angry reactions, go small, go vulnerable, soften up and lead, not with righteousness but with your own open heart. If you're more often avoidant, or an inveterate pleaser, find courage. Dare to rock the boat. If your partner gets mad, so what? Don't collapse, keep going, assert your voice, push through.

A lot of clients who are caught up in an affair come to me wringing their hands and professing anxiety, depression, and utter confusion as they shuttle back and forth between partner and lover. "I have to get to the bottom of this!" they exclaim. "Make a damn choice and get out of this nightmare." Any therapist who takes that remark at face value is someone I'd call *young lunch*. Pulled by the passion, sensuality, and emotional connection of the lover on the one hand and stability, family, and domesticity on the other, these partners ping-pong back and forth for the most part, often lying to both spouse and lover, prolonging the agony and confusion for one simple reason—they want both. I want that for them, both passion and stability. The challenge, of course, lies in having both in one relationship.

Passion had drained from Phil and Liz's marriage not because Liz had buried herself in childrearing but because Phil had not effectively spoken out and been heard in his legitimate need for more.

"Well, Phillip," Liz says toward the end of the session, "I'm certainly hearing you now. You have my full attention."

At that point Phil does something I didn't expect—he bends over and starts to sob with huge, heartrending, raw hurt. He reaches for his wife's hand, but she ignores it. "Don't you see?" he says, mopping his face. "Liz, don't you see? That's all I've ever wanted."

"What, my full attention?" she asks.

"No, you!" he says, exasperated. "You. I don't want anyone else, but I do want you, the real you, awake, alive, here with me."

"Well, I have good news and bad news for you, Phil," I tell him.

"Go on," he says.

"The good news is, you got her. She's fully here with you now. Mission accomplished."

"And the bad?"

"You broke her heart getting here."

Phil and Liz both agree to put aside their hurt feelings—he eagerly, she reluctantly—and work on their marriage. As is universally true in situations like this one, this couple had to face both the underlying cause of Phil's infidelity—their distance—and the overlying crust of hurt caused by his affair.

"Is there hope?" Phil asks me with touching vulnerability. "In your professional opinion, what will we have to deal with?"

"That's easy," I tell him. "Each other."

Taking Each Other On

Dealing with each other. What does that phrase really mean? At its most basic, it signifies taking each other on. Airing your dissatisfactions, articulating your desires, making concrete suggestions about how things might work better for you, and then, if all goes well, working like a team to make things right. Repair demands assertion (not aggression) from the unhappy partner met with care and responsiveness (not defensiveness) in the other. There is a technology to repair, a bundle of skill sets that few learn about in our nonrelational, individualistic culture.

Think for a minute. Where in your own life have you witnessed the skills of repair in relationships? In the culture at large? I doubt it. In that school of relationships we call our families? Not much in evidence there for most of us. The truth is that unless you were very lucky and grew up in a relationally intelligent home, learning the skills of repair means unlearning what you internalized, and doing that under the mentorship of someone like me—either in person, or through workshops, online courses, or reading like this.

Can you learn such skills on your own as a couple, without necessarily seeking professional advice? Yes, many of you will be able to transform yourselves and your relationship through self-study—books like this one, lectures, online workshops. Particularly if you both learn together. Yet if even just one of you masters greater relational skill, the patterns may shift between you. How do you know when you need help? That's simple. You need help as a pair when it's clear that on your own, you cannot work together in this way; you cannot both look at yourselves and take heed. Things don't really get repaired. Nothing much changes.

I counsel couples to take very seriously the cultivation of relational skills in their lives. Drag each other to weekend enrichment programs, listen to thought leaders on relationships, talk together about what you've learned and what you're working on in your own relational practice. And let your children see you repair with each other. If your kids hear the fight—as they will no matter how discreet you may think you are—let them also hear the making up. Teach your children about harmony, disharmony, and repair, as your own parents most likely did not. Arm them with skill; equip them with knowledge.

So what are the skills of repair? You can find them in my last book, *The New Rules of Marriage*, but let me go over them here and update some key points. First, repair is *not* a two-way street. Almost everyone gets this wrong. When you are faced with an upset partner, this is not your turn. This is not a dialogue. Liz doesn't air all her grievances as an invitation for Phil to then air his. *You must take turns.* Repair goes in one direction. When your partner is in a state of disrepair, your only job is to help them get back into harmony with you, to deal with their upset, and to support them in reconnecting. I ask people, when faced with an unhappy partner, to put their needs aside and attend to the other's unhappiness. Why? Because it's in your interest to do so. Remember, from an ecological perspective, if one of you wins and the other is left lacking, both suffer. The "loser" will make the "winner" pay. Phil had gone along to get along, uncomplaining and unfulfilled. Liz had ruled the roost—until the bill came due that afternoon by the river.

To be truthful, most couples are not utterly devoid of repair—they're just not very good at it. Phil did try to tell Liz what he needed—once. Most people do try a few times to talk things through and make life better. But we learn quickly enough that such efforts either yield nothing or elicit defensiveness and escalation.

Like the large guy on the seesaw, shouting at his wife to get down, we frontload our attention on what our partners are doing wrong, not on how we might be contributing. We focus on how unheard we feel, not on how we might speak more effectively. Let me offer an alternative: "I'm sorry you feel bad." Why not start with that—compassion? Compassion doesn't care about who's right and who's wrong. You must let go of the two orientations that toxic individualism pulls you toward. The first focus, so-called objective reality, is often our go-to in such moments: "Well, yes I was late, but the fact is that the traffic was . . ." No one cares about your excuses or explanations. Our second usual focus when faced with an unhappy partner is most usually ourselves. "Oh, come on. How many times have I waited while you . . ." Sorry, no one cares about you right now. They want to know if you care about them.

Think of yourself as being at the customer service window. Someone tells you their microwave doesn't work; they don't want to hear that your toaster doesn't work. Nor are they interested in your reasons. They want a new microwave. Take care of your customer first. Only once they feel satisfied will there be any bandwidth for you and your experience.

Okay, so repair equals skilled speaking met with a skilled response. Let's take each of these in turn.

Let Liz and Phil serve as a cautionary tale. When you're dissatisfied with an aspect of your relationship, it is critical that you say something rather than sweep it aside. But there's a difference between speaking the way most of us do in this culture and speaking in a manner that might actually get you heard. You can start by pulling your accusatory finger away from your partner's face. I can't tell you how many times someone steps into my office saying, "I've got to get some feelings off my chest," followed by "You did this, and then you did that. You never. You always. You, you, you." Whenever that happens, I tilt my chair back, stretch, and say, "Tell me when the feelings are going to start." Stay on your side of the street. Don't accuse them—talk about yourself. Not "Liz, you're avoidant," but rather, "Liz, I don't feel met."

When you start to live relationally, ecologically, you take responsibility for your thinking. Remember, so-called objective reality has no place here. There's my recollection, my construction of events, and then there is yours. On Tuesday, Belinda says, "Have a nice day." I take what she says as being caring. On Tuesday night, we have a fight. When she says,

"Have a nice day" the next morning, I imagine she's being sarcastic. And I have a very different set of feelings about it. *Emotions follow cognition.* How you see something will determine how you feel about it.

What happens between us is just stuff, raw data. Our minds tell us what the data signifies. We tell ourselves a story about what just happened, and our feelings most often follow the story we've constructed. Belinda is being nice. Belinda is being sarcastic. Living beyond individualism requires each of us to take responsibility for our own constructions. "What I make up" is a phrase I ask my clients to use. What I make up is that you're being sarcastic. What I make up is that under your anger, there's hurt. We are not clairvoyant, and neither are we the authoritative voice of objective reality. Keep it subjective; keep it humble. "This was my experience, right or wrong. This is how I recollect it. This is the story I tell myself about it." Here's the trick. For the most part, you cannot violate someone when you speak from the *I*. And with a little practice, there's nothing you need to say that can't be owned as your construction, your experience.

Speaking for Repair

I invite you to use Janet Hurley's *feedback wheel*, a form of speaking that has four parts. It is a structure you can use to organize your thoughts and more skillfully speak up when you are hurt.

1. This is what I recollect happened.
2. This is what I made up about it.
3. This is what I felt.

And that all-important fourth step most speakers leave out:

4. This would help me feel better.

In other words, this is what repair might look like.

You have to help your partner come through for you. Tell them how you'd like them to be. Help them win. Help your partner succeed, because it's in your interest to act like a team. In our individualistic culture, your partner either comes through for you or they don't. But when you begin thinking relationally, ecologically, you realize that you have something to say about how things go between you. "What can I do to help you come through for me?" is an entirely relational question. Thinking like a team is the clear antidote to thinking like two individuals. It's a shift from "I don't like how you're talking to me" to "Honey, I want to hear what you're saying. Could you please lower your voice so I can hear it?" A shift from "I need more sex" to "We both deserve a healthy sex life. What should we do about it?"

Soft Power:
Strong and Loving Simultaneously

Quite often, by the time we do decide to speak up, so much has been festering that we speak from a place of both anger and authority. I want you to lose both. I teach both men and women to speak up with love, to exercise *soft power.*

Within the culture of individualism and of patriarchy, you can be connected or you can be powerful—but you cannot be both at the same time. Remember that. Power is *power over,* not *with,* so you break the thread of mutual connection when you move into power. Dominance does not breed intimacy. In the gender binary of patriarchy, affiliation is "feminine" and power is "masculine." Cooperation is nowhere in sight. This is a critical point for women in particular to understand. Too often when women (or anyone inhabiting the "feminine" side of the equation) shift from accommodation to assertion, they simply move from the "feminine" side to the "masculine." They assert the *I,* but the *us* is forgotten. Finding their voices, powerful women often look an awful lot like powerful men. Here's the great feminist psychologist, Carol Gilligan:

> *Selfish is still the opposite of good for many women, meaning that for them a we does not include a me (or admits only a very toned down me). To the extent that feminism came to see progress in women acting more like privileged men, reclaiming their "I" along with natural rights a la the Enlightenment rugged Individualism you*

*describe, it encouraged women to exchange the selfless
"we" for the selfish "me."*

After fifty years of feminism, many women have earned the
right to be as unrelational as men have always been. I want
more: not what we family therapists call *first-order change*, a
rearrangement of the furniture, but *second-order change*, a
revolution in fundamental structure. I want us to blow up the
gender binary, moving beyond the false dichotomy of power
or belonging. Soft power gives voice to the *I* and cherishes the
we at the same time.

My first exposure to soft power came one spring afternoon
when I was sitting on the porch of my friend Alan. Alan had
done something that enraged me—we needn't go into the details. The point is that I let him have it. "I can't hang with you
as if everything was okay when I'm carrying this," I said. "I
need to tell you—" And off I went.

Alan was furious. As our kids played on the lawn and his
fresh-caught bluefish rested in his smoker, he leaned into me,
and although he didn't raise his voice, his body was trembling
with emotion.

"Terry," he said, "the first and most important thing to say
here is that I love you. You are one of my dearest friends, and I
expect to stay friends for the whole of our lives." He squared his
shoulders. "Having said that, let me say this. You come to my
house as my guest, and in this family gathering, you level an
energy at me that, as you know, I have spent a good part of my
life getting away from. Here in my house. Now listen, I can't

control you and I don't want to. I can't stop you, but I will let you know each and every time you choose to bring that energy to me and my family that I really don't like it, which I don't—at all. Not one bit. Am I making myself clear?"

I sat slack-jawed, regarding my friend. As I've said, I am a fighter. My first automatic response, in *you and me* consciousness, is to fight. If Alan had started with "Who do you think you are?" my scrappy teenage Adaptive Child would have known just what to do. But the son of a gun had me with "Terry, I love you." For that, I was utterly unprepared. It slipped right past the sentries of my heart, to paraphrase Leonard Cohen. It touched me.

Alan's professed love for me left me feeling ashamed of my grandiose anger. It woke me up. *Right*, I thought, remembering it was Alan I was talking to. *My friend.* In my rage, I had lost the thread of our connection. His explicit recollection of love jolted through my body. I was taken aback, disarmed. In that moment of security and felt respect, I could relax my indignant guard and come down off my high horse. I even found myself apologizing for my poor timing and worse delivery. By asserting in virtually the same breath his own needs and also the value of our connection, Alan had an enormous impact— much more than if he had asserted either his needs or our connection by themselves.

They were a strikingly handsome couple. Alex was tall, Black, and imposing in his stillness, while his partner, Martin, small,

White, blond, quick, and sharp, seemed always in motion. Despite being Millennials, Alex and Martin were a classic pair, "killing each other," as they put it, over sex. Alex wanted it virtually all the time; Martin wanted it virtually none of the time. As any good therapist would do, I draw from each of them not just their respective positions but also their interpretation, their narrative, of what sex means to each of them.

Like a great many men, young Alex filtered many (if not most) of his emotional needs through sex. It was how he connected, felt desired, approved of, loved. There's an old cliché in family therapy: one partner talks to the other in order to get them into bed with them. The other partner drags them into bed in order to get them to talk. Like a great many people, both women and men, Martin needed to feel emotionally connected in order to relax into his sexuality. Floating all this to the surface felt like a relief to the couple, and so I was pleased. Truth be told, though, I wasn't certain I'd been of much help.

They came back two weeks later all smiles, eager to share their success. Right after the session, that night in fact, Alex had "moved in," as Martin put it, "for sex." Rather than pull back, Martin gave his husband a passionate kiss, looked deeply into his eyes, and said the following:

"I want you to know I think you are so hot. I just love you so much and I desire you and I feel close to you and I think you're great. By the way, I don't feel like sex tonight, but let me tell you again what a joy it is to . . ." And to their mutual amazement

Alex stared, his mouth ajar, and had said simply, "Ah, okay." No hurt over his "rejection," no coercion, no anger. Because, you see, he felt so loved by Martin, that he could hear his no.

Soft power. When you need to speak up, be artful. Take care of your partner as best you can by explicitly cherishing them and your relationship. Start by letting them know you need repair, is this a good time? If your partner agrees to talk, thank them, start off with an appreciation—something you are thankful for that your partner has said or done, even if it's just that you appreciate their willingness to sit down and talk. Then state your intentions—a good thing to do generally: "I want to clear the air between us *so that I can feel closer to you*." Center yourself in your Wise Adult, prefrontal cortex, and *remember love*. Recall that the person you're addressing is someone you love, or at least care for, and in any case, you will have to live with them. Remembering love is a recentering practice. You're speaking to someone you care about in the hopes of making things better. If that is not your intention, you are probably in your Adaptive Child. Stop! Take a walk around the block, journal, and splash some water on your face. This won't go well until you are self-regulated.

Now that you're centered and your partner is attentive, go through the four steps of the feedback wheel: what happened, what you made up about it, how you felt about it, and finally, what you'd like now.

Back when our kids were little, Belinda might have said to me, for example:

1. Terry, you said you'd be home by six and you arrive at 6:45, no message or text, while I sat with the kids waiting for dinner.
2. What I make up about that is that you still have some narcissistic traits and that you value your time over ours.
3. I felt sad lonely, fearful of the impact on our children, hurt, and angry.
4. What I'd like now is for you to apologize to the kids, and to me for that matter. And tell me what you're going to do to not repeat this pattern.

Notice that each step of the wheel is complete in just a few sentences. Be concise. And here are two more important tips. First, when you share your feelings, be sure to share your feelings, not your thoughts—keep them separate. "I feel like you're angry" doesn't cut it. Better would be "I make up that you're angry and about that I feel." I once had a Boston Southie say to his girlfriend, "I *feel* like you're an asshole." Then he looked at me. "Better, doc?" Hmm.

There are seven primary feelings: joy, pain, anger, fear, shame, guilt, love. Stick with those.

The second tip takes a bit of practice to execute. When you share your feelings, skip over the emotion that first comes to you, your go-to emotion, and lead with others. Belinda and I are both fighters. Our knee-jerk response will be anger. But recall that when Belinda gave me feedback about my being late, she put her anger last, not first. More specifically, if you are used to leading with big, powerful feelings, like anger, or indignation, soften up—reach for and lead with your vulnerability. Find the hurt. Conversely, if you lead with small, timid, insecure feelings, find your power. Where is your anger, the part of you that says "Enough"?

Here's the principle: Changing your stance changes the dance between you. The shift from indignation to hurt, like the shift from tepid complaint to empowered assertion, will quite often evoke a different response than the usual. Try it. Change what you do on your side of the seesaw, and watch what happens. Take the risk of leading with a different part of you—vulnerability for the righteous, assertion for the timid—and then step back and observe.

Once you've given your feedback, you're finished. Let go. Detach from outcome, as they say in Alcoholics Anonymous. On Tuesday your partner answers with generosity and accountability. On Thursday he tells you he's in no mood for your bullshit. Tuesday is a good day for you, for your partner, and for your relationship. Thursday is a terrible day for your partner, a mixed day for the relationship, and still a great day for you. You did a fine job of speaking. That's all you're in charge of. Don't focus on results. Instead, focus on how well you handle yourself. Focus on your own relational performance.

Listening with a Generous Heart

Okay, so let's say you're the one hearing feedback from your partner—now what? Yield. Don't get defensive, or go tit for tat, or any of that Adaptive Child behavior. You, the listener, also need to be centered. You too need to remember love. What can you give this person to help them feel better? You can begin by offering the gift of your presence. Listen. And let them know they've been heard. Reflect back what you heard.

If you're at a loss, just repeat your partner's feedback wheel. In the case of my lateness, I might say to my wife, "Belinda, what I hear is that you waited with the kids while I came home late; you imagine it's my narcissism; you had a lot of feelings about it—hurt, concern for the kids, anger—and you'd like an apology and a plan." Is that reflection comprehensive and perfect? No. Some couples therapies call for exquisite reflecting. We don't. If you are the speaker, and the listening partner has left out important things or gotten something seriously wrong, help them out. Gently correct them, and then have them reflect again. But don't be overly fussy. Serviceable is good enough.

Now that you've listened, you need to respond. How? Empathically and accountably. Own whatever you can, with no *buts*, excuses, or reasons. "Yes, I did that"—plain and simple. Land on it, really take it on. The more accountable you are, the more your partner might relax. If you realize what you've done, if you really get it, you'll be less likely to keep repeating that behavior. And conversely, not acknowledging what you did—by changing the subject, or denying, or minimizing—will leave your partner feeling more desperate.

Now, here's an interesting thing to notice. If you are the speaker, it pays to keep it specific. The feedback wheel is about this one incident, period. Most people go awry when they escalate their complaints, moving from the specific occurrence to a trend, then to their partner's character. For example: "Terry, you came late." (Occurrence.) "You always come late." (Trend.) "You're never on time." (Trend.) "You really are selfish!" (Character.) When the speaker jumps from a particular event to a trend (*you always, you never*) to the partner's character (*you are a . . .*), they render their partner ever more helpless, and each intensification feels dirtier.

Now, notice that if the speaker escalates from incident to trend to character, each move makes things worse. If, by contrast, the listener moves up the ladder, outing himself, each move up feels wonderful to his partner: "I did this. It's not the first time I've done it. It is a character flaw I'm working on." On a good day I might answer Belinda, "Yes, I was late. I've kept you and the boys waiting on several occasions. I think it's a vestige of my narcissism that I need to work on." Now, that's a satisfying apology.

Once you've reflectively listened and acknowledged whatever you can about the truth of your partner's complaint, give. Give to your partner whatever parts of their request (the fourth step in the feedback wheel: *what I'd like now*) as you possibly can. Lead with what you're willing to give, not with what you're not—another simple practice that can help a lot. In my case, Belinda would say, "Terry, I want you to apologize to me, apologize to the kids, go back on medication, and go into psychotherapy three times a week to deal with your narcissism." I *want* to say, or at least my Adaptive Child wants to say, "That's ridiculous. I'm not doing all that." In other words, faced with a bunch of requests, my first instinct is to argue. So here's the thing—if you lead with argument, the odds are great that you will wind up in an argument. Instead, I take a breath and my Wise Adult answers, "Okay, Belinda. I will apologize right now to the kids and to you. I take this issue seriously and will conscientiously work on it. If I can't change it on my own, we can talk about next steps and my getting help." All the stuff I'm unwilling to do? I'm just going to leave that alone.

If your partner requests that you do X, Y, Z, you respond with, "Honey, I'm going to X and Z to beat the band." Sell it. Put some *oomph* in it. You think, of course, that your partner will turn around and say, "Hey, what about Y?" But you might be surprised. Most often, if you put some energy into what you're willing to give, it disarms our partners, and sometimes they're even grateful.

And finally, for you both, let the repair happen. Don't discount your partner's efforts. Don't disqualify what's being offered with a response like "I don't believe you" or "This is too little too late." Dare to take yes for an answer. If what your partner is offering you is at all reasonable, take it, as imperfect as it may be, and relent. Remember, there's a world of difference between complaining about what you're not getting and having the capacity to open up and receive it. Allowing your partner to make amends and come back into your good graces is more vulnerable for you than crossing your arms and rejecting what they're offering. Let them win; let it be good enough. Come into *knowing love.*

Once, back in the day, Belinda and I had been fighting for the better part of twelve hours. I was out of the house at a coffee shop. I called her one more time, hoping for a break in our dance. "Belinda," I said, "are we okay? Should I come home?"

"You really are an asshole," she replied, and I knew right away by her tone that we were all right.

We have a saying in Relational Life Therapy: "Tone trumps content." Tone reveals which part of your brain you're in, *us* consciousness or *you and me* consciousness. Belinda's words were on their face abusive and name-calling. But her tone let me know that I was her little asshole, endearingly impossible. She had moved into knowing love, with no illusions and no minimizing of my faults, but acceptance, faults and all. It was time to come home.

9

Leaving Our Kids a Better Future

How does one transform a legacy? How do we give to our children an experience of the world that is richer, kinder, less individualistic, and more relational than the one we grew up with in our own families? Even the intensely personal work of your own relational recovery is not for you as a lone individual. The great couples therapist Hedy Schleifer asks her clients to bring to their sessions pictures of their kids. One by one she lays out the pictures on chairs, one per chair. The chairs are circling Hedy and her clients as they work together.

"Just remember," she tells her troubled couples, "they're watching."

What is the great American dream, after all, if not the wish to afford our kids a better life than our own? We most often think of that materialistically. But I talk to my clients about being upwardly mobile psychologically—daring to live in a happier, more connected world than that of our parents and perhaps even theirs.

Ted

Ted is a chronic philanderer. At fifty-two and on his third marriage, he is, for the first time in his life, considering monogamy. Sitting with five other guys in a men's group I am running, he talks about his lifetime of lies and deceit. A large white man, workingman handsome in a plaid flannel shirt, looking rawboned and rough-hewn, Ted wants to tell me in lurid detail what a shit he's been to the women in his life.

I want to talk with him about his father.

"What do you want to know?" he asks. "I hardly knew him."

"What does that mean?"

"Well, most every night after dinner, my father would push back his chair, look us over, and say, 'I'm going to see a man about a horse.' And then he'd leave."

"Where'd he go?"

Ted shrugs, shakes his head ruefully. "Don't know, really. Some messed-up woman or other. He'd never say. Showed up in the mornings, though, ready for breakfast."

"And your mom?"

Again, the rueful head shake. "She'd take to her bed, mostly. Sometimes she'd cry. I'd hear her cry."

"And where would you be?"

"I'd be in my bed," he tells me. "You know, reading. Comic books and stuff."

I consider him for a minute. "And what was it like for that little boy? That boy sitting in his room at night, listening to his mother cry?"

Ted's tall thick body seems for a second to fold in on itself. "I tried not to listen," he tells me, his voice soft, almost frail. He has done a lot of not listening in his lifetime. Not listening to the women he's hurt, not listening to the voice of his conscience, his guilt. Not listening to his children when they ask him to stay home, just as he had asked his own father to in his day. There's an old line in AA: "Pass it back or pass it on."

They say it's the height of presumption to quote oneself, but I will anyway. This is from my first book, *I Don't Want to Talk About It*: "Family pathology rolls from generation to generation, like a fire in the woods, taking down everything in its path until one person in one generation has the courage to turn and face the flames. That person brings peace to his ancestors and spares the children that follow." A big old tough guy like Ted might not do the hard work of relational recovery for his own sake or even for his "bitchy" wife. But guys like that will pick up the mantle of this work in order to not damage their children. I routinely ask the men who step into my office: "What kind of father did you have growing up?" and "What kind of father would you like to be?" And then "Will you let me help you?"

Goodbye, Dad

I ask Ted if he'd be willing to try a different, more experiential kind of work. He agrees, and I instruct him to pick up a wad of tissues in his large hands.

"See that empty chair there?" I nod toward the other end of our little semicircle of men, where a chair has been left unoccupied.

"Yup," he says.

"I want you to close your eyes and invite your father to come and sit in that chair so you can talk to him."

"He's dead, ya know," Ted tells me.

"Doesn't matter," I answer. "If anything, that makes this work more important."

Eyes shut, Ted squares his shoulders.

"Ask him out loud," I tell him.

He does. Ted contemplates through closed eyelids his imagined father in the chair set across from him. He takes his time.

"What are you feeling as you look at him?"

"Mostly sick to my stomach," he answers.

"That's shame. That nauseated feeling? That's most often sexual shame."

"Son of a bitch," Ted mutters to no one in particular. He begins to rock slightly; tears appear in the corners of his closed eyes. "Son of a bitch." The rocking is more emphatic now. "You know what he did? He used to take me to his fucking girlfriends."

"What?"

"He'd park me there with a video or a game."

"How old?"

"I'd sit in the living room." Ted ignores me. "I'd hear them in the bedroom."

"What was that like?"

"Scary," he remembers, reexperiencing. He's thoroughly inducted as he speaks; he's back there. "The noises." Again, the rueful smile. He shakes his head. "I was so young, so innocent. I was scared he was hurting her." And now tears track down his face. "I was alone."

"I'm sorry, Ted."

"Then he'd come out and say, 'Now, this is just between us.' Son of a bitch. 'Us *men*,' he'd say."

Don't tell your mother, I reflect.

"'Nobody, don't tell nobody.'" Ted lowers his head. "Who does that? Who does that to a little boy?"

"Tell him," I say.

"What?"

"Tell your father." Through closed eyes, Ted regards the empty chair facing him.

"Son of a bitch, Dad, you—you—" But tears stop him. He bends over, cradling his head in his big hands. "How could you?" he snarls through his tears. "You taught me this, Dad. You taught me this. Some fathers teach their kids how to hit a ball. You taught me how to . . ." He bends over and heaves dry tears.

"Let it go, Ted." I reach over and put a hand on his shoulder. "Just grieve."

As the big man cries, racking tremors shake his frame.

We wait, the other men in the group and me. Wait for the waves to wash over him.

"Your father was a sex addict?" I ask Ted.

"I believe so, yes sir," he says, not looking up.

"And you're a sex addict."

"Yes sir, I know that to be true."

"How's that sick feeling in your gut?"

"It's bad."

"Ted, what was your father's name?"

"William."

"Ted and William." I make like I'm reading from a marquee. "Sex Addiction R Us."

He opens his eyes and looks up at me.

"Ted, you're in the family business."

"I don't want to be."

"You'd like to resign?"

"Yes, I would."

We regard each other for a moment. "Okay. Close your eyes again, and look at your father."

He does.

"Tell him," I urge.

"Tell him what?"

"Whatever you want to," I say. "What he needs to hear. What that little boy needs you say to him."

"I loved my father," he tells me.

"Did you? Did you? Okay then, start with that. Tell him that."

Ted squares his broad shoulders, his voice small. "I love you, Dad," he says, holding back tears. "I miss you. I really miss you, Dad." He bends down, coiled, looks up through closed eyes. "But I'll tell ya this, old man. I sure as hell don't want to be you."

We all let that sit for a moment.

"It's over," I double for him, speaking as his inside voice, "It's over, Dad." And then a smile. "Our little *escapades*."

"And what is he doing?"

"He's listening. Just listening."

"He knows," I guess. "He knows it's over."

Ted "looks" deeply at his imagined father. "You know," he tells me, "I believe he might."

Later in the session, I tell Ted, in his mind's eye, to gather up all the sexual shame that was poured into him as a child. "Your father behaved shamelessly. He radiated the shame he did not feel, and it went right into you."

"Oh my god," Ted says.

"It went into you, Ted, and you've lived with it your whole life."

"It's true," he tells me. "I was mortified. He was so embarrassing, the way he'd be with waitresses and all. My mom, she'd be sitting right there, and he'd . . ."

"Tell him," I urge. "Father," I model, "when you dragged me through your sordid life, you shamed me. I took up your sexual shame, and it's been with me ever since."

Ted repeats virtually every word. "I ran from my shame by acting out." He repeats my words, his voice strong, as he faces his father.

"Just like you did," I say.

"Just like you did," he repeats.

"I will not be your companion anymore," I say.

"Ugh," he utters.

"Good," I say, "feel that."

"I will not—" Ted begins. "Son of a bitch, Dad. I will not be your little pal any longer. I've played out your sexual shamelessness, and it's hurt everyone I love," he tells his father with my coaching.

"I give you back your shame," I prompt.

"I give you back your shame."

"I give you back your entitlement," I say.

Ted shakes his head, no more tears now, just resolve. "Dad," he says, clear and firm, "I can't do this anymore. I'm sorry."

"I give you back your shame," I direct Ted.

"What?"

"I want you, in your mind's eye, to gather up all the shame and all the sexual compulsion that you took in, all that gunk that's lodged in your body, and roll it up into a big ball and hand it back to him."

Ted sits quietly for a moment, then stretches out his hands, as if they held something. "Take it, Dad. Take it back. It's yours." His eyes fill, but he remains steady. "It's always been yours."

"It's never been who you really are, Ted," I tell him. We pause. "Is there anything else you want to tell him for now?"

Ted regards his father for a long moment. "I miss you, Dad," he says finally, softly. "I love you, Dad."

I watch. We watch.

"Goodbye, Dad," says Ted.

That interview was seven years ago. With the help of Sex Addicts Anonymous, a good sponsor, and recovery buddies, Ted has remained sober. He expects to stay so for the rest of his life. I see no reason to doubt him.

Embracing Our Inner Orphans

How do we transform a legacy? By facing with compassion our own orphaned parts, the little boys and girls inside us that we, in our shame and judgment, have abandoned, locked away behind closed doors. By embracing our shadow. In Chapter 3, I detailed the two pathways by which your particular *you and me* consciousness gets formed—through reaction and through modeling.

Reaction means you re-form yourself, contort yourself into whatever you need to be in order to preserve the greatest level of freedom and maturity you have at hand. Was one of your parents intrusive? In reaction, you erect thick protective walls. Was someone controlling? In reaction, you develop a black belt in evasion. Were they needy? You become expert in giving care. For decades, psychology has been centrally concerned with trauma and victimization, and it has recognized adaptation through reaction.

Clinicians have kept their focus on reaction, but social psychologists also stress the equally important role of modeling. Children learn what they live. You become what you see.

Modeling is particularly important when it comes to issues of grandiosity, of traits and behaviors that are victimizing, like the force uniting William and Ted, what one of the creators of family therapy, Ivan Boszormenyi-Nagy, called *the multigenerational legacy of destructive entitlement.* A father transgresses. Shamelessly, he brings his young son to his secret mistress, a terrible thing to do to any child. On the receiving end of the father's behavior, Ted was massively shamed, made to feel small, dirty, and alone. Yet on another level, he was falsely empowered. He received the message that this is the way a grown man behaves. Shame lay at the rotten core of Ted's link to his father, but they were equally fused by entitlement. William poured into his son, like a waiting vessel, all the skewed beliefs and rationalizations that fueled his own sexual "escapades." And Ted, a loyal son, loving his dad, became him.

Unlike reaction, children's modeling of a parent is often unconscious. It's my job to bring it to the surface, to break open those wired-together neurons. Once the replay is explicit and acknowledged, how I work with it depends on how the client regards the parent they've modeled themselves after.

Waking Up

Ernesto had been a rager for more than twenty years, all the while saying his rages came over him too quickly to stop them. In our session, I ask him who the angry one was in his family, and he regales me with stories of his cruel stepmother, whom he loathes. With my help he sees, for the first time, that he has become, in his current family, the very person he most despised growing up. His recoil is forceful and immediate. "For someone to paint me with that brush—to see me as like—ugh, I'm just sick." That sickness Ernesto feels all of a sudden is the guilt he should have been feeling all along, feeling it strongly enough, in fact, that it would have stopped his bad behavior.

That's the way we all work. You don't verbally abuse someone you love, because you'd be mortified; it goes against your value system. What stops offensive behavior is healthy guilt. When Ernesto's stepmother tortured him, she overtly shamed him and *covertly falsely empowered him*. The message: "When you grow up, you can haul off and do this to someone too; it's normal." This is what so many therapists fail to take on or even acknowledge. Too many clinicians would home in on Ernesto's shame but soft-pedal his grandiosity, even though his superior attack was about to cost him his marriage.

I call this first phase of Relational Life Therapy *waking up the client*. The therapist "pops" the balloon of grandiosity, and suddenly therapist and client are seeing the grandiosity together, as if sitting side by side. Again, show me the thumbprint, and I'll tell you about the thumb. We learn our relational stances, like cheating, or rage, or anxious dependence, in relationship. And we resurrect the relationship every time we reenact the stance. Although he didn't realize it at the time, Ted never felt closer to his father than when he sexually acted out.

I'd invite you to do some thinking, maybe even try writing a journal entry. If you're like most of us, what will come to you most easily will be your childhood experiences of shame—the ways you've been hurt. Now, see if you can locate some particular incidents or an ongoing relational theme of false empowerment, in which a parent elevated you as a child (saying "No one understands me the way you do") or modeled entitled behavior for you ("This hurts me more than you").

If the relationship in which you originally learned your characteristic reaction, your stance, was negative, as was true of Ernesto, the result can be an immediate kick that can be used to great advantage. And change can occur quickly, deeply, and with support, permanently. Relational Life Therapists routinely see people like Ernesto swear off a troublesome behavior they've engaged in their whole life, stand up from the couch—and it's gone. We set our bar high for our clients. We expect rapid dramatic change, and to a surprising degree, we get it.

Ask yourself what you might be replaying from a childhood sense of overt or embedded entitlement. Whose behavior might yours line up with—an angry father, an aggrieved mother, an abusive sibling no one controlled?

If, like Ernesto, you are attempting to unhook from unconscious modeling of a despised parent, you can do so swiftly once you see it, either with a therapist or on your own. For someone like Ted, whose sexual acting out is embedded in a relationship with a parent he loves, breaking free is more challenging. The often-unconscious replay of the parent's dysfunction represents a way of being in the relationship. For many clients, keeping spiritual company with their problematic beloved parent is their only way of feeling close to the parent. Repetition of the parent's dysfunction is a form, sometimes the only available form, of attachment. But as you free yourself from this form of attachment to a parent, you must allow yourself to grieve the loss. When someone like Ted stands on the brink of giving up his dysfunction, grief comes pouring out of him: "Goodbye, Dad. You're on your own. I will no longer provide you company."

Can you identify some trait or behavior in you that comes from false empowerment as a child? Were you invited into a superior position, or did one or both parents model a superior position for you? If you have difficulty identifying a repeating grandiose pattern, here's a tip: ask your partner. The odds are they will have plenty to say about it! Listen with an open mind.

Now, if a calamitous behavior that you repeat was embedded in your relationship with someone you despised, it won't be hard to wake up from it, to realize, often with a sense of shock, that you are repeating it, and to knock it off—even permanently. But if the behavior is a way you join with an idealized or beloved parent, in their resentment, or sadness, or despair, beware. Shifting away from the accustomed stance can feel like you are betraying the parent, even abandoning them, triggering grief and sometimes even guilt. Who are you to dare to be happier than the dear ones you grew up with and whom you now leave behind?

Julie and Georgina: That Would Be Nice

In a session with Julie and Georgina, Georgina has just promised to quit her eighty-hour-a-week job, to set her alarm for five a.m. so she and her wife can do yoga together, and generally show up for Julie and their kids in ways she hasn't for well over a decade. Julie is skeptical. I don't blame her, but she's wrong. Georgina means it. I can feel it. Georgina is offering her everything that Julie's been asking for for years, but Julie wraps herself in a self-protective cloak of disbelief and steadfastly remains in complaint mode.

So, thoughtful reader, as you can imagine, my question to Julie is, "Who was the resentful one in your family growing up?" By asking that question, I'm fishing for the model that her Adaptive Child used to form itself. Sure enough, Julie's chronically unhappy mother complained loudly and bitterly about her husband to all and sundry—including her little daughter who, predictably, felt sorry for her mom.

"All relationships," I tell Julie, "are an endless dance of harmony, disharmony, and repair." She looks up at me. "Georgina has just offered repair. Will she follow through? Time will tell. But if you were to relent and allow your wife to repair, Julie, you will leave your unhappy mother behind."

"That would be nice," Julie tells me and, in an apparent incongruity, bursts into tears. "I would like that," she says, crying copiously.

Goodbye, Mom. Goodbye, Dad. This, I believe, is the real meaning of psychological individuation, of "separation," as many psychologists would say. The real work of leaving your parental matrix and becoming your own person is sorting through the legacy, passing on consciously, deliberately, the positive traditions and beliefs you are proud of, and laying to rest the negative traditions lodged in your body's reactivity, your Adaptive Child, the unique contours of your *you and me* consciousness.

According to individualistic myth, adulthood demands separating from one's family of origin, particularly one's mother. In place of that myth, I'd offer a new paradigm. For a child to achieve maturity, the parent-child relationship must be renegotiated, such that the new relationship is roomy enough to allow for the child's increased capacities. But no one needs to leave anyone. From Parsifal to Bambi, boys' adventure stories notoriously begin with the death of their mothers. That's unnecessary. Mothers, hold close to your sons—just not so tightly that they cannot grow.

Family pathology rolls on from generation to generation until someone finally has the courage to turn and face the flames. What does that mean exactly? It means turning toward, surfacing, giving voice to, loving, and ultimately demoting our many inner children. We achieve maturity when we deal with our inner children and don't foist them off on our partners to deal with. When your inner child kicks up (i.e., when you are trauma-triggered), put your arms around it, hoist it up onto your lap, listen to what it has to say, be empathic and loving—and take its sticky hands off the steering wheel. Demote it. "You are not driving the bus. I am, the Wise Adult."

When Belinda and I fight, I literally visualize little Terry, a composite inner child around eight years old. In my mind's eye, I place him behind me; he can hold on to the back of my shirt. I make a deal with him: between the angry energy Belinda is throwing my way and little Terry stands me, the grown-up. "My big body, my strong back, will protect you. Like Superman, spreading his cape to absorb the blast, I will absorb Belinda's energy and spare you. On the other hand, little Terry, you let me deal with Belinda. Don't you try to do it. I can do it better than you can."

Loving, hearing out, being empathic toward, and ultimately demoting our inner children, our adapted or wounded selves — it sounds like a tall order. How do we actually do it?

Desiree and Juan: "You Cannot Rage at My Husband"

With spiky black hair, tight ripped jeans, and a white T-shirt against paler skin, Desiree looks to be about thirty going on sixteen. At first glance, she appears tough and sexy, two qualities I file in the back of my mind for possible exploration.

Beside her, her partner, Juan, Latinx, late thirties, waits attentively, leather notebook opened on his lap, pencil poised to jot down anything said or done of significance. I peek and find that the pages of his waiting journal are made up of little squares, graph paper, in case he might have an impulse to break with words and jot down a formula or a quick grid. Juan, I learn later in our session, is an engineer.

I wonder if they are a complementary couple; she provides the fizz, and he, the stability. I wonder if Desiree is about to complain that her husband is shut down and not cherishing. In my mind, I'm already imagining working with him, opening him up.

The great Italian therapist Gianfranco Cecchin used to say, "Love your hypothesis, feel passion toward your hypothesis—but don't marry it." My first instinct was completely off base. Juan wasn't the problem, Desiree was, by both of their estimations. Desiree was, with little to no real provocation, a rager: she created boisterous scenes in restaurants and high drama at home, storming off, slamming doors, shouting epithets, throwing things.

"You can be quite a handful," I venture.

"Oh yeah." She nods enthusiastically. Like most abusers, both physical and verbal, Desiree is a love dependent. Like most highly reactive partners, she has poor boundaries and little self-protection. She is thin skinned, easily triggered, and easily offended. Whenever Juan tries to distance from her—to break their connection, to make excuses for her enemies—to shut her down, she meets it with a moment or two of intense distress, followed by what could be several hours of screaming attack.

"Yelling?" I ask her.

"Oh yeah."

"Slamming things around, throwing things?"

"At times."

"Name-calling?"

She leans in toward me. "Yes, to all. In other words, exactly the way my mother treated me."

I sit back, take a breath.

"She still does," Desiree says. "In those rare times I see her."

"She calls you—" I begin.

"'Bitch, whore, slut,'" Desiree tells me. "Some others we needn't get into."

I let out my breath. "I'm sorry. How long?"

"Till I was fourteen," she says, her voice flat, matter-of-fact, "when I left home."

I take a minute to let that sink in.

"So," Desiree continues, "when Juan pulls away somehow, or I feel like he crosses me, I just—"

"You feel abandoned is what I'd guess," I tell her.

"Yup, abandoned and betrayed."

"So, there's a little girl in you—" I start.

"Yeah, she's five, the hurt one," Desiree says, preempting me. "I've worked with her a ton in therapy over the years. It's the other one."

"Which?"

"The fifteen-year-old."

"Oh, the angry one."

"Yeah," she says. "The bitch that makes all the trouble."

"You've worked with her?"

Desiree shakes her head no.

"Spoken to her?"

Again, the head shake.

I look at her awhile. "Can I stay with this, Juan?"

He eagerly gives me permission to work with his wife.

I regard Desiree, who looks right back at me, waiting.

"You don't like her very much," I tell her.

"Who?" she asks.

"That fifteen-year-old."

She laughs loudly and bitterly. "No, I don't like her very much."

"Can I tell you why that's a shame?"

She nods.

"Because," I say, "because she saved your ass."

"Oh, I know that," Desiree answers quickly. "It's just that— look, by the time I was fifteen, I had already endured—" She pauses, takes a deep breath. "There'd already been all manner of sexual abuse."

"I'm sorry to hear that."

"The end of high school way into college, I had already slept my way through—I was looking for something, Daddy maybe, who knows, but that girl . . ." Desiree scrunches her face.

"Costly," I say. "She's costly. A really immature little girl."

"To say the least," she allows. "Look, the plain truth is, I despise her."

"That girl?"

"Yes." Her lips are curled. "That one."

"Uh-huh," I say.

Desiree and I look at each other for what seems a long moment.

"I'd like to meet her," I tell her. She groans. "Will you ask her?" I press. I ask her to close her eyes, look down into the cavity of her body, and find that fifteen-year-old girl who lives inside her.

"I'm not sure she'll even—" Desiree begins.

"Let me worry about that. Close your eyes."

Reluctantly, she surrenders to the exercise. She invites her imagined fifteen-year-old self to come up out of her body and join us in the room.

"How does she look?"

Desiree takes a long time. "I don't know. She looks . . . detached. Cut off from herself."

"Right. She is, Desiree. Now tell me, how do you feel as you look at her?"

She shakes her head; unbidden tears appear at the corners of her eyes. "I hate her."

"Ask her if there's anything she wants to say to you," I instruct.

She hesitates for only a second, then makes a face and nods. "She says, 'I don't need your judgment. I did the best I could with the parents I had, *bitch!*'" More nodding, as if to say, *Hmm, she does have a point.*

"You can see that?"

She nods and says yes.

"Then why, Desiree? Why are you so hard on her?"

She pauses, collects herself, and thinks before she answers my question, speaking through tears. "Because she—she—"

"What, Desiree?"

"She wasn't . . . she didn't hold up her end of the bargain. She—"

"What, Desiree? She wasn't a grown-up?"

"She didn't have the strength," Desiree tells me. And now tears come in earnest.

"The strength to . . . ?"

"To push them off of her," she wails. "To get them off!" And now she doubles in on herself and cries.

Juan reaches out to comfort her, but I shush him away. I want her to feel the full brunt of it.

"So now it's clear what all the rage is about."

She looks up at me, questioning.

"Desiree, I think the rage is her way of trying to find enough strength to push them off her. The strength to protect herself."

Hearing this, she bends her head.

I lean in close to her bowed head. "But she didn't have that strength, did she? And you know why she didn't have that strength? Because she was just fifteen, sweetheart." I can hear her cry. "She's just a child."

Desiree stays with her head bent down a long time. Still looking down, she says quietly, "She can lose the 'bitch' part."

"Yes." I'm smiling, though she can't see me. "Good idea. Tell her that, Desiree. Let her know you want to hear her, but—"

Desiree leans forward on the sofa, brushing me aside, an annoyance, and peers at her teenaged self. She nods, hands dangling between her legs. She looks off into some middle space in the distance. "It's time," she says at last. "It's time."

"Tell her what you're feeling now."

Desiree leans in toward her imagined self. "You never asked for—" A wave of grief washes over her. "You didn't deserve it, okay? You just . . . all of it . . . all of it. You just didn't deserve it at all."

"How does she respond?"

Desiree nods. She waits awhile and finally says, "She's taken hold of my hand."

"She has?" I'm gently elated. "Take hers back, Desiree. Hold it tight. She needs you, just as much as the five-year-old."

"I'm sorry," Desiree tells her Adaptive Child. "I'm so sorry." With more raw tears, she is sobbing.

"Let it go. Feel the grief and let it go. You're sorry for . . . ?" I prompt.

"For all of it," she answers. "You never asked for any—"

"And how does she respond?"

"She's crying too," she tells me. "I guess we're crying together."

"Good. That's good. Be with her, hold her in her grief."

After a moment, I double for Desiree, speaking for what I imagine is inside her. "I'm sorry for all you went through," I model.

"Yes." Desiree repeats my words.

"And I'm sorry," I forge on, "that I have been so hard on you all these years."

Desiree's head snaps back as she smiles, unhappily.

"I'm sorry," I repeat.

"I hear you." Desiree lapses into silence. I wait. "I'm sorry," she allows at long last. "I'm sorry I left you on your own. I'm sorry you've been so alone."

"Is she alone now?"

"What do you . . . ?"

"Do you have her?"

She looks down at her clasped hands. "Yes," she says slowly. "Yes. I have her."

"And she?"

Desiree shrugs. "She's just holding on."

"Good."

"She . . ."

"Yes?"

"She says she's sorry she called me a bitch," Desiree tells me.

A broad smile breaks over my face. "One more thing I'd like you to tell her."

"Sure."

"Tell her to come to you when she's angry. You will hold her. You will love her. But she will no longer rage at Juan. That's over."

To my surprise, Desiree grins.

"What is she . . ."

"She gets it," Desiree says. "She's nodding."

"Really?"

"Yup. She's smiling."

"Well, I'll be," I say. "You know, you set limits on a fifteen-year-old, and while they may buck a bit, down deep they're relieved."

Desiree's grin now matches my own. "She can sure raise hell."

"Good," I join with her. "That fight kept you emotionally alive."

"But it's time now. I think she might start to breathe again."

"Yes," I say softly. "I think the fight is over."

Desiree nods, still staring at the chair that her imagined child inhabits, in no rush to break contact. "Is there anything more you need to say to her right now?"

Desiree shakes her head. We wait a moment together.

"Is there more she needs to say to you?" I begin. "And she can lose the chip on her shoulder when she talks to you."

Desiree nods, smiling, two steps ahead of me. "She says thank you."

"Tell her she's welcome."

We sit quietly together, all of us, for a moment. "In your mind's eye," I tell Desiree, "shrink her down so she can fit in the palm of your hand and place her back in your heart where she can rest with you. And then, when you're ready, open your eyes. I've got something to show you."

Slowly, her eyes open.

"How are you doing?"

She nods. "I'm good. I feel good."

"Look at his face," I say, indicating Juan, who sits soundlessly, pencil still poised, tears streaming down his face.

At first, Desiree thinks he's laughing and chuckles to herself uncertainly.

"No," I say, redirecting her. "Look at his face. That's for you. That's called compassion."

She turns to me. "He always gets scared when I show—"

"Desiree," I interrupt, "look at your husband. Be here now."

Nodding to herself, childlike for a moment, she takes Juan's hand. "I just—"

Juan cuts her off. "No, I love that little girl in you, that fighter, that spirit. I want to hold her. And I will. I'm so sad she—" Tears stop him. I can see a splash appear on his graph paper. "I just—"

As I watch, their two bodies strain toward each other.

"You want a hug?" I ask Desiree, who looks up at me. "A hug from the guy?"

She nods and throws out her arms wide for him.

Juan smiles, a little sheepish. He puts down his notebook, unclips his mic, pats his hair, and goes to his wife. They rock together gently, both crying.

"I'm so sorry," Desiree mutters.

"It's okay, baby," he tells her. "I'm right here."

Pass it back or pass it on. Desiree's own daughter, from a previous relationship, was headed toward thirteen herself. For years before Juan, she'd been Desiree's pal, her confidante and implicit caretaker. I tell Desiree that the days of her daughter suffering through another round of her rage are, I hope, over. Desiree readily agrees. "We need a family meeting," she says. Juan groans, but says he's game if she is. "We need to announce the inauguration of a new administration," says Desiree.

Juan now grins, along for the ride. "Nonviolent protests will be heard," he intones with mock solemnity.

"But violence," Desiree warns, "will not be tolerated. You agree?"

He vigorously nods assent.

"And *she* agrees?" I ask Desiree about her younger self.

Desiree stops, tilts her head a bit as if listening, and then smiles. "Reluctantly and begrudgingly," she announces.

"That's fine," I say quickly before anyone can make a fuss. "We'll take it."

Someone once called Relational work "deconstructing patriarchy one couple at a time." I was flattered by that description. As you and your partner step into real intimacy, you both step beyond the contours of patriarchy. Throughout this discussion I have referenced the toxic culture of individualism. But where and how do such cultural forces impinge on someone's personality? Culture is not some bloodless abstraction. Culture is primarily transmitted through people. Culture spoke through the abuse of a mother like Desiree's who conflated normal sexual interest with out-of-control promiscuity. Culture spoke in the voice of a client's father who, on the boy's third birthday, ceremoniously gathered the whole family to watch his son throw his beloved blanky in a fire, too old for that now.

One day, when my kids were still little, I saw the transmission of toxic individualism play out in real time before my eyes. I was at my son's hockey game. A father—mercifully on the other side—was screaming full-voiced at his own woebegone son, about nine years old. In front of everyone in the stands, this father excoriated his boy for not playing well, then excoriated him further for crying. The boy slumped up into the stands and plunked himself beside his waiting mother. She murmured a soothing word or two and tried to put her arm around him. At that point, the boy leaned back and punched his mother in the face.

Hurt people hurt people. Such is the transmission of violence, patriarchy, toxic individualism. The well-meaning mother had tried to comfort her son, but did she stand up for him and set limits on her husband? Somehow I doubted it. Women's silence and men's violence. This boy made a performance—in front of the crowd—of rejecting and despising vulnerability. A ritual act of contempt. No mama's boy, he. And so it rolls, from one generation to the next.

Children look up at their parents and wonder, "Should I be like this one or that one?" Hammer or anvil? Perpetrator or victim? It's a lose-lose choice, but having said that, which would you pick? This boy, at nine, internalized his father's contempt and emulated his violence. He has already come to despise "weakness." His sense of well-being rests on two matching delusions—the delusion of invulnerability coupled with the delusion of dominance. As humans, we are neither. But within the culture of individuality, we are both.

In Europe and in America, in the villages and small towns of generations past, citizens relied on one another's neighborliness to cut through the sheer selfishness of Enlightenment rugged individualism, the insistence on one's rights. But no longer. How does the boy of nine grow into the man enraged when he's told to wear a mask? Who insists on his right to put his neighbors' health at risk? The man who becomes allergic to being told what to do, even by his own family? Through the transmission of culture in the form of a screaming father.

In Senate hallways, in the clenched fist of a young boy, in fighting marriages and silent ones, the same force of rampant individualism severs connection at multiple levels, psychological, familial, and societal. We stand, proud, defended, violent, and alone. Unbridled individualism, whether in your community, your state, or your living room, crashes against the seawall of the need for human intimacy. Dominance eats love. Contempt for vulnerability erodes connection. The Adaptive Child is like a hard drive that internalizes all these cultural messages, transmitted by the very people we look up to, even love. In the heat of the moment, the Adaptive Child discharges all that internalized contempt—toward oneself, toward others, toward the rules—creating misery in our present lives.

Escaping the Great Lie

How can we as individuals escape the contempt that lies at the heart of the Great Lie, the myth of individual superiority or inferiority, when it surrounds us all like the air we breathe? The answer: we cannot escape *as individuals*. Our trauma, with rare exception, is relational, a rupture in the intrapersonal field. And so too our healing must incorporate the relational—a healing of the torn field between us. Healing demands that we learn how to be intimate with one another. We must also start listening and responding to the various clamoring parts of ourselves. But to respond in the present, we need to learn not to be overtaken by past traumas. Our traumas can either teach us or run us, depending on how we handle them.

Getting centered in your Wise Adult self is half the battle. If your Adaptive Child has grabbed the wheel, take a breath, take a break, take a walk. Recall that the real work of intimacy is not day by day but rather minute to minute. In this moment, which will you choose: vulnerable closeness or protected distance, your right to express yourself or our duty to find a workable solution? Will you choose you or us? As the German mystic Thomas Hübl says, in such moments, urgency is our enemy and breath is our friend. Slow down, dear reader. Slow down enough to catch up with yourself. Slow down enough to think for a moment of your partner's experience—beyond right and wrong, beyond "objectivity," and beyond you and your self-centered concerns.

For some of us, taking good care of our relationships will mean standing up with love for ourselves. For others, it will mean learning to stand down. Both require stepping into increased vulnerability. Really mastering this relational technology, speaking with some fluency, takes a good two to five years. But don't despair. These techniques and this new way of thinking are both so powerful and so superior to the mores of the culture at large that even doing them badly has the power to utterly transform your life and your relationships. And guess what? You can start doing them badly today.

Start with this. Swear off unkindness; swear off disrespect. Before you open your mouth, ask yourself: "Does what I am about to say fall below the line of basic respect? Is there a chance my the listener will experience it that way?" I would like you, dear reader, here and now in this moment, to take the following pledge: "Come hell or high water, short of outright physical self-defense, I will not indulge in words or behaviors that are disrespectful to any other human being. And neither will I sit passively by if someone is disrespectful to me. I will ask them to speak differently to me, and if that doesn't work, I will break the interaction and leave. But I won't just be silent and absorb it. In either direction—dishing it out or taking it—I am right now today swearing off disrespectful behavior. I don't need it. I am developing the skills of soft power, speaking up and explicitly cherishing at the same time."

Remember, there is no redeeming value in harshness.

There is nothing that harshness does that loving firmness doesn't do better. When you speak, lose the chip on your shoulder. Angry complaint will most likely get you nowhere. The research is clear: hard emotions—anger, indignation— predictably evoke anger back or else withdrawal.

In your relationship, you may need bold assertion to get your partner's attention. The unflinching exercise of soft power is critical in that first phase of getting what you want— the daring-to-rock-the-boat phase. But once your partner has heard you and is willing to try, then stop thinking of yourself as an individual, and pitch in like a good team member. Help them. Show them what you like, and reward their efforts. Centered in the best part of you, reach for and connect with the best part of your partner. Love demands democracy— between us and others and between our ears.

Start by stepping into your own citizenship, your *virtue*, your *us*. Start by taking this pledge to practice full-respect living. At my ripe age, with thirty-five years of marriage behind me, I have a deal with the universe: if it's unkind, I'm not interested, whether it's unkind between others, between others and me, or between me and me. You may have a point, and I'll try to listen to it even in the midst of a bad delivery. But I don't have much bandwidth for anything said unkindly, so do us both a favor and think about how you want to talk to me. I will do the same for you. As they say in medicine, first do no harm.

Let us start by standing up to contempt and putting it in its place. I'm inviting you to live a nonviolent life in your relationships and with yourself. The next time you are triggered, take a breath. Get centered in your Wise Adult—if it takes one moment or twenty—and use your skills:

Lead with appreciation.

State your intention (e.g., "I want to clear the air so I can feel closer to you").

Use the feedback wheel if you can, or at the least stay on your side of the street.

Give your partner an avenue of repair; tell them what they could do to help you feel better.

And then—and this is a hard one—let go of outcome. You have done a good job no matter if your partner responds to it well or poorly.

Focusing on our own relational practice optimizes our chances of making the relationship work, which is not the same as saying we always get what we want. Digest each other's imperfections, and grieve the things you wanted in your relationship that this partnership will not afford. Embrace what you do have, and allow it to be enough, to be an occasion for joy. These are the grown-up skills of intimacy: skills potent enough not only to transform your relationship but ultimately to heal and remake yourself.

10

Becoming Whole

*"I have three chairs in my house; one for solitude,
two for friendship, three for society."*

—HENRY DAVID THOREAU, *WALDEN*

One phrase.

I almost lost him over a phrase. It appeared to have been a great first session, our therapy off to a fine start. And then it came close to a crashing halt. Over what? Compact, with short gray hair and glasses, Charles, a Black man in his mid-fifties, looked every inch the distinguished academic he was. The dean of a highly regarded local college, he was used to cocking an eyebrow and then watching a student begin to stutter. From time to time, he'd be called upon to, as he once put it, "spread a little constructive terror." Charles never raised his voice. He never had to. At work, he was a force. But at home, he simply collapsed. He was Eeyore in *Winnie the Pooh*. He was, as his wife, Diane, put it succinctly, "slouchy, grouchy, and pouty."

"Could be a law firm," I quip, to no one's apparent amusement.

Diane, also Black, looks a good ten years her husband's junior. Tall and fit, in a gray skirt and sleeveless gold top, she describes their life at home. Charles, she says, has slouched and pouted his way through the recent years of their marriage. He pouts if he is sexually "rebuffed," as he puts it. He pouts if she ignores him too long while phoning her girlfriends. He seems to have the abiding relational stance of *disgruntled customer*.

After years of putting up with it, Diane is angry. Angry at his self-preoccupation; angry that no matter what she does, it never seems enough or quite right. Charles says he supports her career as a community organizer, but when it all comes down, if she isn't immediately available when and how he wants, there'll be slouchy, grouchy payback.

One afternoon Diane found herself enjoying early drinks with an art teacher Charles had hired, a handsome young man full of an ease that invited sharing. His ease almost, though not quite, led her to open up about her frustrations in her marriage. Sharing confidences, and then—what more? She'd decided on the spot that this was all starting to seem just a bit *too* angry at Charles. She took herself home to her husband, informed him of what happened, and added, "this boat needs a good rocking."

Then she found her way to me. Charles didn't know what hit him. Wasn't he a good man? Wasn't he a good husband? He really didn't understand Diane's problem.

Diane and Charles: Rocking the Boat

Diane rests her arm on the side of the couch they share and stretches her long legs. "The word for Charles that you may be searching for here, Terry," she informs me, "might be *depressed*. As in chronic, low grade, lifelong."

"Oh, please." Charles makes a face. "Look at what I've accomplished. Look at where I came from."

"That might be just what I'm talking about," she persists.

"You grew up rough? Where?"

"North Philly," he tells me.

"Hey, Camden, New Jersey." I raise my hand, and he regards me anew.

Finding herself in the pull of a young man's confidences, Diane explains to me, woke her up. Telling Charles about it made her realize that she wanted more: more from the marriage and more from Charles. He said he was game, but in this first session, his caved-in energy is not riotously convincing.

As he slumps out the door at the end, I barely resist the temptation to give his arm an encouraging squeeze. "Cheer up," I say instead. "This can get better. Smile."

And that was the phrase that almost drove him from the therapy: Cheer up, I had instructed him. Smile.

Charles does manage to come back the following week. But he is steamed and, I sense, under that, hurt. Before we are all even seated, he reminds me of what he calls our last session's "parting shot." Then he stares me in the face. "Look," he tells me. "I know you meant well. But do you have any idea how many Black men have been told to smile over the decades, centuries? Act like they were just enjoying the hell out of themselves?" His body vibrates slightly, and I can feel my face flush.

Enslaved people, as described by Isabel Wilkerson in her extraordinary book *Caste*, brought a higher bid on the selling block if they looked happy and docile rather than sullen or sad. Men were whipped into smiling, even dancing—their children and wives, their families, broken apart and sold while they watched.

"I can understand why that might have been triggering," I begin.

"Triggering," he stops me, no Eeyore now. "Now, don't put this on *me*."

"I'm sorry I was insensitive," I continue. "I didn't mean to be patronizing."

"He's just mad because you sounded like me," Diane says, trying to come to my rescue.

"What's annoying from her might just be prejudice when it's coming from you, or ignorance," Charles replies, not budging.

Was he saying I was a racist? Was I? Had that been a racist comment I'd made? Out of context, no, I wouldn't call it racist on its face. The problem is that we aren't stripped of context and can't be. Given the racial history, my comment, while meaning no harm, was insensitive. Charles wasn't my minstrel, and he could damn well feel any way he chose to.

"I don't know, Charles." I find myself growing defensive. (*Why?* I think. *What needs defending?*) "I'm not sure I'd go to 'prejudiced,' but it certainly was—"

"May I ask a couple of questions?" he interrupts. Before I answer, he asks, "You've read a lot of articles, books even, on doing therapy with people of color?"

"Well, I—"

"Sought consultation with someone who knows the issues?"

I find myself unsure as to whether I should feel angry or embarrassed. The truth is, I try to keep up, sporadically, but I would hardly say I'm an expert.

We sit together, the three of us, in rather uncomfortable silence. Finally, having gotten into trouble with one phrase, I decide to try another, a phrase I teach all my couples to use. A phrase I would like you, dear reader, to add to your lexicon.

"So is there anything I can do," I ask Charles, "to move us toward repair?"

At this, Charles smiles.

"Uh-oh," Diane groans softly as her professor husband withdraws from his inside blazer pocket a neatly folded paper and hands it to me.

"And this is . . . ?" I ask, unfolding it.

"A *preliminary* reading list," he answers, amused. Suddenly I feel empathy for Charles's stuttering students. The list is mostly literary, thank goodness: James Baldwin, Malcolm X. Some titles I don't recognize. But there was more that Charles didn't have on his list—articles and books on race and therapy, particularly therapy across racial lines. I commit to pursuing these as well and tell Charles so.

"But," I say, "since you raise it, I would like to ask. Tell me what it's like for you to work with a white therapist."

He shakes his head, glances at Diane. He asks me not unkindly, "And what do you think I've been doing?"

Daring to Name the Truth

Racism. The backbone of the American system. When I was a child in school, racism was about slavery in the bad Old South. Lincoln freed the slaves, and now all men were free! Let's have a Thanksgiving feast with the Wampanoag and Pilgrims celebrating altogether! This is America!

Discordant evidence, however, lies in plain sight all around us. America was taken from the indigenous people who lived here, with bribery, guns, and germ warfare. The Thanksgiving story is one in which Native Americans generously taught white settlers how to live in the new world and then somehow graciously disappeared, peacefully ceding the land under their feet to the Europeans. In fact, a brief alliance between Pilgrims and Wampanoags in Plymouth deteriorated quickly to become one of the bloodiest, nastiest confrontations to take place between the two nations.

Having secured land through genocide, white America imported another group of people to work it. Slavery was not an aberration; it was essential to American prosperity. Ten of the first American presidents owned slaves. Racism is not an anomaly in American history. Steeped in the doctrine of Manifest Destiny, racism *is* American history. In today's America, slavery has morphed into mass incarceration. Two and a half million Americans live behind bars. Although Black people account for slightly over 13 percent of the general population, they make up just under 40 percent of the incarcerated population. And their labor? Inmate labor is worth $2 billion a year. The Thirteenth Amendment grants freedom to all men *except* those found guilty of crime. What follows from that exemption is a shameful history of deliberate, pervasive attempts to equate criminality with color and law and order with whiteness. From the Southern Strategy to Willie Horton, America's right wing went from dog-whistle racism to virulent open white supremacy. Racism brought Donald Trump to power. Racism stormed the Capitol. Racism fuels sheer hatred in many right-wing conservatives.

From lynching and torture to everyday microaggressions, hypertension, and early death, the cost of racism to its objects is unspeakable. As a white psychotherapist, I am also interested in the cost of racism to the racist.

In *Dying of Whiteness*, Jonathan Metzl tells the story of two Southern states, Kentucky and Tennessee, the first with Obamacare, the second without it. In 2016 Metzl encountered a man he calls Trevor, who happened to live on the wrong side of the state line. Had Trevor lived a mere thirty-five-minute drive north, in Kentucky, he would have been eligible for life-prolonging drugs and a desperately needed liver transplant. When Trevor was asked if he would now support Obamacare, he scoffed, "No way I want my tax dollars paying for Mexicans or welfare queens." Metzl points out that Trevor preferred death to betraying his white cohort. Near death, Trevor is no doubt on disability himself, getting health care, Social Security, and perhaps food aid from the government. If I had been talking to Trevor, I would have pointed out that he *was* a "welfare queen."

Racism lies in the poisoned heart of America. So does patriarchy. Both are children of the Great Lie, the delusion of individualism, that one can be essentially superior or inferior to another human being. In a brilliant article, the psychiatrist Heather Hall deconstructs the psychodynamics of racism as a narcissistic disorder. Narcissism, the disorder of our time, is rooted in a misunderstanding—the difference between real self-esteem, which comes from the inside out, and its reflection, the outside-in forms of self-esteem, like the value one derives from performance, or from one's possessions, or from others' esteem. In the myth, remember, Narcissus dies not from an overabundance of self-love but from its opposite. He falls in love with his reflection, over which he bends, sighing, until thirst and hunger slay him. Narcissus is an addict who kills himself.

Better than, less than. One-up or one-down. Superior or inferior—and inferior not just about one attribute, not an inferior farmer, for instance, or tennis player, or writer. No, you are inferior as a human being. This is how *you and me* becomes *us and them*. Because in the toxic cult of individuality, it isn't enough simply to be an individual—like everyone else. No, one must distinguish oneself, one must be special, one must be above average in all things. How quickly and effortlessly that glides into holding oneself above not merely individuals but whole groups of people, whole swaths of humanity. Indigenous people, immigrants, Jews, Latinx, Asians, LBGTQ, the disabled, anyone of color. You assert your individuality by depriving others of theirs.

Upward Mobility and Damage

Charles, in his demands, particularly for sex, and in his consequent sulky retaliation, holds himself aloof and apart. As a Black man, he is the object of our culture's collective grandiosity through racism, while at the same time, in his marital relationship, he is a personal example of narcissism in his demands on and retaliation toward his wife. While at home he has a depressive, passive-aggressive style—he only rarely becomes overtly angry—he nevertheless punishes Diane with his moodiness and ill-temper.

He does that particularly male routine that my wife, Belinda, calls *putting out a stink*. You don't say a word, but the people around you wind up with a headache. Passive-aggression means punishing people by what you don't do, by how little you give. In his public life, Charles has been the soul of maturity, balance, and leadership. At home, as Diane puts it, he reverts from Wise King to Put-Out Prince.

I think to myself that it must be hard to be a Wise King all day long. And then I call to mind Charles's race and I amend that thought. It must be hard to be the Wise King all day, every day, unrelentingly, for how long?

I ask Charles about his meteoric rise from the streets of North Philly to the boardrooms of New England. Listening to his tale of academic achievement, excellence in athletics, and community leadership, I wonder where he ever got to be a big baby. It's an open secret among couples therapists that many powerful people regress in their relationships. President Ronald Reagan called his wife Nancy "Mommy." High-powered couples routinely have babytalk nicknames for each other, often secret words, even a language. Out in the world, Charles measures every word, always has, always needed to. So I wonder where he ever got to be a big old bratty boy.

"You remind me," I tell Charles, "of a famous session in the annals of family therapy." They both look up at me, cautious but open. "Paul Watzlawick, one of the creators of family therapy, was famous for his one-session cures. So here's the tale: A guy comes to him from D.C., African-American, about your age. Like you, this guy was a super-performer, up from poverty, straight As, merit scholar, the whole thing. He's now a highly successful lobbyist in Washington, has a loving wife, three kids in private school, fancy cars. His life is perfect, except for one detail. He suffers from debilitating anxiety attacks.

"'Of course, you're anxious!' Watzlawick is said to have exclaimed. 'You're haunted by your own imperfection, which even you cannot fully escape. There's a fundamental privilege,' he told the guy, 'that all through your growing up and even to this day you've never had. A privilege the lowliest white kid in town possesses in abundance. You know what it is? The privilege to fail, to screw up, to make a perfect fool of yourself.' " I look at Charles and Diane.

"I get it," Charles tells me. "One false step—"

"And it's a long drop down," I agree with him.

"So?" Charles prompts.

"Okay," I say. "So Watzlawick gives him an assignment. He has to know that he can fail spectacularly and still survive. There was a well-known watering hole of the powerful elite in D.C., a fancy steakhouse. Watzlawick tells this guy he has to go to this restaurant and insist on a cheese enchilada. Insist on it so vociferously that he gets himself removed."

"And so?" Charles prompts.

"So," I go on, "he does it. He's so obnoxious he gets himself bodily thrown out the front door, where a small group of family and friends are waiting. Witnessing his ejection, they burst into applause and take him to lunch at the second most prestigious joint in Washington, to celebrate his liberation."

Charles wrinkles his face. "So all I have to do is get thrown out somewhere—"

"And your wife will whip you up a great enchilada!" I say.

"Wife doesn't cook," Diane deadpans.

"Right." I plow on: "Like I said. She'll order you a great enchilada."

"I'm not exactly sure what we're saying here," Charles starts.

"I'm saying everybody needs to be a kid somewhere," I tell him. "Did you get to be much of a kid growing up?"

He shakes his head.

"Your needs, your emotions, were all well-tended to?"

"My parents were dealing with one special needs kid and my brother on drugs. He's okay now," Charles adds.

"But you were the good one?" I ask, knowing the answer.

Charles nods.

Dean's list, football star, I recall him saying. What Charles is, in my assessment, is a lost child: hero type. After thirty-plus years as a family therapist, I find myself drawn to the simplicity of the three family roles first described in AA: hero child, scapegoat child, lost child.

I explain it to Diane and Charles. "The hero is the good one," I tell them. "The scapegoat is the bad one, or the sick one, the family problem."

"That's both my brother and sister in different ways," Charles allows.

"Your sister was the problematic one and your brother was the bad one, the rebel?"

"Pretty much," Charles agrees.

"And you were the one who was left on your own," I venture.

"Well," Charles corrects, "I was praised."

"Right," I tell him. "I subdivide the lost child into two types, depending on why the child is neglected. You can be left alone because you're bad, not worth it. That's lost child: scapegoat type. Or you can be neglected because you're the good one; your parents are busy with something, or someone—"

"That would be my brother," Charles interjects.

"—and, hey, you seem fine on your own. Lost child: hero type, the neglected good one."

"I don't really like being pigeonholed—" Charles winds up.

But I interrupt. "How many games did your parents go to?" I hazard a guess. "How many teacher conferences?"

Charles bridles. "Hey, my dad worked two jobs so my mother could stay at home."

"I'm not saying it's anyone's fault," I tell him. "It just is. You were on your own, Charles. None of your emotional needs was met, particularly, not in that family. You grew up good, and you grew up hungry."

Charles shifts in his chair.

"How old is that pouty boy? The one that drives Diane crazy?"

Charles shrugs warily. "I don't know."

"Make it up," I press on.

"Seven, eight, I guess."

"In your mind's eye, when you look at him, where is he? What's he doing?"

"Nothing," Charles says. "I mean, he's in his room most likely, studying. Doing homework."

"Lonely," I add for him.

"I don't know about that," Charles objects. "Alone, perhaps but—"

"You didn't feel lonely," I posit.

"Not really, that's just the way it was."

"It was normal."

"Yes."

"Being alone."

"I mean there were people—"

"Emotionally alone," I correct. "Psychologically alone."

"Well." Charles takes his time, considering.

"You didn't feel alone," I guess. "It was just normal."

"How it was," Charles agrees.

"No," I say, gathering momentum. "You didn't feel lonely then. You pretty much never feel lonely."

"Not really."

"Until Diane does something you read as uncaring."

"Oh, here it comes."

"Isn't it true, though?" I ask. "You hardly ever feel lonely, until Diane somehow turns her back?"

"It can feel that way."

"Then it all comes out," I guess. "All your loneliness. All his loneliness, that seven-year-old."

"Which is about how old I act, according to my wife," Charles agrees. He claps his hands together. "Okay, so go. Now what?"

"If I may, I want to tell you what Belinda and I used to tell our then four-year-old."

Charles looks up.

"Use your words," I intone.

"As in?"

"As in walking over to your wife and saying, 'Hey. I could use a hug.'"

Charles sits back, amused. "Can you see me doing that?" He turns to Diane. "You'd like that?"

Diane smiles. "Better than flouncing around like a child," she tells him, dismissive.

But Charles really looks at her. "You'd be okay with me being weak?" he asks with what seems real vulnerability— vulnerability I sense in him for the first time.

Diane picks up steam. "You don't think I know that you're weak already? Honey, we're all a mixture of weak and strong. Who do you think you've been fooling?"

Charles seems unconvinced.

"You know," I say, "the same guy who won't ask his wife for comfort is the one who makes her pay when she doesn't give it."

Charles harrumphs without much conviction.

"Here's a bitter pill for you," I say to Charles. "You ready?"

He nods.

"You really can't be mad at not getting what you never asked for."

"But when I do ask—"

"I'm not just talking about sex," I quickly add. "Charles, you have more emotional needs than just sex. A lot of men are a one-note song. You feel insecure, you want sex. Lonely? Sex. Scared about something?"

"Okay," Charles says. "I get the drill."

"So, baby," Diane says, turning to her husband. "You'll talk to me? Tell me who you are? What you're feeling?"

"I *feel*," Charles emphasizes, "like I'd like to get close to you, you know, physically."

"*Other* feelings?" she says.

"There *are* other feelings," I reassure.

"Yeah, like being ganged up on." He asks, "Is that a feeling?"

"It *is*, Charles," I mock-congratulate him.

He purses his lips, looks at Diane. "So if I come to you . . ."

"Yes, Charles," she says.

"With real vulnerability . . ."

"Yes, Charles."

"Sharing my feelings . . ."

"Yes, Charles."

"We'll be closer, I mean, more intimate?"

"Jesus," Diane exhales.

"Well, wait," I tell her, turning to Charles. "If you lay off. If you actually do the work of identifying other feelings and needs besides sexual desire. If you stop pressuring her through your nonverbal complaining . . ."

"Yes?" says Charles.

"You might be surprised," I tell him. "You might actually render yourself more attractive."

"Nothing promised," Diane quickly interjects.

"It's not a quid pro quo," I tell Charles. "No more complaining, no pressure."

"I got that part," Charles tells me.

"But you never know," I chide him. "Grown men are usually sexier than seven-year-olds."

Charles takes a long glance at Diane. "You fell in love with my strength," he tells her. "You told me so."

"I fell in love with all of you, Charles. You're not hiding anything from me. I see what you're trying to hide, and I see you hiding it."

"What do you see?" He bridles a little. "What am I trying to hide?"

She reaches over and grabs his chin, turning his head so he's looking right at her. "I see you, you fool. I see that boy."

Charles frowns.

"I like that little boy," she tells him. "I love that boy."

"But—" Charles coaxes her.

She leans back, quiet for a moment. "It can be tough."

"What's that mean?" he asks.

"It means you tell her what that hurt boy feels when she says no, Charles," I interject, "but you don't drop him off at her doorstep."

Charles takes a long time to look at his wife. "You really do love me, don't you?" he says quietly.

Diane nods. "Hard to take in," she says.

"Sometimes," he tells her.

"A lot of times," Diane answers as they gaze at each other.

"Sometimes," answers Charles, holding her gaze.

I register the soft way they look at each other. "How about now?" I ask Charles. "Can you take it in now?"

Charles looks for a long moment at his wife. When he answers, still locked on Diane, his voice is tender. "Now's all right."

Invulnerable and dominant. If that's the pose all men adapt, for Black and brown men in this country, it may seem like a matter of survival itself. It's easy for a privileged white therapist to say, "Go, be vulnerable." Isabel Wilkerson describes a time when she was flying to a speaking engagement. She was due to sit next to a little white girl, no more than seven or eight. The girl was surprised to see a woman who looked like Wilkerson in first class. Her bewilderment escalated into consternation and then frank upset. "Don't worry," the mother soothed her daughter. "You take my seat on the aisle; I'll sit next to her."

Now, reader, I ask you to stop and think for a moment about what that would feel like. Cooties. Wilkerson has a whole section in her book on cooties. In the early 1950s, Cincinnati, under pressure, attempted to integrate its municipal swimming pools. Whites threw nails and broken glass into the water. In 1960 a Black activist attempted to integrate a public pool simply by swimming in it. After swimming his laps, as he toweled off, he watched the city completely drain the pool and replace it with fresh water.

How dare I, as a therapist, challenge someone to be more vulnerable, knowing that such humiliation or worse can erupt anywhere, anytime? And yet I do, indeed I must. Because intimacy is intimacy—it requires vulnerability, it requires us to sort out and put out our wants and needs, our feelings. Even in resistance. Even in flight.

Over time Charles learned to be a gladiator when need be in the world and at the same time a lover at home. He learned to complain less about what he wasn't getting and, instead, to tend more to Diane's needs, what warmed her up, turned her on. Together, over time, the couple settled into a routine of sex about once or sometimes twice a week, which was "okay" for Charles and "plenty enough" for Diane.

They left therapy soon afterward. They thanked me. I wished them both luck.

As they stood to go, I thanked Charles for helping me "raise my racial consciousness" at the beginning of our work. He reached out his hand, and I shook it with that odd happy-sad feeling I often get when someone "graduates."

"You just keep smiling," he tells me.

Wiseass, I think, but don't say, ceding him the last word.

Grandiosity Damages the Grandiose

Apart and above. We define ourselves against the fantasied backdrop of the Great Lie, as superior to those we deem lesser than us. We assert our individuality by depriving others of theirs. The first act in marginalizing someone is to take aim at their identity as an individual. We deprive enslaved people of their names, we shave imprisoned people and take their clothes, we turn Jews into the numbers on their arms, we tell ourselves that we are privileged, not Black, not poor, not gay, not female. We hold fast to our perceived rung on the ladder by stepping on the faces of those just below us.

And herein lies a huge cost, not just to those we step on but also to us. Because we do the same things to ourselves. We deem this part of us as okay but that part as revolting. We lash ourselves with negative self-talk when we don't measure up. We live harsh lives, both inside and out. Here is a difficult truth: although I want to be crystal clear that the toxin of privilege pales in comparison to the systemic torture, depredation, and humiliation of those who are not privileged, nevertheless, if we as a society are to move beyond these ancient fissures and wounds, we must come to realize that toxic individuality is a culture that flays everyone—those at the top as well as those at the bottom. Recent research indicates wealth impairs one's empathy toward others. Think about that. Would you consider that a favor? Maintaining the system requires blunted empathy, dissociation, compartmentalization, and even faulty thinking.

When I was in college, I was obsessed for a time with J. Robert Oppenheimer, the father of the atomic bomb. As I read about the Manhattan Project, I kept asking myself, How could this man have lived with himself? How could he have brought this atrocity into the world, knowing the planet-endangering consequences of his monstrous invention? The answer I came to, after plowing through several essays and biographies, was shocking: He didn't much think about the consequences. We were at war. He had a commission. Like men for millennia before him, he had a job to do, and he did it. The cost to Oppenheimer lay precisely in what he would not allow himself to think about, in splitting himself through dissociation. Dissociation—the core motif of reaction to trauma. Trauma victims dissociate; in many cases, they must to preserve themselves. Could it be that perpetrators also must dissociate? That a whole, integrated human being cannot so easily harm another?

Once we allow ourselves the privilege of not thinking, we become dangerous. Thirty-eight-year-old Rudy had unprotected sex with prostitutes during the COVID epidemic and then went home to dine with his family. In our session, I asked him, did he not realize the risk he was exposing his wife and kids to? He shrugged. "I told myself I wouldn't get anything." *Sheer grandiosity*, I reflected. "Truth is, I didn't really think about it." We are sickened sometimes by what we can't stop thinking about, but we can be even more damaged by what we refuse to think about.

Superiority Operates in the Dark

"Stars, hide your fires," Macbeth prays before murdering his king; "Let not light see my black and deep desires." Superiority operates in the dark. Grandiosity rarely sees itself. Holding oneself apart and aloof has consequences to others, of course, but it also does damage to the grandiose individual. The field of trauma psychology has recently articulated what it calls *moral injury*, a particular—and quite virulent—form of PTSD that assaults the psyche of the perpetrator. For example, a soldier who commits atrocities, behaving in ways that fall outside the scope of their own morality, will experience moral injury. In war, men rape, murder, and kill innocent people.

In those who commit such criminal acts of grandiosity, healthy guilt is replaced by dread and power. They assuage their guilt by dehumanizing their victims. The psychiatrist Heather Hall writes, "The most malevolent perpetrators insist that the victim admit that they deserve the abuse. . . . The victim realizes that the only way to minimize the pain's intensity is to help the perpetrator assuage the guilt by saying that yes, I did deserve it. That is the final soul-crushing blow to the victim."

Such are the lengths we go to, but the guilt still haunts. In 1997 the psychologist Na'im Akbar coined the term *posttraumatic slavery syndrome* to refer to the adverse effects of slavery transgenerationally on the children of slaves, and their children, and theirs. In recent years, we have begun to learn more and more about epigenetics, the way trauma affects the DNA of the next generation and perhaps beyond. Can I wonder about the legacy of moral injury to whites without somehow minimizing the unspeakable criminality of our actions? Could it be that white Americans collectively carry in our bodies the shame, the psychic injury, that previous generations did not feel but passed on through generations of denial and reenactment? Can I say, without minimizing the atrocities leveled by whites, that the intrapsychic costs of racism to the racist lie precisely in the tortured mechanisms of denial and distortion that attempt to dehumanize the victim but that in fact dehumanize both?

When it comes to gender, I ask men and women to unite, despite the damage men have inflicted on women for thousands of years and still do. Nevertheless, it is in our interest, all of us, to understand the system of patriarchy. It is in everyone's interest to dismantle a superstructure that holds both sexes hostage. In the same way, I believe it is in everyone's interest to remember that we all make up the relational biosphere we inhabit. It is in everyone's interest to once and for all step beyond the Great Lie of superiority and inferiority, shame and grandiosity, victim and perpetrator. We live as a culture with unhealed collective trauma.

We will never experience collective healing until we undo the dissociation and compartmentalization that is required of us to do collective harm.

In his classic 1991 work *Faces of the Enemy*, Sam Keen detailed the process of *otherization*, the methods and tropes people employ to leach humanity from depictions of the enemy, whoever that might be. A body of literature details what it takes to get soldiers to empty their bullets into human bodies. Each war seems to do a better job at otherization and yields a broader percentage of combat compliance. But the question remains: Can a person kill another while feeling their humanity, maintaining an empathic connection to them? The jury is out.

Internally, many of us engage in a somewhat analogous process directed to parts of our own psyche. We otherize parts of our own selves. We banish, fight with, and torture the parts of ourselves we deem unacceptable. Traditionally patriarchal women otherize their self-assertion or selfishness. Traditional men otherize their vulnerabilities. The field of psychology was born from Freud's discovery of repression, the means by which we humans exile that which we deem uncivilized. It is time to pull back the curtain and embrace the untouchable, both in others and in ourselves.

Individualism asserts itself through disassociation. Oppression is omnipresent to the oppressed and lurks in the shadows for the oppressor. How many of us are racists to ourselves? A 2020 study showed that people who admitted to behavior they labeled racist nevertheless denied that they were racist. I'm interested in the psychological gymnastics these subjects went through to acknowledge their behavior and, at the same time, deny the attribute. Individualism exists through disconnection, and the cost of disconnection is disconnection. Virtually everyone in the West feels superior to someone and inferior to someone else. Virtually everyone in the West sees the group they belong to as superior to some other group and inferior to another. None of this sees air or daylight, while in reality, the pain of disconnection sweeps the Western world in an epidemic for all to see. We have never been a lonelier people.

We will not heal as a body politic until we remember what we have dismembered—the despised inferior, in ourselves and in others. All around us, community fractures, as individualism rallies to protect its freedoms and entitlements. In the demands of some for the right to go maskless during a pandemic, or in the strong voice of a left-leaning woman so liberated from accommodating others that she's now abrasive, or in the claims of a therapy patient rounding his fifteenth year of self-improving treatment—individualism thrives. We have never held ourselves as more apart and above, while our epidemic of loneliness, like a rising tide, threatens to engulf us all.

Studies reviewed by Vivek Murthy, the surgeon general of the United States, in his sobering, inspiring book, *Together*, indicate that 22 percent of all American adults say they often or always feel lonely or socially isolated. One in three American adults over the age of forty-five is lonely. In one national survey, one-fifth of respondents said they rarely or never feel close to people. And studies in other countries echo these findings.

"Individualism," Alexis de Tocqueville wrote of America in the 1830s, "is a calm and considered feeling which disposes each citizen to isolate himself from the mass of his fellows and withdraw into a circle of family and friends; with this little society formed to his taste, he gladly leaves the greater society to look after itself." But almost two hundred years later, in today's atomized culture, one's small circle of family and friends may be neither rich nor stable. These days, as the sociologist Robert Putnam discovered, we bowl alone.

Racism may be the Great Lie at its purest—superior and inferior, white and Black. But the same dynamic manifests as masculine and feminine, straight and gay, wealthy and poor.

Poison privilege, like the knife that is all blade, cuts the hand that wields it.

The first step in recovery, coming into right relationship with our privilege, is to see it. To feel its near ubiquitous protection. To acknowledge whatever racist, misogynist, prejudiced views we've internalized. To be willing to confront the unconscious biases we carry. But more than all that, *we must come to understand that holding oneself as fundamentally superior to another is sickening to both parties.*

A driver cuts me off on the road, then reduces his speed, making me slow down. I instinctively hate him: "Who the hell does he think he is? Boston driver!" But then I catch myself. I breathe myself down from the contempt that courses through my body, down from superiority, from grandiosity. I don't do it for the sake of the other driver. I do it for me. I remember that I grew up in a contempt-drenched family. I internalized contempt and turned it on myself for years; I played it out in relationships and made a mess of things more than once. But not now. Today I don't need contempt in my life. I try to practice democracy in my day-to-day life, *same-as*, neither better nor worse. Neither apart nor aloof.

Individualism stands on the backs of its exiles—the chronic, pervasive guilt that haunts the privileged, coupled with the degrading oppression of those without it. To work, individualism requires repression. We tell ourselves that the other is less human than we are, and we behave in ways that suggest that we ourselves have lost our humanity. Not content simply to turn the Great Lie on others, many of us turn it in on ourselves as well. We spend our days habitually tugged by better-than-less-than, harshly judging our own imperfections.

The Great Lie is a frightening, nasty dream from which we might awaken. Emerging from the dream of shame and grandiosity, we come into connection, *same-as*. Just like you. We come into intimacy. Personal democracy. We come to ourselves. And the possibility of lasting, sustained relational joy.

The Everyday Practice of Love

Remember, intimacy—the thing we all long for, if we're really honest with ourselves, the touch of human connection that heals, that fulfills, the only thing in our lives capable of rendering us truly happy, intimacy is not something you have; it's something you do. And you can learn to do it better.* You can learn to do a better job of asserting your rights with love, cherishing the relationship even as you stand up for yourself. You can learn to let go of the trap of "objective" reality and tend, instead, to your partner's subjective hurts or longings, listening, really listening, with compassion and generosity rather than defensiveness and self-centeredness. "I'm sorry you feel bad. Can I say or do anything now that might help?" will often point you toward repair instead of escalated distance or warfare. Self-protection; self-assertion—there is a golden door to

---

* For anyone who wishes to learn more about relational skills to see the new rules of marriage and my online course Staying in Love, they are available on my website, TerryReal.com.

walk through that takes us beyond me, me, me. Not that there shouldn't be a me. Traditionally, women have been taught to submerge their me to the we. But we is not relationship. Intimacy is not some blended egoless amalgam. Intimacy is an endless dance of I and US, the needs of each vital part of the relationship called myself or yourself as those individual wants filter through the needs of the relationship itself. In this moment, perhaps my individual assertiveness takes precedence: "No, please stop treating me like that. I much prefer it this way instead." Other times, you yield, giving your partner what they desire. You ask yourself, "Why not? What will it cost me?" You remember that generosity pays off. As you think more and more ecologically, it begins to appear self-evident that it is in your interests to behave skillfully in, to be a good steward of, your own relational biosphere. Why? Because you're in it, dear reader; it is the air you breathe, the atmosphere you depend upon. Wake up. Wake up and take care.

Epilogue: Broken Light

Sister, mother
and spirit of the river,
spirit of the sea,
suffer me not to be separated,
and let my cry come unto Thee.

T. S. ELIOT, "ASH WEDNESDAY"

Individualism bids us to see ourselves as separate and dominant. Ecology, relationality, invites us to see ourselves as neither dominating nor dominated but part of. But what does it mean to no longer be separate, to be truly a part of the world we inhabit? The anthropologist Gregory Bateson, husband of Margaret Mead, is commonly considered the father of family therapy. In his iconic 1972 work *Steps to an Ecology of Mind*, he called the delusion that we are separate entities, divorced from nature and from one another, "mankind's epistemological mistake." We can temporarily correct this unhappy mistake, according to Bateson, with drugs like alcohol and psychedelics, which is why we find pleasure in them. Research has been building for some years now to show that psychedelics can decrease the fear of death in terminal patients — precisely because they afford many a vision of life beyond the boundaries of the body, the individual.

As a psychotherapist, I find myself often in the position of being a kind of boundary merchant. Couples who have weak or missing psychological boundaries are marked by reactivity or volatility. But with practice, they can work on their psychological boundaries, thicken their skin, and become less reactive.

On the other hand, those who live behind walls—particularly emotional walls, letting out or taking in too little—need to practice *intentional receptivity*, deliberately relaxing, breathing, and taking in what's presented to them.

A healthy psychological boundary, like healthy self-esteem, lies in the middle—neither too open and porous nor too closed and walled off. How we take in, or keep out, others' judgments is a huge psychological issue. But while many boundaryless states—like enmeshment and love addiction—are pathological, others seem available to us that are not merely normal but superlative. We relax self-other boundaries in eroticism, in that unique collaboration between craft and inspiration that is making art, in the exuberance of scientific intuition, and most utterly, in mysticism.

The Wise Adult and Spirit

What is it like not merely to understand that we are a part of a living whole but to actually feel it? When we step out from our Adaptive Child into our Wise Adult, we move beyond individualism, hubris, and the delusion of power and control. Some release control and allow for natural process, including our own mortality. Others turn their ears toward a different music. The legendary psychoanalyst Carl Jung observed that the cure for addiction had to be spiritual because in essence the hole that intoxication was meant to fill was an existential hole. I agree. Psychologists speak about basic trust, a capacity that supposedly develops at two or three years of age, an essentially optimistic belief that the universe is friendly enough and that things will work out.

But how much basic trust do you have at three, four, eight, when someone twice your size periodically lashes out and acts like they hate you? Psychotherapists are keen to ask clients to "let go." But let go into what? You won't jump if there's no water in the pool where you dive. For those of us who come from traumatic backgrounds—and in my estimation, that is millions of us—trust may not be an easy thing to come by.

In my third decade of regular meditation practice, I often felt expanded, that the boundaries of me and other had relaxed and that I was, as they say, at one with the universe. It was a thrilling, liberating experience. But not until somewhere in my fourth decade of meditation did I begin to feel loved. Basic trust came to me only in my sixties. My spiritual practice led me to experience myself as merged with nature that was alive, intelligent, benevolent, and loving. When some—artists, mystics, exquisite lovers—relax their individualistic selves and allow themselves to be at one with nature, it turns out that nature answers back. When we hold ourselves aloof from and superior to nature, we hold ourselves back from the experience of surrender to the numinous—to whatever form of the sacred speaks to us.

———

Perhaps the next step in our evolutionary process is not forward but back to the wisdom of ancient traditions. Perhaps the ultimate wisdom of our Wise Adult selves is not ours as individuals but draws from the collective wisdom of humanity over centuries.

It's been called by many names—Chi, the Tao, Buddha Nature, and if you haven't slept through decades of *Star Wars* films, the Force. Some Zen Buddhists call it Big Mind, the broader whole, the state of oneness with all. Little Mind, our ordinary consciousness—apart and above—is a breeding ground for suffering. No matter how we may try to grasp hold of it, everything in our lives is impermanent, changing. As long as we stay in Little Mind, we experience one loss after another. But that is not our only option. We can also choose to die: that is, to die as our ego-driven, separate selves, and to awaken to our true condition. As Suzuki Roshi wrote:

> To live in the realm of Buddha nature means to die as a small being, moment after moment. When we lose our balance we die, but at the same time we also develop ourselves, we grow. Whatever we see is changing, losing its balance. The reason everything looks beautiful is because it is out of balance, but its background is always in perfect harmony. This is how everything exists in the realm of Buddha nature, losing its balance against a background of perfect balance.

To be at one, to be spiritually awake. The ultimate move beyond the individual: the Master ". . . steps out of the way / And lets the Tao speak for itself."

But the Master doesn't step entirely out of the way. She doesn't disappear. The Tao speaks through her. The metaphor I like best is art. The artist masters her craft. She paints and paints, expanding and deepening her technique, until one day, inspiration passes through her and her work comes alive. She is not the greatness in the painting, and if she takes it as her own, she will become arrogant. But neither is she a mere midwife. A great artist is proud of her craft and grateful for the inspiration that passes through her. It is a collaboration.

Our relationship to nature, I believe, should be artful. We are neither above nor below; we are partners. In his 1956 masterwork *The Forge and the Crucible*, the Romanian historian Mircea Eliade explored ancient man's beliefs about one of humankind's earliest forms of technology: metalworking. Eliade conducted a cross-cultural exploration of the roots of what developed in the Western Middle Ages as alchemy, the forebear of Western science. Eliade chose metalwork as a prototypical technology, and as such, he hoped that the myths and narratives concerning it would offer a window into early man's relationship to technology itself.

What Eliade found was remarkable. Many cultures in the Middle East, India, and China that he studied viewed ancient metalworkers either as sacred shamans or as criminals. Sometimes he found both views within a single culture. Metalworkers were universally seen as reaching into the earth's womb and extracting that which was held there in gestation. The universe tended toward perfecting itself, most of the cultures he studied believed. Gold and other precious gems and metals were the final stage of the earth's subterranean "embryos." By "turning" ore into precious gems and gold, metalworkers therefore took the place of time, accelerating the process of the earth's maturation. Some cultures saw them as midwives, others as violating vandals, and still others, as either. What was the deciding factor? What distinguished between wisdom and criminality?

The answer may be surprising. The element determining whether a practitioner was seen as a saint or a felon was *the internal state of the practitioner.*

Metalworkers who wanted only gain or reward, who imposed their personal will on nature, were portrayed as thieves, a kind of rapist. But those whose spirituality was developed enough that they could work in congruence with the larger whole were regarded as saints or mages. Alchemy was not only a science but also a form of contemplation of the Divine, in which inside and outside were not separate. Early scientists who made fundamental discoveries—Giordano Bruno, Francis Bacon, even Isaac Newton—interspersed their accounts of their scientific observations and experiments with quotations from mystical tracts. A practitioner who was able to achieve inner harmony would, by definition, be capable of transmuting the earth's materials. And conversely, the alchemist who was able to transmute material in his laboratory would, by definition, achieve a state of spiritual enlightenment. The transformation of metal and the transformation of mind were one and the same.

In my own tradition, Judaism, one finds the idea of correspondents in the age-old concept of *tikkun olam*. Our manifest world is shattered, and shards of Divine light have been trapped in broken fragments throughout the cosmos. Only humans can mend the broken world through their own personal transformation.

Is technology blessed or demonic? It depends on the heart and soul of the one wielding the technology. We can, in our actions, in the consciousness we choose to live by, restore our world or plunge it further into darkness and strife. The question is simple. How are we to live on this planet? In control, as you and me? Or in harmony, as us?

The great Taoist master Lao-tzu wrote presciently around six thousand years ago:

> *In harmony with the Tao,*
> *the sky is clear and spacious,*
> *the earth is solid and full,*
> *all creatures flourish together,*
> *content with the way they are,*
> *endlessly repeating themselves,*
> *endlessly renewed.*
>
> *When man interferes with the Tao,*
> *the sky becomes filthy,*
> *the earth becomes depleted,*

the equilibrium crumbles,
creatures become extinct.

The Master views the parts with compassion,
because he understands the whole.

I confess to particularly being fond of that last line: "The Master views the parts with compassion, / because he understands the whole."

Compassion comes from that part of us that can grasp the whole, our Wise Adult self. Our wiser self, our bigger mind, must surround, befriend, and ultimately contain the zero-sum world of *you and me* consciousness, our Adaptive Child. Whether we are loving each other in our bedrooms, playing games with our kids, learning to be more respectful when we think of those who are unlike us, or striving to be kinder when we speak to ourselves, we welcome the dispossessed within us and without. We emerge from the Great Lie of individuality and turn toward our wounded planet, toward our wounded neighbors; we restore, in relationship, our own wounded selves. This is our work, our calling. With luck, it is our destiny. The stakes could hardly be higher.

The idea of the individual is a construct of landed white men. As we learn more about how social our brains are, it becomes clear that the ideal of a freestanding individual is myth. Our brains act in consort with one another, not separately, individually. Once we remember those we have dismembered, once we credit the voices of the dispossessed—women, indigenous peoples, people of color—the narcissistic and deluded nature of the Great Lie at the heart of individualism becomes clear.

We need a new paradigm, one that is ecological and relational, one that moves us from exclusive to inclusive, from independent to interdependent, from dominant to collaborative with one another, with the earth, and within our own selves. Nature has neither rewards nor punishments; it has consequences. In this moment, right here, right now, our actions matter. How we think, how we see ourselves in the world, matters. With our partners, our children, our neighbors, within our own minds—we can redeem or we can violate. The choice is ours.

Acknowledgments

How could a book on the ecology of relationships ever expect to be written by a single mind? It wasn't.

I'd like to thank Gwyneth Paltrow and the folks at Goop for instigating this madness. Jeffrey Perlman, branding maestro, helped conceive the idea of a critique of individuality. Thanks to my so-much-more-than-agent, Richard Pine, who's been with me through every idea, every title, every word. And to my quiet superpower, Donna Loffredo, my editor at Penguin Random House, who rolled up her sleeves and waded into this work with a level of engagement that I'd never seen in an editor before. Chapter by chapter, sentence by sentence, we shaped this book together. Donna, you have been a gifted co-conspirator. To Kiki Koroshetz for many thoughtful notes. And a special, heartfelt thanks to Bruce Springsteen for his profound reflections and good company.

I bow to my teachers, too numerous to name, but I must pay first homage to the legendary trauma and recovery pioneer Pia Mellody, whose work ripples through my own. Thanks to Olga Silverstein, who taught me how to dislodge stuck positions, including mine. And to my fellow faculty at the Family Institute of Cambridge, who still inspire.

I am grateful for my forever colleague and friend Carol Gilligan, who pushed me toward a more radical perspective over and over again. This would not be the same book without your voice. And thanks to Jane Fonda, who also reminded me of my political roots and commitment.

Tremendous thanks to Juliane Taylor Shore, who combined a gifted understanding of Relational Life Therapy, matched with brilliance as a teacher of neurobiology. You are the evidence we're based on. To Emma Clement, for invaluable help with research and notation. To Brian Spielmann and Richard Taubinger, internet wizards. To Lisa Sullivan, who kept the ship afloat. To Jack Sayre, who kept my writer's spirits up long after there was reason to go home. To Rich Simon, still here in my heart, who cheered me on as a writer like no other.

To the friends who put up with me, even feigning interest at times: Dick Schwartz, Jeanne Catanzaro, Jette Simon, Liz Doyne, Thomasine McFarlind, Mel Bucholtz, Esther Perel, Jack Saul, Scott Campbell, Doreen and Bob, Jay and Francoise, Denise and Stefan, Zach Taylor, Richard Macmillan, David Hochner, and so many more who supported me during this time.

I pay homage to the men, women, and nonbinary clients who have trusted me over many years. It has been a great privilege to be with you, courageous group, together on the threshing floor, this crucible of pain and transformation. It has been an honor to have been a part of your work.

Finally, and most important, thanks to Justin and Alexander: you never fail to quicken me with joy. And to my darling Belinda, my greatest teacher, heart of my heart, breath of my breath. Thank you for this thirty-plus-years opportunity to work on myself.

With appreciation and love,
Terry Real
Newton, Massachusetts

Notes

Chapter 1: Which Version of You Shows Up to Your Relationship?

2 those who fight and those who distance: A common observation among couples therapists.

2 Hailstorm and tortoise: Hedy Schleifer (therapist), personal communication to author.

4 journey toward wholeness and intimacy: Real, "High Impact Couples Therapy."

5 particularly the amygdalae: When the prefrontal cortex is not connected to and soothing the subcortical system, we lose a pause between what we feel and what we do. The prefrontal cortex doesn't really shut down; if it did, we couldn't talk or think or come up with arguments at all. It's more that the connection between the two is shut down. When we perceive safety and kindness, the prefrontal cortex watches, soothes, and integrates the information it receives from the subcortical systems in the brain (such as the limbic system). When we perceive danger, our instincts of self-protection take over, and the prefrontal cortex has a much harder time regulating *those* lower systems. In such a state, the prefrontal cortex and the subcortical systems are not in connection with each other, and we are likely to make moves to protect ourselves both verbally and physically. Cozolino, *Neuroscience of Psychotherapy*; Van der Kolk, *Body Keeps the Score*; Siegel, *Mind: A Journey*; Siegel, *Developing Mind*; Siegel, *Mindsight*.

6 I win, you lose: The limbic/subcortical system is actually quite advanced and new in our human version. Other animals have this part as well, but ours is far more complex even at the subcortical level. Other ways of referring to it could be: the feeling system, the fast system, the subcortical, the subconscious, the limbic, the brain that holds our old learnings, the reactive brain. Our survival as a species is deeply linked both to our connection with others and to our ability to move away from dangerous situations. When these two instincts come into conflict, the parts of our brains that we share with other phylogenetically older species may instinctually choose to sacrifice connection in order to save us physically. Panksepp and Biven, *Archaeology of Mind*; Porges, *Polyvagal Theory*.

6   the more compelling you and me becomes: Van der Kolk, *Body Keeps the Score*; Fisher, *Healing Fragmented Selves*; Fisher, *Transforming Legacy of Trauma*.

7   fundamentally confusing the mind: Van der Kolk, "Body Keeps Score"; Levine, *Trauma and Memory*; Siegel, *Developing Mind*.

8   compensating part of us as the Adaptive Child: Many similar three-part descriptions of the human psyche have been offered by psychology over the decades: Berne and McCormick, *Intuition and Ego States*; Schwartz, *Internal Family Systems*; Mellody, Miller, and Miller, *Facing Codependence*. Stan Tatkin speaks of the difference between one's "Primitives" and one's "diplomats" two different parts of the brain in *Wired for Love*. Dan Siegel, in *Developing Mind*, speaks of two neurological states: responsive prefrontal cortex, and reactive.

8   "kid in grown-up's clothing": Mellody, "Post-Induction Training."

8   distinct from the Wise Adult: Chart adapted from Mellody, Miller, and Miller, *Facing Codependence*.

9   those associated with emotional maturity: Erikson and Erikson, *Life Cycle Completed*; Arnett, *Emerging Adulthood*; Wrightsman, *Adult Personality Development*.

12 "There appears to be precipitation": This phrase is adapted from Hammett, *Continental Op*.

17 true liberation is freedom: Michael Mendizza, dir., *Krishnamurti: With a Silent Mind* (film). Krishnamurti Foundation of America, 1989.

18 urgency is your enemy: Hübl and Real, "Evolutionary Relationships."

18 Breath can change your heart rate: Porges, *Polyvagal Theory*; Russo, Santarelli, and O'Rourke, "Physiological Effects of Slow Breathing."

18 corrective emotional experience: *Memory reconsolidation* is a term neuroscientists have given to the phenomenon in which long-term memories change their consolidated structure in the face of new information. Old memories can become flexible shift previous "emotional knowings" in the face of new information if three elements are present: (1) There is enough safety for the brain to maintain an integrated state, sharing information across various neural networks, (2) The expectation of the original knowing is in the conscious awareness and embodied at the time of the new experience, and (3) An experience provides a disconfirmation of the original "knowing" or expectation. While some corrective experiences will create memory reconsolidation, not all will. The timing of the experiences is essential, as is the identification of a mismatch. Ecker, "Memory Reconsolidation"; Ecker, Ticic, and Hulley, *Unlocking the Emotional Brain*; Schwabe, Nader, and Pruessner, "Reconsolidation of Human Memory."

19 from reactivity to responsibility: Siegel, *Mind: A Journey*; Siegel, *Developing Mind*; Siegel, *Mindful Therapist*; Siegel, *Mindsight*; Mellody, Miller, and Miller, *Facing Codependence.*

Chapter 2: The Myth of the Individual

20 individual comes from the term indivisible: The Merriam-Webster dictionary provides the etymology of *individual*: Medieval Latin *individualis*, from Latin *individuus* indivisible, from *in-* + *dividuus* divided, from *dividere* to divide.

20 the example of a blind man: Bateson, *Steps to an Ecology of Mind*, 251.

21 "The subjects observed a rubber hand": Metzinger, *Ego Tunnel*, 3.

21 we experience the world: How much of our knowing is a priori and how much is absorbed has been a matter of hot debate since the time of Kant. See Kant, *Critique of Pure Reason*; Chomsky, *Language and Mind*; Whittaker, *Theory of Abstract Ethics*; Singer, *Does Anything Really Matter?*; Steup and Sosa, *Contemporary Debates in Epistemology*; Thurow, "Implicit Conception and Intuition Theory."

21 see the world as a newborn baby: Eagleman, *Brain*; McGilchrist, *Master and His Emissary.*

22 changing tapestry of self-representations: Damasio, *Descartes' Error*; Eagleman, *Brain*; McGilchrist, *Master and His Emissary*; Panksepp and Biven, *Archaeology of Mind*; Siegel, *Developing Mind.*

22 The discovery of neuroplasticity changed: Ecker, Ticic, and Hulley, *Unlocking the Emotional Brain*; Levine, *Trauma and Memory*; Radiske et al., "Prior Learning of Relevant Non-Aversive Information"; Schwabe, Nader, and Pruessner, "Reconsolidation of Human Memory"; Yang et al., "Novel Method."

22 "Neurons that fire together": Hebb, *Organization of Behavior.*

22 "States become traits": Siegel, *Mindful Therapist.*

22 neuroplasticity is currently the name: Badenoch, *Heart of Trauma*; Cozolino, *Neuroscience of Psychotherapy*; Doidge, *Brain That Changes Itself*; Ecker, Ticic, and Hulley, *Unlocking the Emotional Brain.*

24 some sort of recoil: For recoil to take place, the person must experience two things that cannot be simultaneously true. Ernesto's two things were that rage was a justified way to discharge anger and other unpleasant emotions *and* that he was justified in hurting people like his stepmother hurt him, which was in fact inexcusable. Neuroscientists speak of such experiences as "embodied disconfirming experiences" or "embodied mismatches." Ecker, "Memory Reconsolidation"; Ecker, Ticic, and Hulley, *Unlocking the Emotional Brain*; Exton-McGuiness, Lee, and Reichelt, "Updating Memories."

25 the relationality of the right brain: Badenoch, *Heart of Trauma*; McGilchrist, *Master and His Emissary*.

25 Interpersonal neurobiology: Siegel and McNamara, *Neurobiology of "We."*

26 Insecure relationships stress you out: Badenoch, *Heart of Trauma*; Felitti et al., "Relationship of Childhood Abuse"; Murthy, *Together*; Sbarra and Hazan, "Coregulation, Dysregulation, Self-Regulation"; Sels et al., "Emotional Interdependence"; Szalavitz and Perry, *Born for Love*.

26 stimulating social interaction: Badenoch, *Heart of Trauma*; Cozolino, *Neuroscience of Psychotherapy*; Panksepp et al., "Neuro-Evolutionary Foundations"; Phillips, Wellman, and Selke, "Infants' Ability to Connect Gaze"; Swain et al., "Brain Basis of Parent-Infant Interactions"; Tronick and Gold, *Power of Discord*.

26 "good enough holding environment": Winnicott, "Theory of Parent-Infant Relationship."

26 "Child developmental researchers": Tronick and Gold, *Power of Discord*, 30.

28 "still face" experiments: Tronick, "Still Face Experiment."

30 If you inject a mouse's paw: Langford et al., "Social Modulation of Pain"; Sapolsky, *Behave*, 224–25.

31 interpersonal nature of our brains and nervous system: Badenoch, *Heart of Trauma*; Badenoch, *Brain-Wise Therapist*; Beckes and Coan. "Social Baseline Theory"; Cozolino, *Neuroscience of Psychotherapy*; McGilchrist, *Master and His Emissary*; Murthy, *Together*; Panksepp, *Archaeology of Mind*; Porges, *Polyvagal Theory*; Szalavitz and Perry, *Born to Love*; Sapolsky, *Behave*; Siegel, *Mind: A Journey*; Siegel, *Developing Mind*; Siegel, *Mindful Therapist*; Siegel, *Mindsight*.

31 "The brain is a social organ": Siegel, *Mindsight*, 211.

31 orphanages with unusually high death rates: Spitz, "Hospitalism."

32 "The conditions of confinement": Dingfelder, "Psychologist Testifies."

33 All manner of new research: McGilchrist, *Master and His Emissary*; Overall, "Attachment and Dyadic Regulation"; Sapolsky, *Behave*; Sels et al., *Emotional Interdependence*; Siegel, *Mind: A Journey*.

33 Social Baseline Theory: Beckes and Coan, "Social Baseline Theory."

34 economy of action: Ibid.

34 made up of billions of neurons: Herculano-Houzel, "Remarkable."

34 But it's energetically costly: Clore and Ortony, "Cognition in Emotion"; Gailliot and Baumeister, "Physiology of Willpower"; Kurzban, "Does the Brain Consume"; Van der Kolk, *Body Keeps the Score*; Sapolsky, *Behave*.

34 prefrontal cortex not only offloads: Beckes and Coan, "Social Baseline Theory."

34 people seek others for co-regulation: Overall, "Attachment and Dyadic Regulation"; Panksepp, *Affective Neuroscience*; Reis, Clark, and Holmes, "Perceived Partner Responsiveness"; Sbarra and Hazan, "Coregulation, Dysregulation, Self-Regulation"; Sels et al., "Emotional Interdependence"; Uchino, Cacioppo, and Kiecolt-Glaser, "Relationship Between Social Support."

34 "close proximity to social resources": Beckes and Coan, "Social Baseline Theory," 976; Gross and Medina-DeVilliers, "Cognitive Processes Unfold," 378.

35 multitasking is a yuppie: Sapolsky, *Behave*.

35 prefrontal cortices almost always slow down: Beckes and Coan, "Social Baseline Theory."

35 Their revolutionary insight: Ibid.; Coan, "Social Regulation of Emotion"; Cozolino, *Neuroscience of Psychotherapy*; Overall, "Attachment and Dyadic Regulation"; Panksepp, *Affective Neuroscience*; Porges, *Polyvagal Theory*; Siegel, *Developing Mind*; Sbarra and Hazan, "Coregulation, Dysregulation, Self-Regulation"; Sels et al., "Emotional Interdependence"; Uchino, Cacioppo, and Kiecolt-Glaser, "Relationship Between Social Support."

37 Holding a friend's hand: Astbury, "Hand to Hold"; Berscheid, "Human's Greatest Strength"; Ciechanowski et al., "Influence of Patient Attachment Style"; Coan, "Social Regulation of Emotion"; Cozolino, *Neuroscience of Psychotherapy*; Younger et al., "Viewing Pictures of a Romantic Partner."

37 question the wisdom of singling out: Badenoch, *Heart of Trauma*; Beckes and Coan, "Social Baseline Theory"; Keverne, Nevison, and Martel, "Early Learning and Social Bond"; Cozolino, *Neuroscience of Psychotherapy*; Kern et al., "Systems Informed Positive Psychology"; Sbarra and Hazan, "Coregulation, Dysregulation, Self-regulation"; Szalavitz and Perry, *Born for Love*; Siegel, *Developing Mind*; Siegel, *Mind: A Journey*; Wang, "Why Should We All Be Cultural Psychologists?"

38 logic and instrumentality reign: McGilchrist, *Master and His Emissary*.

39 holding oneself above nature was hubris: "Because Greek has a word for error (*hamartia*) but not for sin, some poets—especially Hesiod (7th century bce) and Aeschylus (5th century bce)—used *hubris* to describe wrongful action against the divine order. This usage led to the modern sense of the term and its assertion of impiety." "Hubris," *Encyclopaedia Britannica*.

40 the Great Watchmaker: Paley, *Natural Theology*; Abersold, "Words to Live By."

45 "rapport talk": Tannen, *You Just Don't Understand*.

49   shifting from an individualistic: Badenoch, *Heart of Trauma*; Siegel, *Developing Mind*.

Chapter 3: How *Us* Gets Lost and *You and Me* Takes Over

53   we feel "taken over": A more precise way of saying this is that the prefrontal cortex and the subcortical limbic system stop communicating with each other. Without the modulation, the soothing, of the prefrontal cortex, emotions seem overwhelming, at once instantaneous and endless. Badenoch, *Heart of Trauma*; Siegel, *Mind: A Journey*; Stevens, Gauthier-Braham, and Bush, "Brain That Longs to Care for Itself."

53   ultimately befriend it: The embrace of disowned parts of us by our Wise Adult selves has always been a feature of relational life therapy. I especially owe to my colleague and friend Richard Schwartz a heightened sensitivity to the uselessness of fighting with parts of ourselves and the usefulness of coming into loving firm relationship with every aspect of our personality.

54   offending from the victim position: Mellody, Miller, and Miller, *Facing Codependence*.

57   circumscribed catastrophic events: Fisher, *Transforming Legacy of Trauma*; Basham and Miehls, *Transforming the Legacy*; Johnson, *Emotionally Focused Couple Therapy*; Ogden, Minton, and Pain, *Trauma and the Body*.

57   every day of your childhood: Basham and Miehls, *Transforming the Legacy*; Felitti et al., "Relationship of Childhood Abuse"; Fisher, *Transforming Legacy of Trauma*; Johnson, *Emotionally Focused Couple Therapy*; Ogden, Minton, and Pain, *Trauma and the Body*.

61   Trauma Grid: The Trauma Grid is taken from Real, *New Rules of Marriage*.

62   Here's how to tell: This discussion of passive abuse and the five psychological domains I owe to Mellody, "Post-Induction Training."

64   falsely empowering them: Mellody, Miller, and Miller, *Facing Love Addiction*.

64   we call that enmeshment: Minuchin, *Families and Family Therapy*; Minuchin and Nichols, *Family Healing*; Adams, *Silently Seduced*.

64   The energy goes from the child: Mellody, Miller, and Miller, *Facing Love Addiction*.

68   "All happy families are alike": Tolstoy, *Anna Karenina*, 1.

68   "holding environment": Winnicott, "Theory of Parent-Infant Relationship."

70 modeling, tends to internalize it: Frey, "Stockholm Syndrome"; Dewey, "Stockholm Syndrome"; Danylchuk, and Connors, *Treating Complex Trauma*; De Bellis and Zisk, "Biological Effects of Trauma"; Perry et al., "Childhood Trauma."

71 five losing strategies: Real, *New Rules of Marriage*, 293.

72 people classed as narcissistic: Akıncı, "Relationship Between Types of Narcissism"; Brookes, "Effect of Overt and Covert Narcissism"; Howes et al., "When and Why Narcissists"; Rose, "Happy and Unhappy Faces"; Zajenkowski et al., "Vulnerable Past, Grandiose Present."

73 The early pioneers of family therapy: Bowen, *Family Therapy in Clinical Practice*; Whitaker and Malone, *Roots of Psychotherapy*; Boszormenyi-Nagy and Framo, *Intensive Family Therapy*.

74 Multigenerational legacies: Mellody, Miller, and Miller, *Facing Love Addiction*.

74 When my father laughed: For more on this, see Real, *I Don't Want to Talk About It*.

74 Freud regarded all neurotic symptoms: Freud, *History of Psychoanalytic Movement*.

78 our narcissistic, individualistic society: Lasch, *Culture of Narcissism*; Putnam, *Bowling Alone*.

Chapter 4: The Individualist at Home

83 rugged individualist: Hoover, "Principles and Ideals."

83 freestanding, self-determining individual: Hinchman, "Idea of Individuality," 773; Binkley, *Concept of the Individual*; Locke, *Two Treatises of Government*; Lukes, *Individualism*.

83 "Aristocracy links everybody": Tocqueville, *Democracy in America*, 508; Arieli, *Individualism and Nationalism*, chap. 10; Lukes, *Individualism*, 26.

83 meaning "each man": "Individualistic self-conception and social interpretation, however, prevent men from appreciating the extent to which their freedom, independence, and happiness depend on women's unrequited sacrifices." Turner, "American Individualism and Structural Injustice." For more on individualism and freedom, see Beres, "Commentary"; Grabb, Baer, and Curtis, "Origins of American Individualism"; Winthrop, "Tocqueville's American Woman."

84 a second wave of individualism: Bellah, *Habits of the Heart*; Hinchman, "Idea of Individuality."

84 the Romantic individualist: Beiser, *Romantic Imperative*; Berlin and Hardy, *Roots of Romanticism*.

84 "All that is alive tends": Goethe, *Wisdom and Experience*, 134; Goethe, *Zur Farbenlehre*.

84 horses about to be rendered: Serge Sobolevitch, Ph.D. (Rutgers University), personal communication, January, 1974.

85 A new ideal type: Dye, "Goethe and Individuation," 159–72; Goethe, *Sorrows of Young Werther*.

85 of deep feeling, of sensibility: "The chief aim of aesthetic education, whether in the romantic or Leibnizian-Wolffian tradition, was the cultivation of sensibility. Normally contrasted with reason, sensibility was defined in a very broad sense to include the powers of desire, feeling and perception. The underlying premise behind the program of aesthetic education was that sensibility could be developed, disciplined and refined no less than reason itself." Beiser, *Romantic Imperative*, 100.

85 unique expression of individuality: "Expressive individualism holds the each person has a unique core of feeling and intuition that should unfold or be expressed if individuality is to be realized." Bellah, *Habits of the Heart*, 333–34. See also Lukes, *Individualism*, 30–33; Siedentop, *Inventing the Individual*; Simmel, *Sociology of Simmel*; Vareene, *Americans Together*.

85 discover and express one's "voice": Gilligan, *In a Different Voice*.

87 "You did this today": Real, *New Rules of Marriage*; Real, *Fierce Intimacy*.

87 "You hurt me, so I have": Mellody, "Post-Induction Training."

88 That's what joining with them means: Real, "Matter of Choice."

94 one's unique stamp, spirit, personality: Bellah, *Habits of the Heart*, 333–34; Beiser, *Romantic Imperative*; Lukes, *Individualism*, 30–33; Simmel, *Sociology of Georg Simmel*.

94 the Romantic individualist's great fear: Bellah, *Habits of the Heart*, 75–80.

95 was synonymous with gentry: "Individuality, after all, is a luxury afforded the dominant caste. Individuality is the first distinction lost to the stigmatized." Wilkerson, *Caste*, 142. See also Beres, "Commentary."

96 the myth of the self-made man: Gerth and Mills, "Introduction," 59–60; Gustavsson, *Problem of Individualism*; Turner, "American Individualism and Structural Injustice."

96 distinct physiological circuits: Sapolsky, *Behave*, chap. 14.

97 The Triumph of the Therapeutic: Dworkin, "Rieff's Critique of Therapeutic"; Rieff, *Triumph of Therapeutic*.

98 One's development, one's Bildung: "It is no exaggeration to say that *Bildung*, the education of humanity, was the central goal, the highest aspiration, of the early romantics. All the leading figures of that charmed

circle—Friedrich and August Wilhelm Schlegel, W. D. Wackenroder, Friedrich von Hardenberg (Novalis), F. W. J. Schelling, Ludwig Tieck, and F. D. Schleiermacher—saw in education their hope for the redemption of humanity." Beiser, *Romantic Imperative*, 88.

98 while Romantic expressive individualism: Bellah, *Habits of the Heart*; Veroff, Douvan, and Kulka, *Inner American*, 529–30.

99 "In the absence of any": Bellah, *Habits of the Heart*, 77.

99 "collectivism in a smaller group": Grabb, Baer, and Curtis, "Origins of American Individualism"; Daniels, "Brief History of Individualism"; Lukes, *Individualism*, 7.

99 "public good is not a term": Paine, *Dissertations on Government*; Lukes, *Individualism*, 53.

102 "We must all hang together": More, *Benjamin Franklin*, 110.

Chapter 5: Start Thinking Like a Team

115 subjective sense of safety or its lack: Badenoch, *Heart of Trauma*; Van der Kolk, *Body Keeps the Score*; Porges, *Polyvagal Theory*; Siegel, *Mindsight*; Tronson et al., "Fear Conditioning and Extinction."

116 tongue is mightier than the sword: Kerner, *She Comes First*.

117 core negative image of the other: For further information, see Real, *New Rules of Marriage*, 83–92; Real, *Fierce Intimacy*.

118 "I just don't want to have sex with you!": Real and Perel, "The Relate 2 Day Workshop."

127 we call this redistribution: Papp, *Process of Change*; Silverstein, *Who's Depressed?*

Chapter 6: You Cannot Love from Above or Below

143 grandiosity—feeling superior: Gilligan, *Violence*; Pincus, and Lukowitsky, "Pathological Narcissism"; Fanti et al., "Unique and Interactive Associations"; Mellody, Miller, and Miller, *Facing Love Addiction*.

145 In our daily lives: Badenoch, *Heart of Trauma*; McGilchrist, *Master and His Emissary*; Pankseep, *Archaelogy of Mind*; Porges, *Polyvagal Theory*; Siegel, *Mindsight*; Stevens, Gauthier-Braham, and Bush, "Brain That Longs to Care for Itself."

145 an antirelational, narcissistic society: Lasch, *Culture of Narcissism*; Joiner, *Mindlessness*; Campbell, Miller, and Buffardi, "United States."

154 entitled privilege is like a knife: Tagore, *Stray Birds*.

154 the same feeling: For a fuller discussion of shame and grandiosity, see Real, *New Rules of Marriage*.

155 microaggression: The term was coined by Chester Pierce, a Harvard psychiatrist. See Pierce, "Offensive Mechanism," 280.

155 full-respect living: Real, *New Rules of Marriage*, 236–79.

157 "Each person has inherent worth": Mellody, "Post-Induction Training."

157 You are perfectly imperfect: Mellody, "Community Lecture."

157 behavior and the person: Spock and Needlman, *Dr. Spock's Baby and Child Care*.

158 The great feminist family therapist: Silverstein, *Who's Depressed?* See also Ecker, "Memory Reconsolidation"; Ecker, Ticic, and Hulley, *Unlocking the Emotional Brain*; Schwabe, Nader, and Pruessner, "Reconsolidation of Human Memory."

161 giving brings much longer-lasting happiness: O'Brien and Kassirer, "People Are Slow to Adapt."

163 "There is a field": "Out Beyond Ideas," translated by Coleman Barks, Rūmī, *Essential Rumi*.

Chapter 7: Your Fantasies Have Shattered, Your Real Relationship Can Begin

166 Death by a thousand cuts: Perel and Real, "Dialogue on Infidelity."

166 an influential book on trauma: Janoff-Bulman, *Shattered Assumptions*.

168 "I expect to have six marriages": Perel and Real, "Dialogue on Infidelity."

168 Two-thirds of marriages survive the hit: Carey and Parker-Pope, "Marriage Stands up for Itself"; Marin, Christensen, and Atkins, "Infidelity and Behavioral Couple Therapy"; Moritz, "If You Cheated."

168 the day you turn to: Framo, "Reality of Marriages."

169 Harmony, then disharmony, then repair: Much of the following discussion is in line with or derived from the pioneering work of child developmental researcher Ed Tronick. For further discussion, see Tronick and Gold, *Power of Discord*.

169 a baby is molded: Tronick, "Still Face Experiment."

169 "uninterrupted oceanic bliss": Freud, *Future of an Illusion*.

169 the real story of finding connection: Tronick and Gold, *Power of Discord*; Tronick, *Neurobehavioral and Social-Emotional Development*; Lester, Hoffman, and Brazelton, "Rhythmic Structure of Interaction"; Nugent, Lester, and Brazelton, *Cultural Context of Infancy*.

170 hormones that create the quickened pulse of lust: Acevedo, "After the Honeymoon"; Seshadri, "Neuroendocrinology of Love."

170 romance or love addiction: Fisher et al., "Intense, Passionate, Romantic Love"; Mellody, Miller, and Miller, *Facing Love Addiction*; Seshandri, "The Neuroendocrinology of Love"

174 "marital contract": Perel, *State of Affairs*; Real, "Working with Infidelity in Couples Therapy."

182 a fresh new stage of development: Making a permanent shift in the Adaptive Child involves what neurobiologists call *memory reconsolidation*. Relational Life Therapy uses the term *Adaptive Child* to refer to the early ways each person learned to keep themselves as safe and well as they could. In Angela's case, her previous emotional knowing—"If I stay passive and accommodating, I will keep myself safe"—was shattered by the discovery of the affair. This made her emotional knowing extraordinarily pliable and ready to be updated with new information for a brief period of time. Discord is an opportunity for such *memory reconsolidation*. Angela's new emotional knowing is: *Standing up for myself will keep me safe, I will not depend on accommodating Mike to keep me safe*. Accommodation *and* standing up for herself cannot keep her safe at the same moment, so her experience of disconfirmation is achieved. Now she has new emotional knowing about safety and standing up for herself in her limbic brain. This represents a change to the Adaptive Child directly (the lower brain, which runs on implicit memory) rather than to the Wise Adult (the prefrontal cortex, which is run by compassion, curiosity, and courage). The change makes it much easier for the Wise Adult to run the show because it has less to regulate. Angela perceives less threat because she has built trust in herself and in the relationship in her lower, limbic brain. In these ways, close intimate relationships have the power to heal even, in some instances, severe trauma, if the conditions are right. We heal by repeated experiences of having our negative expectations disconfirmed by real life encounters. Kindness can heal. Empathy can heal, if indirectly. The best way to open another's heart, it turns out, is to open your own. Ecker, "Memory Reconsolidation"; Ecker, Ticic, and Hulley, *Unlocking the Emotional Brain*; Exton-McGuiness, Lee, and Reichelt, "Updating Memories"; Schwabe, Nader, and Pruessner, "Reconsolidation of Human Memory"; Tronick and Gold, *Power of Discord*; Tronson et al., "Fear Conditioning and Extinction."

185 EMDR: Eye Movement Desensitization and Reprocessing (EMDR) is a therapy designed by Francine Shapiro. For more information see Shapiro and Forrest, *EMDR*.

187 "Rather than a sense of helplessness": Tronick and Gold, *Power of Discord*, 43.

188 Seventy-thirty is the principle: Ibid.

188 the felt experience of safety: When a person perceives that they are in safety, their brain does not have a reaction of judgment and agenda.

They don't think of their partner as the enemy or try to get them to be different than they are. But when a person, on a low and automatic level, perceives danger, the brain's normal responses are agenda and judgment. They are likely to think of their partner as wrong or bad and to try to get their partner to be different. If you stay in a state of safety, you can influence your dance with your partner by responding with kindness and boundary and your Wise Adult, even when they are not in the same space. If your partner is in a judgmental space toward you, you'll feel danger for a second, but if you let go of the outcome of this moment and lean into collaboration instead of winning, you won't stay in a sense of danger. You do not have to stay in perceiving danger just because your partner is perceiving danger. Letting go of it allows you to rock the boat or to lean in with vulnerability and *stay in safety while doing so.* This is a relational technology: the stance of relational mindfulness is a second-to-second stance of relationship first. Let go of winning, let go of control, and give in to kindness toward yourself and collaboration and connection with others. It is a practice. As with all practices, you do it better over time, but even doing it badly will transform your relationship with yourself and with others. This stance is a hack for the autonomic nervous system. Relational mindfulness has the power to shift us from reactive (staying in danger: agenda and judgment) to responsive (flexible, vulnerable, empowered, regulated) while facing a person who is maybe not in their most Wise Adult self. This is true empowerment: You can choose relational mindfulness on purpose. You are in charge of your emotional safety. You hope your partner shows up and helps out. If they don't show up for you today, you'll be okay. Badenoch, *Heart of Trauma*; Dana, *Polyvagal Theory*; Porges, *Polyvagal Theory*; Tronick and Gold, *Power of Discord.*

189   the absence of judgment: Badenoch, *Heart of Trauma*; Porges, *Polyvagal Theory.*

192   "Why don't you just come on in?": In this discussion I was inspired by Robert Bly's poem "The Resemblance Between Your Life and a Dog":

I never intended to have this life, believe me—
It just happened. You know how dogs turn up
At a farm, and they wag but can't explain.

It's good if you can accept your life—you'll notice
Your face has become deranged trying to adjust
To it. Your face thought your life would look

Like your bedroom mirror when you were ten.
That was a clear river touched by mountain wind.
Even your parents can't believe how much you've changed.

Sparrows in winter, if you've ever held one, all feathers,
Burst out of your hand with a fiery glee.
You see them later in hedges. Teachers praise you,

But you can't quite get back to the winter sparrow.
Your life is a dog. He's been hungry for miles,
Doesn't particularly like you, but gives up, and comes in.

Chapter 8: Fierce Intimacy, Soft Power

197 their Bildung, as the German Romantics: Beiser, *Romantic Imperative.*

198 has no needs of her own: Jack, *Silencing the Self*; Brown and Gilligan, *Meeting at Crossroads.*

198 Hey, I could use a hug: Levant and Wong, *Psychology of Men and Masculinities.*

200 type-one love avoidants: A type-one love avoidant hails from a family in which everyone lived behind walls and avoided the expression of emotion, as if it were poor taste or a burden. Attachment theory describes type-one avoidants as having an "avoidant dismissive" attachment style. In contrast, what I call type-two love avoidants avoid closeness for fear of being overrun or smothered. Such partners have, in some ways, the opposite trauma from that experienced by type-one avoidants. Type-one avoidants live out of an Adaptative Child part that is driven by often covert neglect; they internalized a contempt for intimacy through modeling. Type-two love avoidants live out of an Adaptive Child part driven by enmeshment, boundaryless intrusion, or exploitation. See Mellody, Miller, and Miller, *Facing Love Addiction*; Siegel, *Mindsight.*

200 "Our marriage wasn't hellish": Real, *I Don't Want to Talk About It,* 140; Segell, "Pater Principle," 121.

201 You go off looking for a different you: Perel, *State of Affairs.*

201 the essential capacity to confront issues: Real, *Fierce Intimacy.*

207 school of relationships we call: Perel, Real, and Faller, "Learning from the Affair."

207 skills of repair: Real, *New Rules of Marriage.*

211 Janet Hurley's feedback wheel: Mellody, Miller, and Miller, *Facing Codependence*; Real, *New Rules of Marriage,* 292.

213 Selfish is still the opposite of good for many women: Carol Gilligan, personal communication to author, June 2021.

Chapter 9: Leaving Our Kids a Better Future

224 "Just remember": Hedy Schleifer, personal communication, September 2020.

226 "Family pathology rolls": Real, *I Don't Want to Talk About It*, page 262.

232 By embracing our shadow: For more on shadow work, see Ford, *Dark Side of Light Chasers* and Ford, *Secret of Shadow*. For more on exiling parts, see Schwartz, *Internal Family Systems*, and Schwartz, *No Bad Parts*.

233 multigenerational legacy of destructive entitlement: Boszormenyi-Nagy and Framo, *Intensive Family Therapy*.

234 "about to cost him his marriage": In the last three decades a revolution has occurred in understanding and treating trauma, a revolution akin to the drug revolution a few decades ago that transformed the lives of millions suffering with psychological conditions.

I've been struck by how readily the general public has adopted the idea of having been traumatized.

It does beg the question though: Where are all the traumatizers?

In psychotherapy these days it seems everyone is a victim. One wonders why so little attention has been paid to the victimizers. Surely there must be millions of them. Hurt people hurt people. It's time we took aggression more seriously as we look so carefully at its consequences.

240 "Love your hypothesis": Boscolo, *Milan Systemic Family Therapy*.

249 "deconstructing patriarchy one couple": Marvin, "Therapy Master Class."

252 urgency is our enemy: Hübl and Real. "Love, Trauma and Healing."

254 Angry complaint will most likely: Schoebi, "Coregulation of Daily Affect"; Butner, Diamond, and Hicks, "Attachment Style"; Gottman et al., "Predicting Marital Happiness"; Jarvis, McClure, and Bolger, "Exploring How Exchange Orientation"; Keltner and Kring, "Emotion, Social Function"; Salazar, "Negative Reciprocity Process."

Chapter 10: Becoming Whole

259 Men were whipped into smiling: Wilkerson, *Caste*, 137; Brown, *Narrative and Life of Brown, a Fugitive Slave*, 45.

261 bloodiest, nastiest confrontations: Messina, "America's Most Devastating Conflict."

261 Ten of the first American presidents owned slaves: "Slavery in the President's Neighborhood," n.d.

262 $2 billion a year: For an excellent treatment, see *13th* (documentary film), directed by Ava DuVernay (Kandoo Films/Netflix, 2016). See also Dyer, *Perpetual Prisoner Machine*, 19.

263 "No way I want my tax dollars": Metzl, *Dying of Whiteness*.

263 "welfare queen": Ibid.

263 racism as a narcissistic disorder: Hall, "Trauma and Dissociation."

263 Narcissus is an addict who kills himself: Real, *I Don't Want to Talk About It*, 270.

265 Paul Watzlawick: Rohrbaugh and Shoham, "Brief Therapy."

273 Invulnerable and dominant: Coates, *Between the World and Me*; Kendi, *How to Be an Antiracist*, 389.

273 "Don't worry": Wilkerson, *Caste*, 115–30.

275 wealth impairs one's empathy toward others: Sapolsky, *Behave*, chap. 14.

275 J. Robert Oppenheimer: Pais and Crease, *Oppenheimer: A Life*; Goodchild, *Oppenheimer*.

276 "Stars, hide your fires": William Shakespeare, "Act 1, Scene 4," *Macbeth* (S.I.: Duke Classics, 2012), 34.

276 moral injury, a particular: Denton-Borhaug, *And Then Your Soul Is Gone*.

277 "The most malevolent perpetrators": Hall, "Trauma and Dissociation."

277 post-traumatic slavery syndrome: Akbar, *Breaking the Chains*.

277 epigenetics, the way trauma effects: For an exploration of the journey of three different types of bodies (Black, white and police bodies) that are carrying the legacy of transgenerational, epigenetic trauma as well as cultural trauma and pain, see Menakem, *My Grandmother's Hands*.

278 otherization, the methods and tropes: Keen, *Faces of the Enemy*, 12–13.

278 Each war seems to a better job: A surprising revelation is that, throughout history, many soldiers do not. In the war of independence a surprising number of men left their rifles unfired. By the Civil War, that number had dropped considerably. Each war led to a better job at otherization and a broader percentage of compliance. "In combat conditions during World War II," observes Sam Keen, ". . . Army psychologists discovered that the percentage of American soldiers who fired their rifle at a seen enemy even once did not rise about 25 percent, and the more usual figure was 15 percent. An amazing finding! Between 75 and 80 percent of trained combat troops would *not* willingly kill an enemy." Keen, *Faces of the Enemy*, 178. See also Barry, *Unmaking War*; Denton-Borhaug, *And Then Your Soul Is Gone*, 111–12; Grossman, *On Killing*, 141–55; Marshall, *Men Against Fire*. New training to promote desensitization and otherization of the enemy, referred to as "reprogramming" by some veterans, "increased the firing rate of the individual infantryman from 15 to 20 percent in World War II to 55 percent in Korea and nearly 90 to 95 percent in Vietnam." Grossman, *On Killing*, 263.

279 Freud's discovery of repression: Freud, *Unconscious*; Freud, *Psychopathology of Everyday Life*.

279 A 2020 study showed: Dolan, "Most Racially Prejudiced People"; West and Eaton, "Prejudiced and Unaware of It."

279 We have never been a lonelier people: "In a 2018 report by the Henry Kaiser Family Foundation 22 percent of all adults in the US say they often or always feel lonely or socially isolated. That's well over fifty-five million people—far more that the number of adult cigarette smokers and nearly double the number of people who have diabetes. A 2018 AARP study using the rigorously validated UCLA loneliness scale found that one in three American adults over the age of forty-five are lonely. And in a 2018 national survey by the US health insurer Cigna, one-fifth of respondents said they rarely or never feel close to people. Studies in other countries echo these findings. Among middle-aged and elderly Canadians, nearly one-fifth of men and around a quarter of women say they feel lonely once a week or more. One-quarter of Australian adults reported being lonely as well. More than two hundred thousand seniors in the United Kingdom 'meet up or speak on the phone with their children, family and friends less often than once a week'; 13 percent of Italian adults report having no one to ask for help; and in Japan, over 1 million adults meet the official government definition of social recluses, or hikikomori." Murthy, *Together*, 10.

280 "Individualism is a calm": Tocqueville, *Democracy in America*, 506.

280 we bowl alone: Putnam, *Bowling Alone*.

Epilogue: Broken Light

285 "mankind's epistemological mistake": Bateson, "The Cybernetics of 'Self': A Theory of Alcoholism," in *Steps to an Ecology of Mind*.

285 psychedelics can decrease the fear of death: Fischman, "Seeing Without Self"; Pollan, *How to Change Your Mind*; Pollan, "Trip Treatment."

287 cure for addiction had to be spiritual: In correspondence with William Wilson, an alcoholic with whom he was working, Jung explained, "You see, Alcohol in Latin is 'spiritus' and you use the same word for the highest religious experience as well as for the most depraving poison. The helpful formula therefore is; spiritus contra spiritum." Jung, *Letters*.

287 Psychologists speak about basic trust: Erikson and Erikson, *Life Cycle Completed*; Erikson, "Reflections on the Last Stage"; Erikson, *Childhood and Society*.

288 "To live in the realm of Buddha": Suzuki, *Zen Mind, Beginner's Mind*, 31.

289 "steps out of the way": Mitchell, *Tao Te Ching*, Verse 45, p. 74.

290 "embryos": Eliade, *Forge and Crucible*.

290 Early scientists who made: McKnight, *Science, Pseudo-Science*.

290 The transformation of metal: Yates, *Bruno and the Hermetic Tradition.*

291 tikkun olam: Berman, Birnbaum, and Blech, *Tikkun Olam*; Teutsch, *Guide to Jewish Practice.*

291 "In harmony with the Tao": Mitchell, *Tao Te Ching*, Verse 39, p. 66.

293 Nature has neither rewards nor punishments Ingersoll, "Some Reasons Why."

Bibliography

Abersold, Bill. "Words to Live By: William Paley Uses Watch Analogy to Argue Existence of God, Intelligent Design of Universe." *El Chicano Weekly* (San Bernardino, Calif.) 56, no. 19 (2018).

Acevedo, Bianca P., et al. "After the Honeymoon: Neural and Genetic Correlates of Romantic Love in Newlywed Marriages." *Frontiers in Psychology* 7, no. 11 (2020): 634, doi.org/10.3389/fpsyg.2020.00634.

Adams, Kenneth M. *Silently Seduced: When Parents Make Their Children Partners: Understanding Covert Incest.* Deerfield Beach, Fla.: Health Communications, 1991.

Akbar, Na'im. *Breaking the Chains of Psychological Slavery.* Tallahassee, Fla.: Mind Productions, 2020.

Akıncı, İrem. "The Relationship Between the Types of Narcissism and Psychological Well-Being: The Roles of Emotions and Difficulties in Emotion Regulation." M.S. thesis, Middle East Technical University, 2015.

Arieli, Yehoshua. *Individualism and Nationalism in American Ideology.* Cambridge, Mass.: Harvard University Press, 1964.

Arnett, Jeffrey Jensen. *Emerging Adulthood: The Winding Road from the Late Teens Through the Twenties.* New York: Oxford University Press, 2006.

Astbury, N. "A Hand to Hold: Communication During Cataract Surgery." *Eye* 18, no. 2 (2004): 115–16, doi.org/10.1038/sj.eye.6700569.

Badenoch, Bonnie. *Being a Brain-Wise Therapist.* New York: W.W. Norton, 2008.

———. *The Heart of Trauma.* New York: W.W. Norton, 2018.

Barry, Kathleen. *Unmaking War, Remaking Men.* Santa Rosa, Calif.: Phoenix Rising Press, 2011.

Basham, Kathryn K., and Dennis Miehls. *Transforming the Legacy: Couple Therapy with Survivors of Childhood Trauma.* New York: Columbia University Press, 2004.

Bateson, Gregory. *Steps to an Ecology of Mind: Collected Essays in Anthropology, Psychiatry, Evolution, and Epistemology*. Northvale, N.J.: Aronson, 1987.

Beckes, Lane, and James A. Coan. "Social Baseline Theory: The Role of Social Proximity in Emotion and Economy of Action." *Social and Personality Psychology Compass* 5, no. 12 (2011): 976–88, doi.org/10.1111/j.1751-9004.2011.00400.x.

Beiser, Frederick C. *The Romantic Imperative: The Concept of Early German Romanticism*. Cambridge, Mass.: Harvard University Press, 2006.

Bellah, Robert Neely. *Habits of the Heart: Individualism and Commitment in American Life*, updated ed. Berkeley: University of California Press, 1996.

Beres, Louis René. "Commentary: The Masses Were Never Intended to Rule." *U.S. News & World Report*, March 20, 2018.

Berlin, Isaiah, and Henry Hardy. *The Roots of Romanticism*. Princeton, N.J.: Princeton University Press, 1999.

Berman, Saul J., David Birnbaum, and Benjamin Blech. *Tikkun Olam: Judaism, Humanism and Transcendence*. New York: New Paradigm Matrix, 2014.

Berne, Eric, and Paul McCormick. *Intuition and Ego States: The Origins of Transactional Analysis: A Series of Papers*. San Francisco: Harper & Row, 1977.

Berscheid, Ellen. "The Human's Greatest Strength: Other Humans." In *A Psychology of Human Strengths: Fundamental Questions and Future Directions for a Positive Psychology*, ed. Lisa G. Aspinwall and Ursula M. Staudinger. New York: American Psychological Association, 2003.

Binkley, Susan Carpenter. *The Concept of the Individual in Eighteenth-Century French Thought from the Enlightenment to the French Revolution*. Lewiston, N.Y.: Edwin Mellen Press, 2007.

Bly, Robert. *Eating the Honey of Words: New and Selected Poems*. New York: HarperCollins, 2009.

Boscolo, Luigi, et al. *Milan Systemic Family Therapy: Conversations in Theory and Practice*. New York: Basic Books, 1987.

Boszormenyi-Nagy, Ivan, and James L. Framo, eds. *Intensive Family Therapy: Theoretical and Practical Aspects*. New York: Brunner/Mazel, 1985.

Bowen, Murray. *Family Therapy in Clinical Practice*. New York: J. Aronson, 1978.

Brookes, James. "The Effect of Overt and Covert Narcissism on Self-Esteem and Self-Efficacy Beyond Self-Esteem." *Personality and Individual Differences* 85 (2015): 172–75, doi.org/10.1016/j.paid.2015.05.013.

Brown, Lyn Mikel, and Carol Gilligan. *Meeting at the Crossroads: Women's Psychology and Girls' Development*. Cambridge, Mass.: Harvard University Press, 2013.

Brown, William Wells. *Narrative and Life of William Wells Brown, a Fugitive Slave*. Boston, 1874.

Butner, Jonathan, Lisa M. Diamond, and Angela M. Hicks. "Attachment Style and Two Forms of Affect Coregulation Between Romantic Partners." *Personal Relationships* 14, no. 3 (2007): 431–55, doi.org/10.1111/j.1475-6811.2007.00164.x.

Campbell, W. Keith, Joshua D. Miller, and Laura E. Buffardi. "The United States and the 'Culture of Narcissism.'" *Social Psychological and Personality Science* 1, no. 3 (2010): 222–29, doi.org/10.1177/1948550610366878.

Carey, Benedict, and Tara Parker-Pope. "Marriage Stands Up for Itself." *New York Times*, June 26, 2009.

Chomsky, Noam. *Language and Mind*. New York: Harcourt, Brace & World, 1986.

Ciechanowski, P., et al. "Influence of Patient Attachment Style on Self-Care and Outcomes in Diabetes." *Psychosomatic Medicine* 66, no. 5 (2004): 720–28, doi.org/10.1097/01.psy.0000138125.59122.23.

Clore, Gerald L., and Andrew Ortony. "Cognition in Emotion: Always, Sometimes, or Never?" In *Cognitive Neuroscience of Emotion*, ed. Lynn Nadel, Richard D. Lane, and Geoffrey L. Ahern. New York: Oxford University Press, 2000.

Coan, James A. "The Social Regulation of Emotion." In *Oxford Handbook of Social Neuroscience*, ed. Jean Decety and John T. Cacioppo. New York: Oxford University Press, 2011.

Coates, Ta-Nehisi. *Between the World and Me*. New York: Spiegel & Grau, 2015.

Cozolino, Linda. *The Neuroscience of Psychotherapy: Healing the Social Brain*, 3rd ed. New York: W.W. Norton, 2017.

Damasio, Antonio R. *Descartes' Error: Emotion, Reason, and the Human Brain*. New York: G.P. Putnam, 1994.

Dana, Deb. *The Polyvagal Theory in Therapy: Engaging the Rhythm of Regulation*. New York: W.W. Norton, 2018.

Daniels, Eric. "A Brief History of Individualism in American Thought." In *For the Greater Good of All: Perspectives on Individualism, Society, and Leadership*, ed. Donelson Forsyth and Crystal L. Hoyt. New York: Palgrave Macmillan, 2011.

Danylchuk, Lynette S., and Kevin J. Connors. *Treating Complex Trauma and Dissociation: A Practical Guide to Navigating Therapeutic Challenges*. London: Taylor & Francis, 2016.

De Bellis, Michael D., and Abigail Zisk. "The Biological Effects of Childhood Trauma." *Child and Adolescent Psychiatric Clinics of North America* 23, no. 2 (2014): 185–222, doi.org/10.1016/j.chc.2014.01.002.

Denton-Borhaug, Kelly. *And Then Your Soul Is Gone: Moral Injury and the U.S. War-Culture.* Sheffield, U.K.: Equinox, 2021.

Dewey, Donald. "The Stockholm Syndrome." *Scandinavian Review* 94, no. 3 (2007).

Dingfelder, Sadie F. "Psychologist Testifies on the Risks of Solitary Confinement." *Monitor on Psychology* 43, no. 9 (2012), http://www.apa.org/monitor/2012/10/solitary.

Doidge, Norman. *The Brain That Changes Itself.* New York: Viking, 2007.

Dolan, Eric. "Study Finds the Most Racially Prejudiced People Tend to Think That They Are Less Racist than the Average Person." *PsyPost,* June 9, 2020.

Dworkin, L. Niquie. "Rieff's Critique of the Therapeutic and Contemporary Developments in Psychodynamic Psychotherapy." *Journal of Theoretical and Philosophical Psychology* 35 no.4 (2015): 230–43, doi.org/10.1037/teo0000024.

Dye, Ellis. "Goethe and Individuation." In *Romantic Rapports,* ed. Larry H. Peer and Christopher Clason. Rochester, N.Y.: Boydell & Brewer, 2017.

Dyer, Joel. *The Perpetual Prisoner Machine: How America Profits from Crime.* Boulder, Colo.: Westview Press, 2000.

Eagleman, David. *The Brain: The Story of You.* New York: Pantheon, 2015.

Ecker, Bruce. "Memory Reconsolidation Understood and Misunderstood." *International Journal of Neuropsychotherapy* 3, no. 1 (2015): 2–46, doi.org/10.12744/ijnpt.2015.0002-0046.

Ecker, Bruce, Robin Ticic, and Laurel Hulley. *Unlocking the Emotional Brain: Eliminating Symptoms at Their Roots Using Memory Reconsolidation.* New York: Routledge, 2012.

Eliade, Mircea. *The Forge and the Crucible,* 2nd ed. Chicago: University of Chicago Press, 1978.

Erikson, Erik H. *Childhood and Society,* 2nd ed. New York: W.W. Norton, 1964.

——. "Reflections on the Last Stage—and the First." *Psychoanalytic Study of the Child* 39, no.1 (1984): 155–65, doi.org/10.1080/00797308.1984.11823424.

Erikson, Erik H., and Joan M. Erikson. *The Life Cycle Completed: Extended Version.* New York: W.W. Norton, 1998.

Exton-McGuiness, Marc T. J., Jonathan L. C. Lee, and Amy C. Reichelt. "Updating Memories: The Role of Prediction Errors in Memory

Reconsolidation." *Behavioral Brain Research* 278, no. 1 (2014): 375–84, doi.org/10.1016/j.bbr.2014.10.011.

Fanti, Kostas A., et al. "Unique and Interactive Associations of Callous-Unemotional Traits, Impulsivity and Grandiosity with Child and Adolescent Conduct Disorder Symptoms." *Journal of Psychopathology and Behavioral Assessment* 40, no. 1 (2018): 40–49, doi.org/10.1007/s10862-018-9655-9.

Felitti, Vincent J., et al. "Relationship of Childhood Abuse and Household Dysfunction to Many of the Leading Causes of Death in Adults: The Adverse Childhood Experiences (ACE) Study." *American Journal of Preventive Medicine* 14, no. 4 (1998): 245–58, doi.org/10.1016/S0749-3797(98)00017-8.

Fischman, Lawrence G. "Seeing Without Self: Discovering New Meaning with Psychedelic-Assisted Psychotherapy." *Neuro-Psychoanalysis* 21, no. 2 (2019): 53–78, doi.org/10.1080/15294145.2019.1689528.

Fisher, Helen E., et al. "Intense, Passionate, Romantic Love: A Natural Addiction? How the Fields That Investigate Romance and Substance Abuse Can Inform Each Other." *Frontiers in Psychology* 7 (2016): 687, doi.org/10.3389/fpsyg.2016.00687.

Fisher, Janina. *Healing the Fragmented Selves of Trauma Survivors: Overcoming Internal Self Alienation*. New York: Routledge, 2017.

_____. *Transforming the Living Legacy of Trauma: A Workbook for Survivors and Therapists*. Eau Claire, Wisc.: PESI Publishing, 2021.

Ford, Debbie. *The Dark Side of the Light Chasers*. New York: Riverhead Books, 2010.

_____. *The Secret of the Shadow*. San Francisco: Harper, 2002.

Framo, James. "The Reality of Marriages." Presentation to the American Family Therapy Academy, 1981.

Freud, Sigmund. *The Future of an Illusion* [1927]. Trans. James Strachey. New York: W.W. Norton, 1989.

_____. *The History of the Psychoanalytic Movement* [1914]. New York: Collier Books, 1963.

_____. *The Psychopathology of Everyday Life* [1901]. Trans. James Strachey. New York: W.W. Norton, 1966.

_____. *The Unconscious* [1915]. Trans. Graham Frankland. London: Penguin Books, 2005.

Frey, Rebecca. "Stockholm Syndrome." In *The Gale Encyclopedia of Mental Health: Q-Z*. Detroit: Thomson Gale, 2019.

Bibliography

Gailliot, Matthew T., and Roy F. Baumeister. "The Physiology of Willpower: Linking Blood Glucose to Self-Control." *Personality and Social Psychology Review* 11 (2007): 303–27, doi.org/10.1177/1088868307303030.

Gerth, H. H., and C. Wright Mills. "Introduction: The Man and His Work." In *From Max Weber: Essays in Sociology*, trans. and ed. H. H. Gerth. London: Routledge & Kegan Paul, 1948.

Gilligan, Carol. *In a Different Voice: Psychological Theory and Women's Development.* Cambridge, Mass.: Harvard University Press, 1982.

Gilligan, James. *Violence: Our Deadly Epidemic and Its Causes.* New York: G.P. Putnam, 1996.

Goethe, Johann Wolfgang von. *The Sorrows of Young Werther* [1774], trans. Burton Pike. New York: Modern Library, 2004.

———. *Wisdom and Experience*, trans. and ed. Hermann J. Weigand. New York: Pantheon, 1949.

———. *Zur Farbenlehre*. Tübingen, 1810.

Goodchild, Peter. *J. Robert Oppenheimer: Shatterer of Worlds.* Boston: Houghton Mifflin, 1981.

Gottman, John M., et al. "Predicting Marital Happiness and Stability from Newlywed Interactions." *Journal of Marriage and Family* 60, no. 1 (1998): 5–22, doi.org/10.2307/353438.

Grabb, Edward, Douglas Baer, and James Curtis. "The Origins of American Individualism: Reconsidering the Historical Evidence." *Canadian Journal of Sociology* 24, no. 4 (1999): 511–33, doi.org/10.2307/3341789.

Gross, Elizabeth B., and Sara E. Medina-DeVilliers. "Cognitive Processes Unfold in a Social Context: A Review and Extension of Social Baseline Theory." *Frontiers in Psychology* 11 (2020), doi.org/10.3389/fpsyg.2020.00378.

Grossman, Dave. *On Killing: The Psychological Cost of Learning to Kill in War and Society*, rev. ed. (Boston: Little, Brown, 2009).

Gustavsson, Gina. *The Problem of Individualism: Examining the Relations Between Self-Reliance, Autonomy and Civic Virtues.* Ph.D. diss., Uppsala University, 2007.

Hall, Heather. "Trauma and Dissociation in the News: Post-Traumatic Slavery Syndrome Revisited." *International Society for the Study of Trauma and Dissociation (ISSTD) News*, January 22, 2021, https://news.isst-d.org/post-traumatic-slavery-syndrome-revisited/.

Hammett, Dashiell. *The Continental Op.* Ed. Steven Marcus. New York: Random House, 1974.

Hebb, Donald O. *The Organization of Behavior: A Neuropsychological Theory.* New York: Wiley, 1949.

Herculano-Houzel, Suzana. "The Remarkable, Yet Not Extraordinary Human Brain." *Proceedings of the National Academy of Sciences*, 109, supp.1 (2012): 10661–68, doi.org/10.1073/pnas.1201895109.

Hinchman, Lewis P. "The Idea of Individuality: Origins, Meaning, and Political Significance." *Journal of Politics* 52, no. 3 (1990): 759–81, doi.org/10.2307/2131826.

Hoover, Herbert. "Principles and Ideals of the U.S. Government" (speech), October 22, 1928, https://millercenter.org/the-presidency/presidential-speeches/october-22-1928-principles-and-ideals-united-states-government.

Howes, Satoris S., et al. "When and Why Narcissists Exhibit Greater Hindsight Bias and Less Perceived Learning." *Journal of Management* 46, no. 8 (2020): 1498–528, doi.org/10.1177/0149206320929421.

Hübl, Thomas, and Terrence Real. "Evolutionary Relationships in Extraordinary Times." Online course, April 7, 2020.

———. "Love, Trauma and Healing." Online course, April 15, 2021.

Ingersoll, Robert G. "Some Reasons Why." In *The Works of Robert G. Ingersoll*, vol. 2, *Lectures 1900*. New York: Dresden, 1902.

Jack, Dana Crowley. *Silencing the Self: Women and Depression*. Cambridge, Mass: Harvard University Press, 1991.

Janoff-Bulman, Ronnie. *Shattered Assumptions: Towards a New Psychology of Trauma*. New York: Free Press, 1992.

Jarvis, Shoshana N., M. Joy McClure, and Niall Bolger. "Exploring How Exchange Orientation Affects Conflict and Intimacy in the Daily Life of Romantic Couples." *Journal of Social and Personal Relationships* 36, nos. 11–12 (2019): 3575–87, doi.org/10.1177/0265407519826743.

Johnson, Susan M. *Emotionally Focused Couple Therapy with Trauma Survivors*. New York: Guilford, 2002.

Joiner, Thomas. *Mindlessness: The Corruption of Mindfulness in a Culture of Narcissism*. New York: Oxford University Press, 2017.

Jones, Kenneth, and Tema Oken. "White Supremacy Culture." In *Dismantling Racism: A Workbook for Social Change Groups*. ChangeWork, 2001.

Jung, Carl. *Letters*, vol. 2, *1951–1961*. Edited by Gerhard Adler, trans. Jeffrey Hulen. Princeton, N.J.: Princeton University Press, 1976.

Kant, Immanuel. *Critique of Pure Reason*, trans. Norman Kemp Smith. New York: St. Martin's Press, 1965.

Keen, Sam. *Faces of the Enemy: Reflections of the Hostile Imagination*. San Francisco: Harper & Row, 1986.

Keltner, Dacher, and Ann M. Kring. "Emotion, Social Function, and Psychopathology." *Review of General Psychology* 2, no. 3 (1998): 320–42, doi.org/10.1037/1089-2680.2.3.320.

Kendi, Ibram X. *How to Be an Antiracist*. New York: One World, 2019.

Kern, M. L., et al. "Systems Informed Positive psychology." *Journal of Positive Psychology* 15, no. 6 (2020): 705–15, doi.org/10.1080/17439760.2019.163 9799.

Kerner, Ian. *She Comes First: The Thinking Man's Guide to Pleasuring a Woman*. New York: Regan Books, 2004.

Keverne, E. B., C. M. Nevison, and F. L. Martel. "Early Learning and the Social Bond." In *The Integrative Neurobiology of Affiliation*, ed. C. Sue Carter, Izja Lederhendler, and Brian Kirkpatrick. Cambridge, Mass.: MIT Press, 1999.

Kurzban, Robert. "Does the Brain Consume Additional Glucose During Self-Control Tasks?" *Evolutionary Psychology* 8 (2010): 244–59, doi. org/10.1177/147470491000800208.

Langford, D. J., et al. "Social Modulation of Pain as Evidence for Empathy in Mice." *Science* 312, no. 5782 (2006): 1967–70, doi.org/10.1126/science.1128322.

Lasch, Christopher. *The Culture of Narcissism: American Life in an Age of Diminishing Expectations*. New York: W.W. Norton, 1978.

Lester, B. M, J. Hoffman, and T. Berry Brazelton. "The Rhythmic Structure of Mother-Infant Interaction in Term and Preterm Infants." *Child Development* 56, no.1 (1985): 15–27, doi.org/10.1111/j.1467-8624.1985.tb00081.x.

Levant, Ronald F., and Y. Joel Wong. *The Psychology of Men and Masculinities*. Washington, D.C.: American Psychological Association, 2017.

Levine, Peter A. *Trauma and Memory: Brain and Body in a Search for the Living Past: A Practical Guide for Understanding and Working with Traumatic Memory*. New York: North Atlantic Books, 2015.

Locke, John. *Two Treatises of Government*. Edited by Peter Laslett. Cambridge, U.K.: Cambridge University Press, 1960.

Lukes, Steven. *Individualism*. 1973; reprint ECPR Press, 2006.

Marin, Rebeca A., Andrew Christensen, and David C. Atkins. "Infidelity and Behavioral Couple Therapy: Relationship Outcomes over 5 Years Following Therapy." *Couple and Family Psychology: Research and Practice* 3 no. 1 (2014): 1–12, doi.org/10.1037/cfp00000.

Marshall, S. L. A. *Men Against Fire: The Problem of Battle Command in Future War*. New York: Morrow, 1947.

Marvin, Carolyn. "Therapy Master Class." Lecture at the Family Institute, Cambridge, Mass., June 2020.

McGilchrist, Iain. *The Master and His Emissary*. New Haven, Conn.: Yale University Press, 2019.

McKnight, Stephen A. *Science, Pseudo-Science, and Utopianism in Early Modern Thought*. Columbia: University of Missouri Press, 1992.

Mellody, Pia. "Community Lecture." Lecture at the Meadows Institute, Phoenix, Ariz., 2003.

———. "Post-Induction Training for Therapists." Lecture at the Meadows, Wickenburg, Ariz., 1987.

Mellody, Pia, Andrea Wells Miller, and Keith Miller. *Facing Codependence: What It Is, Where It Comes From, How It Sabotages Our Lives*. San Francisco: Perennial Library, 1989.

———. *Facing Love Addiction: Giving Yourself the Power to Change the Way You Love*. San Francisco: Harper San Francisco, 2003.

Menakem, Resmaa. *My Grandmother's Hands: Racialized Trauma and the Pathway to Mending Our Hearts and Bodies*. Las Vegas, Nev.: Central Recovery Press, 2017.

Messina, Mike. "America's Most Devastating Conflict: King Philip's War." Connecticut History, August 12, 2020, https://connecticuthistory.org/americas-most-devastating-conflict-king-philips-war/.

Metzinger, Thomas, *The Ego Tunnel: The Science of the Mind and the Myth of the Self*. New York: Basic Books, 2009.

Metzl, Jonathan. *Dying of Whiteness: How the Politics of Racial Resentment Is Killing America's Heartland*. New York: Basic Books, 2019.

Milne, A. A. *Winnie-the-Pooh: The Complete Collection of Stories and Poems*. Edited by Ernest H. Shepard. London: Methuen Children's Books, 1994.

Minuchin, Salvador. *Families and Family Therapy*. Cambridge, Mass.: Harvard University Press, 1974.

Minuchin, Salvador, and M. P. Nichols. *Family Healing: Tales of Hope and Renewal from Family Therapy*. New York: Free Press, 1993.

Mitchell, Stephen, ed. *Tao Te Ching: A New English Version*. New York: HarperCollins, 2004.

More, Paul Elmer. *Benjamin Franklin*. Boston: Houghton Mifflin, 1900.

Moritz, Katie. "If You Cheated, Is There Hope for Your Relationship?" *Rewire*, April 19, 2019, https://www.rewire.org/cheated-hope-relationship/.

Murthy, Vivek Hallegere. *Together: The Healing Power of Human Connection in a Sometimes Lonely World*. New York: Harper Wave, 2020.

Nugent, J. Kevin, Barry M. Lester, and T. Berry Brazelton. *The Cultural Context of Infancy*. Norwood, N.J: Ablex, 1989.

O'Brien, Ed, and Samantha Kassirer. "People Are Slow to Adapt to the Warm Glow of Giving." *Psychological Science* 30, no. 2 (2019): 193–204, doi.org/10.1177/0956797618814145.

Ogden, Pat, Kekuni Minton, and Clare Pain. *Trauma and the Body: A Sensorimotor Approach to Psychotherapy*. New York: W.W. Norton 2006.

Overall, N. C. "Attachment and Dyadic Regulation Processes." *Current Opinion in Psychology* 1 no.1 (2015): 61–70.

Paine, Thomas. *Dissertations on Government, the Affairs of the Bank, and Paper Money*. London, 1817.

Pais, Abraham, and Robert P. Crease. *J. Robert Oppenheimer: A Life*. New York: Oxford University Press, 2006.

Paley, William. *Natural Theology; or, Evidences of the Existence and Attributes of the Deity, Collected from the Appearances of Nature*. London, 1802.

Panksepp, Jaak. *Affective Neuroscience: The Foundations of Human and Animal Emotions*. New York: Oxford University Press, 1998.

Panksepp, Jaak, and L. Biven. *The Archaeology of the Mind: Neuroevolutionary Origins of Human Emotions*. New York: W.W. Norton, 2012.

Panksepp, Jaak, et al. "Neuro-Evolutionary Foundations of Infant Minds: From Psychoanalytic Visions of How Primal Emotions Guide Constructions of Human Minds Toward Affective Neuroscientific Understanding of Emotions and Their Disorders." *Psychoanalytic Inquiry* 39, no. 1 (2019): 36–51.

Papp, Peggy. *The Process of Change*. New York: Guilford Press, 1983.

Perel, Esther. *The State of Affairs: Rethinking Infidelity*. New York: Harper, 2017.

Perel, Esther, and Terry Real. "A Dialogue on Infidelity." Lecture at Annual Psychotherapy Networker Symposium, Washington D.C, March 24, 2012.

Perel, Esther, Terry Real, and George Faller. "Learning from the Affair." Lecture at Annual Psychotherapy Networker Symposium, Washington D.C, March 28, 2015.

Perry, Bruce D., et al. "Childhood Trauma, the Neurobiology of Adaptation, and 'Use-Dependent' Development of the Brain: How 'States' Become 'Traits.'" *Infant Mental Health Journal* 16, no. 4 (1995), doi.org/10.1002/1097-0355(199524)16:4<271::AID-IMHJ2280160404>3.0.CO;2-B.

Phillips, Ann T., Henry M. Wellman, and Elizabeth S. Spelke. "Infants' Ability to Connect Gaze and Emotional Expression to Intentional Action." *Cognition* 85, no. 1 (2002): 53–78.

Pierce, Chester. "Offensive Mechanism." In *The Black 70's*, ed. Floyd B. Barbour. Boston: Porter Sargent, 1970.

Pincus, Aaron L., and Mark R. Lukowitsky. "Pathological Narcissism and Narcissistic Personality Disorder." *Annual Review of Clinical Psychology* 6, no. 1 (2010): 421–46, doi.org/10.1146/annurev.clinpsy.121208.131215.

Pollan, Michael. *How to Change Your Mind: What the New Science of Psychedelics Teaches Us About Consciousness, Dying, Addiction, Depression, and Transcendence.* New York: Penguin Press, 2018.

————. "The Trip Treatment." *New Yorker*, February 2, 2015.

Porges, Stephen W. *The Polyvagal Theory: Neurophysiological Foundations of Emotions Attachment Communication Self-Regulation.* New York: W.W. Norton, 2011.

Putnam, Robert D. *Bowling Alone.* New York: Simon & Schuster, 2000.

Radiske, Andressa, et al. "Prior Learning of Relevant Non-Aversive Information Is a Boundary Condition for Avoidance Memory Reconsolidation in the Rat Hippocampus." *Journal of Neuroscience the Official Journal of the Society for Neuroscience* 37, no. 40 (2017): 1372–17, doi.org/10.1523/JNEUROSCI.1372-17.2017.

Real, Terrence. *Fierce Intimacy: Standing Up to One Another with Love* (CD). Boulder, Colo.: Sounds True, 2018.

————. "High Impact Couple's Therapy: How to Go Deep Quickly." Online at Milton Erickson, Couples Institute, Menlo Park, Calif., June 5, 2021.

————. *I Don't Want to Talk About It: Overcoming the Secret Legacy of Male Depression.* New York: Fireside, 1998.

————. "A Matter of Choice: Deciding: To Be Right or Be Married?." *Psychotherapy Networker*, November–December 2011, https://www.psychotherapynetworker.org/magazine/article/314/a-matter-of-choice.

————. *The New Rules of Marriage: What You Need to Know to Make Love Work.* New York: Ballantine, 2008.

————. "Staying in Love: The Art of Fierce Intimacy." Online course.

————. "Working with Infidelity in Couples Therapy: Conversations with Terrence Real." Webinar course, 2012.

Real, Terrence, and Esther Perel. "The Relate 2 Day Workshop: Taught by Terrence Real and Esther Perel." Workshop at Millennium Harvest House, Boulder Colo., March 3–4, 2017.

Reis, Harry T., Margaret S. Clark, and John G. Holmes. "Perceived Partner Responsiveness as an Organizing Construct in the Study of Intimacy and Closeness." In *Handbook of Closeness and Intimacy*, ed. D. Mashek and A. Aron. Mahwah, N.J.: Lawrence Erlbaum Associates, 2004.

Rieff, Philip. *The Triumph of the Therapeutic: Uses of Faith After Freud.* New York: Harper & Row, 1966.

Rohrbaugh, Michael J., and Varda Shoham. "Brief Therapy Based on Interrupting Ironic Processes: The Palo Alto Model." *Clinical Psychology* 8, no. 1 (2001): 66–81, doi.org/10.1093/clipsy.8.1.66.

Rose, Paul. "The Happy and Unhappy Faces of Narcissism." *Personality and Individual Differences* 33, no. 3 (2002): 379–91, doi.org/10.1016/S0191-8869(01)00162-3.

Rūmī, Jalāl al-Dīn. *The Essential Rumi*, trans. Coleman Barks et al. N.p.: Blackstone, 2018.

Russo, Marc A., Danielle M. Santarelli, and Dean O'Rourke. "The Physiological Effects of Slow Breathing in the Healthy Human." *Breathe* 13, no. 4 (2017): 298–309, doi.org/10.1183/20734735.009817.

Salazar, Leslie Ramos. "The Negative Reciprocity Process in Marital Relationships: A Literature Review." *Aggression and Violent Behavior* 24 (2015): 113–19, doi.org/10.1016/j.avb.2015.05.008.

Sapolsky, Robert. M. *Behave: The Biology of Humans at Our Best and Worst.* New York: Penguin, 2017.

Sbarra, David A., and Cindy Hazan. "Coregulation, Dysregulation, Self-Regulation: An Integrative Analysis and Empirical Agenda for Understanding Adult Attachment, Separation, Loss and Anxiety." *Personality and Social Psychology Review* 12, no. 2 (2008): 141–67, doi.org/10.1177/1088868308315702.

Schoebi, Dominik. "The Coregulation of Daily Affect in Marital Relationships." *Journal of Family Psychology* 22, no. 4 (2008): 595–604, doi.org/10.1037/0893-3200.22.3.595.

Schwabe, Lars, Karim Nader, and Jens C. Pruessner. "Reconsolidation of Human Memory: Brain Mechanisms and Clinical Relevance." *Biological Psychiatry Journal* 76, no. 4 (2014): 274–80, doi.org/10.1016/j.biopsych.2014.03.008.

Schwartz, Richard C. *Internal Family Systems Therapy.* New York: Guilford Press, 1995.

———. *No Bad Parts: Healing Trauma and Restoring Wholeness with the Internal Family Systems Model* (CD). Boulder, Colo.: Sounds True, 2021.

Segell, Michael. "The Pater Principle." *Esquire*, March 1995.

Sels, Laura, et al. "Emotional Interdependence and Well-Being in Close Relationships." *Frontiers in Psychology* 7 (2016), doi.org/10.3389/fpsyg.2016.00283.

Seshadri, Krishna G. "The Neuroendocrinology of Love." *Indian Journal of Endocrinology and Metabolism* 20, no. 4 (2016): 558–63, doi.org/10.4103/2230-8210.183479.

Shapiro, Francine, and Margot Silk Forrest. *EMDR: The Breakthrough Therapy for Overcoming Anxiety, Stress, and Trauma.* New York: Basic Books, 1997.

Siedentop, Larry. *Inventing the Individual*. Cambridge, Mass.: Harvard University Press, 2014.

Siegel, Dan. J. *The Developing Mind*, 2nd ed. New York: Guilford Press, 2012.

_____. *Mind: A Journey to the Heart of Being Human*. New York: W.W. Norton, 2017.

_____. *The Mindful Therapist: A Clinician's Guide to Mindsight and Neural Integration*. New York: W.W. Norton, 2010.

_____. *Mindsight: The New Science of Personal Transformation*. New York: Bantam, 2010.

Siegel, Dan J., and S. McNamara, S. *The Neurobiology of "We": How Relationships, the Mind, and the Brain Interact to Shape Who We Are* (CD). Boulder, Colo.: Sounds True, 2008.

Silverstein, Olga. *Who's Depressed?* Ackerman Institute for the Family, 2012.

Simmel, Georg. *The Sociology of Georg Simmel*. Translated and edited by Kurt Wolff. New York: Free Press, 1950.

Singer, Peter, ed. *Does Anything Really Matter? Essays on Parfit on Objectivity*. New York: Oxford University Press, 2017.

"Slavery in the President's Neighborhood FAQ." White House Historical Association, n.d., https://www.whitehousehistory.org/slavery-in-the-presidents-neighborhood-faq.

Spitz, René A. "Hospitalism: An Inquiry into the Genesis of Psychiatric Conditions in Early Childhood." *Psychoanalytic Study of the Child* 1, no.1 (1945): 53–74, doi.org/10.1080/00797308.1945.11823126.

Spock, Benjamin, and Robert Needlman. *Dr. Spock's Baby and Child Care*. 8th ed. New York: Pocket Books, 2004.

Steup, Matthias, and Ernest Sosa, eds. *Contemporary Debates in Epistemology*. Malden, Mass.: Blackwell, 2005.

Stevens, Larry, Mark Gauthier-Braham, and Benjamin Bush. "The Brain That Longs to Care for Itself: The Current Neuroscience of Self-Compassion." In *The Neuroscience of Empathy, Compassion, and Self-Compassion*, ed. Larry Stevens and Christopher Woodruff. Cambridge, Mass.: Academic Press, 2018.

Suzuki, Shunryū. *Zen Mind, Beginner's Mind: Informal Talks on Zen Meditation and Practice*, ed. Trudy Dixon. Boston: Shambhala, 2011.

Swain, J. E., et al. "Brain Basis of Early Parent-Infant Interactions: Psychology, Physiology, and In Vivo Functional Neuroimaging Studies." *Journal of Child Psychology and Psychiatry, and Allied Disciplines* 48, nos. 3–4 (2007): 262–87, doi.org/10.1111/j.1469-7610.2007.01731.x.

Szalavitz, Maia, and Bruce D. Perry. *Born for Love: Why Empathy Is Essential—and Endangered.* New York: William Morrow, 2010.

Tagore, Rabindranath. *Stray Birds.* New York: Macmillan, 1916.

Tannen, Deborah. *You Just Don't Understand: Women and Men in Conversation.* New York: William Morrow, 1990.

Tatkin, Stan. *Wired for Love.* Oakland, Calif.: New Harbinger, 2011.

Teutsch, David A. *A Guide to Jewish Practice: Community, Gemilut Hesed, and Tikun Olam.* Wyncote, Penn.: Reconstructionist Rabbinical College Press, 2009.

Thoreau, Henry David, *Walden, or, Life in the Woods.* Boston, 1854.

Thurow, Joshua C. "The Implicit Conception and Intuition Theory of the A Priori, with Implications for Experimental Philosophy." In *The A Priori in Philosophy,* ed. Albert Casullo and Joshua C. Thurow. New York: Oxford university Press, 2013.

Tocqueville, Alexis de. *Democracy in America.* Edited by J. P. Mayer. Garden City, N.Y.: Doubleday, 1969.

Tolstoy, Leo. *Anna Karenina* [1878], trans. R. Pevear and L. Volokhonsky. New York: Penguin, 2003.

Tronick, Ed. *The Neurobehavioral and Social-Emotional Development of Infants and Children.* New York: W.W. Norton, 2007.

———. "Still Face Experiment" (video), UMass Boston, November 30, 2009, https://www.youtube.com/watch?v=apzXGEbZht0&ab_channel=UMassBoston.

Tronick, Ed, and Claudia M. Gold. *The Power of Discord: Why the Ups and Downs of Relationships Are the Secret to Building Intimacy, Resilience, and Trust.* New York: Little Brown Spark, 2020.

Tronson, Natalie C., et al. "Fear Conditioning and Extinction: Emotional States Encoded by Distinct Signaling Pathways." *Trends in Neuroscience* 35, no. 3 (2012): 145–55, doi.org/10.1016/j.tins.2011.10.003.

Turner, Jack. "American Individualism and Structural Injustice: Tocqueville, Gender, and Race." *Polity* 40, no. 2 (2008): 197–215, doi.org/10.1057/palgrave.polity.2300088.

Uchino, B. N., J. T. Cacioppo, and J. K. Kiecolt-Glaser. "The Relationship Between Social Support and Physiological Processes: A Review with Emphasis on Underlying Mechanisms, and Implications for Health." *Psychological Bulletin* 119, no. 3 (1996): 488–531, doi.org/10.1037/0033-2909.119.3.488.

Van der Kolk, Bessel. "The Body Keeps Score: Integration of Mind, Brain, and Body in the Treatment of Trauma" Presentation to the Evolution of Psychotherapy conference, Milton H. Erickson Foundation, Phoenix, Ariz., 2013.

_____. *The Body Keeps the Score: Brain, Mind, and Body in the Healing of Trauma*. New York: Penguin Books, 2015.

Vareene, Hervé. *Americans Together: Structured Diversity in a Midwestern Town*. New York; Teachers College Press, 1977.

Veroff, Joseph, Elizabeth Douvan, and Richard A. Kulka. *The Inner American: A Self-Portrait from 1957 to 1976*. New York: Basic Books, 1981.

Wang, Qi. "Why Should We All Be Cultural Psychologists? Lessons From the Study of Social Cognition." *Perspectives on Psychological Science: A Journal of the Association for Psychological Science* 11, no. 5 (2016): 583–96, doi.org/10.1177/1745691616645552.

West, Keon, and Asia A. Eaton. "Prejudiced and Unaware of It: Evidence for the Dunning-Kruger Model in the Domains of Racism and Sexism." *Personality and Individual Differences* 146, no. 1 (2019): 111–19, doi.org/10.1016/j.paid.2019.03.047.

Whitaker, Carl A., and Thomas P. Malone. *The Roots of Psychotherapy*. New York: Brunner/Mazel, 1981.

Whittaker, Thomas. *The Theory of Abstract Ethics*. Cambridge, U.K.: Cambridge University Press, 1916.

Wilkerson, Isabel. *Caste: The Origins of Our Discontents*. New York: Random House, 2020.

Winnicott, D. W. "The Theory of the Parent-Infant Relationship." *International Journal of Psycho-Analysis* 41 (1960): 585–95.

Winthrop, Delba. "Tocqueville's American Woman and 'The True Conception of Democratic Progress.'" *Political Theory* 14, no. 2 (1986): 239–61, doi.org/10.1177/0090591786014002004.

Wrightsman, Lawrence S. *Adult Personality Development: Theories and Concepts*. Thousand Oaks, Calif.: Sage, 1994.

Yang, Y., et al. "A Novel Method to Trigger the Reconsolidation of Fear Memory." *Behavior Research and Therapy* 122 (2019): 1–9, doi.org/10.1016/j.brat.2019.103461.

Yates, Frances A. *Giordano Bruno and the Hermetic Tradition*. Chicago: University of Chicago Press, 1964.

Younger, Jarred, et al. "Viewing Pictures of a Romantic Partner Reduces Experimental Pain: Involvement of Neural Reward Systems." *PLOS ONE* 5 (2010): e13309, doi:10.1371/journal.pone.0013309.

Zajenkowski, Marcin, et al. "Vulnerable Past, Grandiose Present: The Relationship Between Vulnerable and Grandiose Narcissism, Time Perspective and Personality." *Personality and Individual Differences* 98 (2016): 102–6, doi.org/10.1016/j.paid.2016.03.092.

Index

About the Author

Terrence Real is an internationally recognized family therapist, speaker, and author. He founded the Relational Life Institute, offering workshops for couples, individuals, and parents, along with a professional training program for clinicians to learn his Relational Life Therapy methodology. He is the bestselling author of *I Don't Want to Talk About It*, *How Can I Get Through to You?*, and *The New Rules of Marriage*.